PLAYS OF THE YEAR SPECIAL
The Six Wives of Henry VIII

PLAYS OF THE YEAR SPECIAL

EDITED BY
J. C. TREWIN

THE SIX WIVES OF HENRY VIII

Catherine of Aragon
Rosemary Anne Sisson

Anne Boleyn
Nick McCarty

Jane Seymour
Ian Thorne

Anne of Cleves
Jean Morris

Catherine Howard
Beverley Cross

Catherine Parr
John Prebble

FREDERICK UNGAR PUBLISHING
COMPANY
NEW YORK

Published by
PAUL ELEK LIMITED in 1972
54-58 Caledonian Road,
London, N1 9RN

ISBN 0 8044 2886 7

Made and printed in Great Britain

CONTENTS

LIST OF ILLUSTRATIONS

*The above illustrations are reproduced by courtesy of
the British Broadcasting Corporation*

INTRODUCTION

I

The plays in this volume are important, not simply because of their exciting dramatic quality, their technique framed for the television screen, but also because they show us a man who, popularly, has been so overcast by tradition that few people have paused to consider him afresh. A fine writer, in another context, has used the phrase: 'We are a great people for labels, and we furnish them with well-nigh imperishable gum.' Certainly Henry the Eighth, who ruled from 1509 to 1547, is an English monarch too long oppressed by his label. Consider the small-talk of popular history down the years. To practically every reign the glib *aide-memoire*. What of Henry the Eighth? He had six wives. Be ready with the gum-brush.

This is where our television dramatists are now so splendidly restoring. They have written what amounts to a joint biography of a complex figure. Based on the six marriages (and here for once the label has been of use), the plays proved in performance to be acceptable to vast audiences, an example of television at its most enlightened and without routine chatter.

The sequence spans the King's life from the age of eighteen to his death at fifty-five years and seven months. It should be remembered that Henry was not always the daunting square-faced despot of a famous Holbein portrait. In his youth (according to a letter in

1515 from the Venetian Ambassador Extraordinary), he was 'the handsomest potentate ... above the usual height, with an extremely fine calf to his leg, his complexion very fair and bright, with auburn hair combed straight and short, in the French fashion, and a round face so very beautiful that it would become a pretty woman, his throat being long and thick'. He was a linguist and musician as well as a fine horseman and an expert with the bow.

In these plays we watch Henry through the years of his tumultuous reign. Each episode is named for a wife. Thus Rosemary Anne Sisson writes of Catherine of Aragon, Nick McCarty of Anne Boleyn, Ian Thorne of Jane Seymour, Jean Morris of Anne of Cleves, Beverley Cross of Catherine Howard, and John Prebble of Catherine Parr. Clio has collaborated handsomely with them all, and the King himself is governor. There is no sign here of the waxwork-drama in which the expected people, in Max Beerbohm's phrase, 'make remarks highly characteristic of themselves'. On the screen the King was alive: he was, persuasively, the Henry who said: 'I do not choose anyone to have it in his power to command me; nor will I ever suffer it.' For that matter, he was the Henry who said, as reported by a historian: 'Three may keep counsel, if two be away; and if I thought my cap knew my counsel, I would throw it in the fire and burn it.' But there was also the man's strange charm. He could plausibly have written the song I think of when his name is mentioned:

> Pastime with good company
> I love and shall until I die.
> Grudge who lust, but none deny.
> So God be pleased, thus live will I.
> For my pastance,
> Hunt, sing and dance,
> My heart is set.
> All goodly sport
> For my comfort
> Who shall me let?

Youth must have some dalliance,
Of good or ill some pastance.
Company me thinks the best,
All thoughts and fancies to digest.
　　For idleness
　　Is chief mistress
　　Of vices all.
　　　　Then who can say
　　　　But mirth and play
Is best of all?

Company with honesty
Is virtue, vices to flee.
Company is good and ill,
But every man hath his freewill.
　　The best ensue,
　　The worst eschew!
　　My mind shall be,
　　　　Virtue to use,
　　　　Vice to refuse;
Thus shall I use me.

He could also write, I am afraid:

　　As the holly groweth green,
　　And never changeth hue,
　　So I am and e'er have been,
　　Unto my lady true.

　We must think of all sides of Henry the Eighth, not simply of the man Charles Laughton acted, with uncompromising loyalty to his script-writers, in a famous Korda film: Henry, the gross sensual hulk, the comic monster apparently born at the age of forty in flaming Tudor ire. It has never been easy to escape from the Bluff King Hal stereotype. Again and again this Henry has arrived from dramatists prodigal in a form of tushery from which only such a writer as, say, Clifford Bax (in *A Rose Without a Thorn*) could sometimes escape. Bounties have been few. Even when Shakespeare's *Henry VIII*—parts of which are probably Fletcherian—has been revived, an actor, and

there have been many fine ones,* has had always to
fight against the received idea. Maybe casual visitors
remember best such an exchange as this (III.ii):

> Suffolk: I do assure you
>   The King cried 'Ha!' at this.
> Lord Chamberlain: Now, God incense him,
>   And let him cry 'Ha!' louder!

II

These six plays now flash up a Henry more complete, more reasonable, than any we have had on
stage or screen. Seeing them and reading them, I have
recalled my childhood in Cornwall close to one of the
most powerful of English lighthouses. Night by night
in winter I would look out to Brazil (so they told me)
and to the Atlantic, so hidden that one could not see
from the window even to the nearest edge of the
lawn, let alone to the sunken garden, the field beyond,
and the headland above the cove. Then, suddenly, the
light would swing in its arc and the broad blade
would cut a shining path far across the water. So with
these plays: they cut through the mists of tradition.

Leaving them now to work with their own powerful immediacy, I must supply a scaffolding of fact and
date. Henry, born in 1491, succeeded to the throne in
1509 when he was not quite eighteen. Barely six
weeks after his father's death, he was married to his
elder brother Arthur's widow to whom he had been
contracted for some years: Catherine of Aragon,
daughter of Ferdinand, first King of Spain through
the union of Aragon and Castile, and Isabella his
Queen. In 1533 Henry divorced Catherine (mother of
one surviving child, a daughter who would be Mary I
of England) after a long secret union with Anne
Boleyn (Bullen). Three years later, in May 1536,

---

*Celebrated stage and film players of Henry VIII in this
century have included Arthur Bourchier, Lyn Harding, Emil
Jannings, Charles Laughton, Anthony Quayle, Paul Rogers,
Harry Andrews, Donald Sinden and Frank Vosper.

Anne, found guilty of adultery and treason, was executed—she, too, had one surviving daughter, the future Queen Elizabeth I—and Henry turned to a third wife, Jane Seymour, shy and devout, daughter of Sir John Seymour of Wolf Hall on the edge of Savernake Forest in Wiltshire. We find Henry writing to Jane just before their marriage in 1536: 'Advertising you that there is a ballad made lately of great derision against us, which if it go much abroad and is seen by you, I pray you to pay no manner of regard to it. I am not at present informed who is the setter forth of this malignant writing, but if he is found out he shall be straitly punished for it.' That is the voice of the monarch whose 'Ha!' could terrify.

Queen Jane died of septicaemia at Hampton Court in October 1537 after giving birth to the later King Edward VI. A fourth and diplomatic marriage in 1540 was doomed from the first; Henry did not see until it was too late the uncomely and well-meaning Anne of Cleves from a Rhineland Duchy: the matter ended in swift annulment. Soon (1542), and within a year of marriage, a fifth wife, Catherine (Katheryn) Howard, the 'rose without a thorn', daughter of Lord Edmund Howard, had gone to the block; like Anne Boleyn, she had been charged with infidelity, though nothing more than pre-nuptial unchastity could be proved. A sixth wife and third Catherine, who was the daughter of Sir Thomas Parr of Kendal, and who had been already twice widowed, outlived the King (they were married in 1543) by little more than a year. He died in 1547; Catherine, by then the wife of Lord Seymour of Sudeley, in 1548.

Hans Holbein (1497/8-1543), Henry's court painter for seven years from 1536, left several famous portraits. Four of the Queens, Anne Boleyn, Jane Seymour, Anne of Cleves, and Catherine Howard, sat to him; and we think of Henry as he stares, immensely formidable, from a picture—so life-like (it was said) that 'everyone who sees it is frightened'. A later portrait (1542) was painted in the year of Catherine Howard's execution. It is hard to look at it without recalling the ghost story of Hampton Court where, according to legend, the Queen haunts the corridor, or gallery, that leads past Wolsey's Closet to the Chapel Royal. Hearing the King was in the Chapel, Catherine evaded her guards, tried to reach him, and was seized and carried back, shrieking, to her quarters: a scene traditionally still re-enacted in the Hampton Court midnight.

Here now is the story of the reign and its astonishing complexity of character and event:

> Adieu, mine own lady,
>   Adieu, my special,
> Who hath my heart truly,
>   Be sure and ever shall.
>
> Green groweth the holly, so doth the ivy,
> Though wintry blasts blow ne'er so high,
> Green groweth the holly . . .

J. C. TREWIN

Hampstead, London
1971

I have to express warm gratitude to my colleague, Mrs Judith Rayner, for her collaboration in the editing of this volume.

Note: Camera directions from the original productions have been retained wherever they were felt to be vital to the action and atmosphere of the plays.

Catherine of Aragon

ROSEMARY ANNE SISSON

Catherine of Aragon was first presented by BBC Television on 1 January, 1970, with the following cast:

HENRY VII	John Woodnutt
PRINCE ARTHUR	Martin Ratcliffe
DR DE PUEBLA	Ken Wynne
DONA ELVIRA MANUEL	Sally Travers
CATHERINE OF ARAGON	Annette Crosbie
EARL OF SURREY	Donald Bisset
MARIA DE SALINAS	Margaret Ford
FRANCESCA DE CARCERES	Joyce Mandré
DON GUTIERRE GOMEZ DE FUENSALIDA	Peter Stephens
BISHOP FOX	Robert Hartley
HENRY VIII	Keith Michell
TUTOR	Will Leighton
LORD WILLOUGHBY	Valentine Palmer
ANNE BOLEYN	Dorothy Tutin
INEZ DE VENEGAS	Ina de la Haye
CARDINAL WOLSEY	John Baskcomb
PRINCESS MARY	Verina Greenlaw
CARDINAL CAMPEGGIO	Ronald Adam
DUKE OF NORFOLK	Patrick Troughton
DUKE OF SUFFOLK	Raymond Adamson
USHER	Richard Burnett
EUSTACHE CHAPUYS	Edward Atienza
NOBLEMAN	Peter Bennett
ARCHBISHOP WARHAM	Charles Workman
BISHOP FISHER	Geoffrey Lewis

Produced by Ronald Travers and Mark Shivas
Directed by John Glenister
Designed by Peter Seddon
The scene in which Sir Edmund Bedingfield appears was omitted from the play when it was screened.

Characters

ARTHUR, *Prince of Wales*
CATHERINE OF ARAGON
DR DE PUEBLA
THE EARL OF SURREY
THE DUKE OF NORFOLK
DONA ELVIRA MANUEL
KING HENRY VII
MARIA DE SALINAS
DON GUTIERRE GOMEZ DE FUENSALIDA
DR FOX, *Bishop of Winchester*
FRANCESCA DE CARCERES
PRINCE HENRY, *later King Henry VIII*
TUTOR
LORD WILLOUGHBY
ANNE BOLEYN
INEZ DE VENEGAS
CARDINAL WOLSEY
CARDINAL CAMPEGGIO
THE DUKE OF SUFFOLK
ARCHBISHOP WARHAM
BISHOP FISHER
USHER
EUSTACHE CHAPUYS
SIR EDMUND BEDINGFIELD
BISHOPS
NOBLEMEN
LADIES
CLERK

Sets

A gallery in the palace of Greenwich (with alcove)
A room at Greenwich
Dr de Puebla's lodgings
The Council Room and King's Study
Another room in Greenwich
The Queen's bedchamber
Anteroom in the Queen's apartments
The Court at Blackfriars
Outside Blackfriars
The Queen's room at Kimbolton
The hall at Kimbolton
Coronation set piece

Telecine

A field and tent near Dogmersfield

i

Exterior. Field. Night. October. 1501.

(Seen from above, a superb pavilion tent pitched in an open field.

A horseman canters towards it, with a slighter figure on horseback following. As he arrives and swings off the horse, zoom in to find Henry VII.

He is an old forty-four, long ago grown secretive with poverty and danger and feeling his way to an uncertain throne. He has the Tudor rat-trap of a mouth which is later to appear in Henry VIII, Mary and Elizabeth, and he still retains an occasional hint of the Welsh accent of his youth.

Just now he is feeling active and cheerful, having ridden hard to please his own fancy. Henry VII is plainly dressed, except for a gold chain and a ruby ring. He is met outside the Pavilion by the Spanish Ambassador, Dr de Puebla, a rather ugly, common, lame little man, a Spanish Jew who speaks excellent English, and, incidentally, is more richly dressed than Henry VII.

Dr de Puebla, dismayed by the situation in which he finds himself.)

DE PUEBLA : Your Majesty!

(He makes a quick bow, anxious to have his say before Henry VII says what he has come for.)

Your Majesty, I—

HENRY VII *(Apparently blithely unconcerned)*: Doctor de Puebla. I have come with his Royal Highness, the Prince of Wales, to see the Princess Catherine.

7

(*He observes de Puebla's dismay with a bland air. He knows very well.*)

DE PUEBLA: Sir, her Royal Highness' parents have given orders—My instructions are—

HENRY VII (*Quizzically*): Your instructions?

DE PUEBLA (*Putting a brave front on it*): As Spanish Ambassador, Sir—(*He swallows.*) By the laws of Spain, a royal bride may not be seen until after her wedding, even by—even by her bridegroom.

(*De Puebla looks past Henry VII to Prince Arthur, who has dismounted from his horse and stands timidly waiting. He is a slight, fair, delicate boy, looking young for his fifteen years. De Puebla looks nervously back at Henry VII, who looks impassively back for a moment, and then suddenly smiles.*)

HENRY VII (*Very pleasantly*): But, Doctor Puebla, this is England.

(*He beckons to Prince Arthur and steps forward into the tent.*)

ii

Interior. The tent. Night.

(*Henry VII steps into a sort of antechamber, divided by silk hangings from the other half of the tent. He is met by Dona Elvira Manuel, a commanding Spanish Duenna. De Puebla hastily follows Henry VII and Arthur inside.*)

DE PUEBLA: His Majesty, King Henry the Seventh, his Royal Highness, Prince Arthur, to see her Serene Highness, Princess Catherine of Aragon.

DONA ELVIRA (*Curtseying*): Your Majesty, her Royal Highness has retired for the night.

HENRY VII: Then we will visit her in her bedchamber.

(*Henry VII makes a move. Dona Elvira moves even faster towards the curtain.*)

DONA ELVIRA: I—! If you will—! A moment.

(*She disappears. Henry VII looks at de Puebla and grins, and de Puebla smiles back. The curtain moves, and Catherine shyly appears, a trim slender figure, veiled. She curtseys. Henry VII steps forward. Dona Elvira comes out behind Catherine and helps her to raise her veil. She is sixteen years old, well-formed, round-faced, with a mass of russet-gold hair. Henry VII smiles with considerable satisfaction. He comes to take her hand.*)

HENRY VII: Welcome. Welcome to England.

(*She smiles shyly back.*)

CATHERINE: Gracias Majestad, estoy nuy complacio a de Encontrarme ya en Inglaterra.

HENRY (*Slightly embarrassed at the Spanish*): My son—Prince Arthur—your future husband.

(*Catherine's eyes go past him to Prince Arthur. Mix through Arthur to:*)

iii

Interior. Worcester Cathedral. Night.

(*A coffin being lowered into a tomb, to the sound of a heavy tolling of a bell and plainsong. Henry VII,*

9

dressed in black, his face stiff with grief, stands watching it, his arm round the shoulder of a sturdy, fair-haired boy of ten, Prince Henry, also in black. In the throng of nobles, find de Puebla, his face intent. A stone clangs down on the tomb. On it we can read the words: 'Arthur, Prince of Wales, Aetatis 16'. De Puebla looks from the tomb to Prince Henry. Follow his gaze from Prince Henry back to the tomb, and mix through the tomb to Titles.

Catherine of Aragon by Rosemary Anne Sisson.)

1

Interior. A gallery in Greenwich. Day. Autumn, 1505.

(Silence. The camera finds first a small, very shabby pair of embroidered slippers, the toes worn almost away. Above them, the hem of the black velvet gown is frayed. The camera moves up the torn and mended skirt, past a small, heavily-ringed pair of hands holding a book, and lingers on the mended bodice, held together by a rich brooch, before coming to rest on the face of Catherine of Aragon, sitting in an alcove of the gallery, very calm and intent on the book. She is about twenty now, her hair confined in a black head-dress, trimmed with tarnished gold. A murmur of voices in the background draws us—and the camera—further down the gallery, where the Earl of Surrey stands talking to Doctor de Puebla, the Spanish Ambassador. Surrey is a rough, soldierly, but snobbish man of about sixty.)

SURREY: Does she understand her situation?

DE PUEBLA: If you mean, my Lord of Surrey, 'does she know it'? No. She prefers not to know it.

SURREY: You mean, she is stupid.

DE PUEBLA: Ah no. Stupidity is not a matter of choice. This is. The Princess Catherine chooses not to know certain things. It is a royal attribute.

SURREY (*With an unkind laugh*): I am glad there is something 'royal' about her! Come, de Puebla, confess it! Your Princess is a pauper, a widow, and an unsuccessful suitor for the hand of her late husband's brother.

DE PUEBLA (*Quickly*): Her Royal Highness and Prince Henry are betrothed!

SURREY (*With another laugh*): 'Betrothed' is a long way from 'married', as every Ambassador knows! (*Catherine's attention is drawn by the louder voice, though she can't hear the words. She looks up, her eye rests on de Puebla, she frowns a little, and returns to her book.*) Incidentally, I've heard it said that 'her Royal Highness' has no great opinion of *her Ambassador.*

(*He points the last two words at de Puebla.*)

DE PUEBLA (*Drily*): I wonder who told you that.

(*De Puebla glances down the gallery, where Dona Elvira Manuel approaches Catherine. She is dressed more in the Spanish style than Catherine and not so shabby. Surrey follows de Puebla's glance, and they look at each other and smile.*)

SURREY: The Duenna doesn't like you, either. (*Slyly.*) Whose side is she on, I wonder?

DE PUEBLA (*Innocently*): Side?

SURREY: Does Dona Elvira support the claim of Princess Catherine's father or of her sister in their—disagreements?

DE PUEBLA: As a member of the Princess's household, she takes no part in affairs of state.

SURREY: How about Dona Elvira's brother? (*De Puebla glances at him quickly.*) Does it never occur to the Princess that the King might not wish to ally himself to a Spanish Royal family whose members are squabbling violently among themselves?

DE PUEBLA: When the Princess Catherine wants something, she sees no difficulties in the way of achieving it, and wishes to hear of none. It's another royal attribute.

SURREY: An awkward one for you.

(*De Puebla's face softens. He looks lovingly at Catherine.*)

DE PUEBLA: My poor Princess! She's very young, she's motherless, and far from home. I must do what I can for her, though she thinks I do nothing.

SURREY (*Slyly, looking at him*): You'll not make her Queen of England, do what you may.

DE PUEBLA (*Patiently*): We shall see.

CATHERINE (*Off*): Doctor de Puebla!

(*De Puebla turns quickly, and sees Dona Elvira standing behind Catherine, and smiles a little, wryly. He bows slightly to Surrey, and goes towards Catherine.*)

DE PUEBLA: Your Royal Highness?

(*Catherine glances swiftly up at Dona Elvira, showing that she has just been primed by her.*)

CATHERINE (*With fairly heavy Spanish accent*): Have you an audience with the King today?

12

DE PUEBLA: Yes, your Highness. His Majesty commanded me to wait upon him at ten o'clock this morning.

CATHERINE: Then, if you are not too busy discussing matters of interest to *his Majesty,* perhaps you would ask him for some money for me.

(*Her voice and face are calm, but the book is now in her lap, and her hands, resting on it, are tightly clasped. We follow de Puebla's eyes as he sees this, and then see his face soften again.*)

DE PUEBLA: I do ask him, your Highness, every time I—

DONA ELVIRA (*Breaking in violently*): Every time you are not engaged in making jokes, or—

DE PUEBLA (*Breaking in very coolly*): Be glad that his Majesty laughs at my jokes. When he has laughed, then he listens—a little.

DONA ELVIRA: And does nothing!

(*De Puebla takes a breath, lets it go, and spreads out his hands. Catherine has been glancing between him and Dona Elvira, and now makes an effort to assert herself.*)

CATHERINE: Dr de Puebla! (*She stands up, dropping the book. De Puebla quickly stoops and picks it up for her. Catherine is thrown by this out of her intended royal dignity. She speaks brokenly and angrily.*) My ladies—my Spanish ladies—how can they marry without dowries? They are in rags. *I* am in rags! When we are at Court, we are—disgraced. And when we are in Durham House, I cannot maintain my household. I am selling my plate to buy food.

DE PUEBLA (*Suddenly*): Your plate? Part of your dowry? Don't sell that!

CATHERINE: What else can I do? We are hungry! (*Very quietly*). We—are—hungry.

DE PUEBLA: I know. (*Gently*.) I know.

CATHERINE (*Spanish royal temper blazing out*): Then *do* something!

(*The clock begins to strike outside. De Puebla glances towards it, and then at Surrey, who straightens and prepares to leave, glancing at him. De Puebla sighs and bows to Catherine.*)

DE PUEBLA: Your Highness. I must go to his Majesty. (*Coldly, without bowing*.) Dona Elvira.

(*De Puebla walks away, joining Surrey who puts an arm round his shoulders as they walk away together.*)

DONA ELVIRA: He will do nothing, as usual. Can't you speak to the King? While we are staying here at Court—

CATHERINE: What can I say to him? Can *I* ask him for money? Can *I* beg him to let me marry his son, because if I don't, I have no place in the world? (*She puts the book down, and walks away. She is really frightened, and showing it for once...*) What will become of me? Unless I marry Prince Henry, what will become of me? How can I go back to Spain unmarried? My father would never receive me, and even if he did—(*With increasing distress.*)—What will become of me?

(*Behind her, Dona Elvira looks pleased, as though a desired opportunity has just opened before her.*)

DONA ELVIRA: Have you thought of appealing to your sister?

CATHERINE (*Turns*): My sister?

DONA ELVIRA: Queen Juana.

CATHERINE (*Frowning, puzzled*): Would she help me?

(*Dona Elvira is subtly gratified again, as though she has advanced another step.*)

DONA ELVIRA: If she were to come here—with her husband—If she saw and understood your situation, assuredly she would help you.

(*Catherine hesitates, still puzzled. Dona Elvira glances in the direction in which de Puebla has gone.*)

That vulgar, low-bred little man! How can your father employ him as Ambassador? King Henry likes him because he, too, is ill-bred and parsimonious!

CATHERINE (*Slightly on her dignity*): Dona Elvira, my father-in-law—

DONA ELVIRA: Is apt to forget that you are a Royal Princess of Spain. But if he saw you with your sister—

(*She pauses. Catherine glances at her, thinking it over.*)

DONA ELVIRA: Why not write to your sister, and tell her how you long to see her—and her husband—here in England?

(*Catherine looks at her, hesitating, and then suddenly, joyfully, smiles her assent.*)

2

Interior Study/Council Room. Day.

(*Close up of King Henry VII laughing at something de Puebla has just said. He likes de Puebla and they understand each other. They are devious together, rarely deceive each other, but enjoy the exercise.*)

HENRY VII: But then, de Puebla, you know that people would always rather be robbed than pay taxes.

DE PUEBLA: That depends, your Majesty, what the taxes are for.

HENRY VII: True. Very true. If they are for war— good! Everyone is happy. Tell the people they are to be killed and pillaged, their homes destroyed, their women raped, and they must pay for it into the bargain, and they are perfectly agreeable. Give them what I have given them—years of peace and good government, and then say this must be paid for, and they will hate you for ever. So you see—(*Looking at him slyly.*)—since I don't wish to go to war, I have to be as economical as I can. (*Pause. De Puebla is momentarily stymied.*) The Princess Dowager is short of money, is she?

DE PUEBLA (*As though hard of hearing*): The—? Er—? The—? (*Suddenly enlightened.*) Oh! The Princess of Wales.

HENRY VII: Not yet.

DE PUEBLA: She and Prince Henry were betrothed.

HENRY VII (*Casually*): But then, when he was fifteen—

DE PUEBLA (*Casually making his contribution*): The age at which the marriage was to take place—

16

HENRY VII (*Ignoring this*): The Prince protested against the betrothal.

DE PUEBLA (*Startled*): He did?

HENRY VII: On the grounds that it contravened canon law for him to marry his late brother's wife.

DE PUEBLA (*Quickly*): There is a Papal dispensation! (*Henry VII slightly inclines his head, the hint of a smile on his lips. De Puebla eyes him fixedly.*) Was the protest made publicly?

HENRY VII (*Looking at him sideways*): Before a— select—company.

DE PUEBLA (*Comprehending*): So that if, at any time in the future—

HENRY VII: Precisely. (*Pause. Close up of de Puebla endeavouring to conceal his dismay. Henry VII decides on near-candour.*) See here, my good friend. When you persuaded me into this marriage—

DE PUEBLA (*Politely demurring*): Er—

HENRY VII (*After a moment, smiling grimly*): Very well. When you persuaded King Ferdinand of Aragon and Queen Isabella of Castile to allow their daughter to marry my son, Arthur, she brought with her the goodwill of all Spain to be powerful buttress against the enmity of France. But now, Queen Isabella is dead. Her daughter, Juana, is Queen of Castile, and they say she and her husband are plotting to seize Aragon as well. (*De Puebla looks slightly startled. Henry VII smiles, gratified.*) So what benefit could there be now in a marriage between Prince Henry and Princess Catherine?

(*De Puebla opens his mouth to reply. Henry VII swiftly interposes.*)

Especially since King Ferdinand hasn't even paid the second part of her dowry!

DE PUEBLA (*Delicately*): I understand—when Prince Arthur died—there was some question of returning the first part of the dowry.

HENRY VII (*With absolute finality*): There was never any question of returning the first part of the dowry! (*He and de Puebla look at each other, and smile openly. Henry VII stands up.*) Well, you will write to King Ferdinand about the terms on which our merchants may trade with Spain?

DE PUEBLA: Yes, your Majesty.

HENRY VII: And tell him you understand his daughter is in need of money. (*De Puebla opens his mouth, shuts it, and bows and turns away.*) By the way, you had better warn Princess Catherine to be careful how she sells her plate. (*De Puebla looks startled.*) Its value, you may remember, was to form the third part of her dowry. (*De Puebla looks at him hopelessly, bows again, and turns towards the door. As he reaches it—*) De Puebla—(*He turns, Henry VII has sat down at his desk and picked up his pen. He speaks casually.*) I understand Queen Juana, Princess Catherine's sister, has a daughter of marriageable age.

(*De Puebla looks at him, horrified. Henry VII smiles and begins to write his accounts in a small, crabbed hand.*)

3

Interior. The gallery in Greenwich. Day.

(*Catherine, smiling with new hope and pleasure, sits reading through the letter she has just written. She stands up as de Puebla comes into the gallery, and is so happy that she speaks to him as he comes near.*)

CATHERINE: Doctor de Puebla!

DE PUEBLA: Your Royal Highness, I'm afraid his Majesty—

CATHERINE: I have written to my sister!

DE PUEBLA: To your—? To which of your—?

CATHERINE: To my sister, Queen Juana of Castile, suggesting that she and her husband should visit me here.

(*De Puebla stares at her.*)

CATHERINE: You see, Dona Elvira cares what becomes of me, though you do not!

DE PUEBLA: Dona Elvira? Did *she* suggest—?

CATHERINE (*Smiling*): Here is the letter. As soon as my sister receives it—

DE PUEBLA (*Too eagerly*): Let me send it for you!

(*He holds his hand out for it. Catherine draws back, looking at him suspiciously.*)

CATHERINE: No. Dona Elvira will send it for me.

(*She turns and walks past him. De Puebla looks after her horrified.*)

DE PUEBLA: Your Royal Highness! You must believe me! If you send that letter—(*Catherine turns and looks at him coldly. De Puebla is agitated enough to speak the truth.*) The King is considering a marriage between Prince Henry and Queen Juana's daughter, Eleanor!

(*Catherine's face doesn't change, but she looks at him closely and slowly returns.*)

19

CATHERINE: But Dona Elvira said—

DE PUEBLA (*Desperately truthful, still*): Dona Elvira's brother is in Flanders, plotting with your sister against your father.

CATHERINE: Dona Elvira has been my Duenna ever since she came to England with me. She has been— she has been like a mother to me. I would trust her as I trusted my own mother.

DE PUEBLA: Your Royal Highness—did you live for fifteen years in the court of Spain and have lived five years more at the English court—and you still haven't learnt that you can trust nobody?

CATHERINE (*Coldly*): Not even you, Doctor de Puebla?

(*He hesitates. His eyes fall for a moment, and then he looks up.*)

DE PUEBLA: You can trust me in one thing. I've fought for this marriage for nearly twenty years. I won't see it destroyed.

CATHERINE (*Coldly*): There is no question of that. Prince Henry and I are betrothed.

(*De Puebla looks at her hopelessly. Her eyes go past him as Dona Elvira comes into the gallery.*)

DE PUEBLA: Your Royal Highness—

CATHERINE: At your next audience with King Henry, you will please ask him for some money for the expenses of my household when I return to Durham House. (*De Puebla sags, defeated.*) And ask his Majesty to be so good as to supply me with a new Duenna. (*De Puebla looks at her quickly.*) Now, please leave me.

(*De Puebla hesitates, reaching out his hand for the letter.*)

DE PUEBLA : Shall I . . .?

CATHERINE (*Eyes on Dona Elvira*): Leave me! (*De Puebla goes, passing Dona Elvira, who gives him a little smile of triumph, as they pass. Catherine tears up the letter. Dona Elvira sees her do it, and pauses, startled.*) Dona Elvira! (*Their eyes meet.*)

4

Interior. A Study/Council Room. Evening.

(*Henry VII stands in the dusk looking out of the casement window at the river.*)

HENRY VII : So the Princess's Duenna has gone to— visit her brother in Flanders.

(*He speaks without looking round. De Puebla stands eyeing him rather uneasily.*)

DE PUEBLA : Rather unexpectedly.

HENRY VII (*Glancing round at him*) : Very unexpectedly. Will she be gone for long?

DE PUEBLA : Almost—um—indefinitely, I think. That's why her Royal Highness—

HENRY VII : The Princess Catherine certainly can't go on living at Durham House without a Duenna. My mother would be greatly shocked at the idea.

DE PUEBLA : So if some noble English lady could be found who . . .

HENRY VII: But, after all, when she is visiting the Court, she is under the protection of my mother.

DE PUEBLA: Yes, your Majesty, but when she returns to her own household at Durham House—

HENRY VII: Why should she?

DE PUEBLA: Your Majesty?

HENRY VII: She is always complaining of the expense of her household, and here is a way of saving it. (*He turns away from the window.*) Yes. That is the answer. In future she can live at Court all the time. That will save her the expense of her household, and save me the trouble of finding her another Duenna. A very happy solution—don't you think?

(*He eyes de Puebla with an innocent, happy smile. De Puebla looks ruefully back at him.*)

5

Interior. The alcove in Greenwich. Night.

(*Catherine sitting at a table where a candle is burning. Maria de Salinas, her young lady-in-waiting, stands looking at her anxiously. She is as shabbily dressed as Catherine, but a naturally cheerful, warmhearted, attractive Spanish girl. Francesca de Carceres, another young lady-in-waiting, colder and more calculating, is standing on the other side.*)

CATHERINE: So I am to lose my household! I am to live at Court like—like a pensioner! A pensioner without a pension. How am I to pay my servants? All my Spanish servants? I brought them here; I am responsible for them. And my ladies—how am I to find you dowries?

FRANCESCA: Dowries, your Highness? If we could have enough money for a new dress, that would be something.

(*Catherine glances at her, troubled. Maria glares at Francesca.*)

MARIA (*Under her breath*): Francesca!

CATHERINE: I know it's hard for you, but—

MARIA (*Cheerfully*): Don't worry about us, your Highness. If we have no dowries, the Englishmen must take us without!

(*Catherine looks at her desperately troubled. Maria suddenly puts her arm round her and kisses her. Catherine returns her kiss, and then is nearly in tears, but fights them back.*)

CATHERINE: Oh Maria—if I were married, then as Princess of Wales I would have my own income, even during the King's lifetime. The marriage treaty was signed years ago. All de Puebla had to do was to arrange the marriage, and instead of that he accuses . . . ! I believe the whole affair was a plot between him and King Henry to rob me of my household and to save King Henry money! And now de Puebla says he is ill in bed and can't see me! (*Suddenly.*) I shall write to my father. I shall write to my father and beg him to send me a new Ambassador.

(*She pulls a piece of paper towards her and begins to write in large, angry writing.*)

6

Interior. De Puebla's lodgings. Day.

(*Close up of Don Gutierre Gomez de Fuensalida, chest swelling and gold-chained, looking highly pleased with himself. He is a large, self-satisfied Spaniard, richly dressed, the sort of upper-class character who moves triumphantly from diplomatic post to diplomatic post, making a dreadful hash of them all, but much too self-satisfied ever to realize it.*)

FUENSALIDA: The English are like children—only docile when they're roughly treated. (*The camera moves round to receive de Puebla's reaction to this. De Puebla is in bed with gout. The bedroom is shabby, and de Puebla, short of money, as usual, looks dirty and ill-kempt. Fuensalida looks round the room distastefully.*) You have to show them who's master.

DE PUEBLA: And when you've done that Don Fuensalida?

FUENSALIDA: Then they give in.

DE PUEBLA: King Henry will give nothing until he receives the second part of the dowry.

FUENSALIDA: I've brought that with me.

(*De Puebla sits up suddenly, hurts his foot, and sinks back.*)

DE PUEBLA: King Ferdinand sent the money? In full?

FUENSALIDA (*Surprised*): Naturally.

DE PUEBLA (*Smiles ruefully*): Does the Princess know?

FUENSALIDA: I haven't seen her yet. I am told it is not etiquette for me to visit any member of the royal household before I see the King. (*De Puebla looks slightly incredulous. Fuensalida swells contentedly.*) I am seeing the English King tomorrow. I shall tell him that we have kept our part of the bargain and expect him to fulfil his obligations without delay.

(*He turns away.*)

DE PUEBLA (*Softly, to himself*): I hope King Henry laughs at your jokes as he did at mine.

(*Note: This and the ensuing scenes, 7—13, are intended to form a sort of swiftly-moving montage of Fuensalida's disastrous embassage. The settings are unimportant, and it could almost be played against black. No recording breaks are intended.*)

7

Interior. Study/Council Room. Day.

(*Henry VII is sitting in a large chair to receive Fuensalida. He is ill, and still suffers from rheumatism and bad temper, but is struggling to be amiable.*)

HENRY VII: I am delighted to know that my dear friend, King Ferdinand, can now meet his obligations in the matter of Princess Catherine's dowry. The Princess is—

FUENSALIDA (*Loudly interrupting*): His Majesty, the illustrious King of Aragon will be glad to hear that you are prepared to keep your word—at last.

(*Henry VII stiffens and looks at him in silence for a moment.*)

HENRY VII: I always keep my word.

8

Interior. Study / Council Room. Day.

(Doctor Fox, Bishop of Winchester, sits presiding with the Earl of Surrey and three or four other Lords and Clerics. Opposite them sits Fuensalida.)

FOX *(Reading from a paper)*: Don—Gutierre—Gomez de Fuensalida.

(Evidently pleased to have got it right, he smiles and nods his head to Fuensalida.)

FUENSALIDA: I have brought sixty-five thousand ducats of Aragon—

SURREY *(Quickly)*: Of Aragon?

FUENSALIDA: Which are worth more than the escudos of Castile mentioned in the treaty.

(Surrey glances at Fox, who nods, and Surrey subsides.)

FUENSALIDA: I now claim, on behalf of his Serene Highness King Ferdinand of Aragon, the fulfilment of the said marriage treaty.

FOX *(Smoothly)*: This is what we all desire, Ambassador, and King Henry, who dearly loves the Princess, desires it more than anyone. *(Fuensalida looks highly gratified. Stay on his face, as Fox continues.)* You have brought the 65,000 ducats—and, I trust, also the jewels and plate which were to form the third part of the dowry?

(Fuensalida's face changes.)

FUENSALIDA: You know very well, Bishop, that the Princess brought the jewels and plate with her in fifteen hundred and one!

FOX: We know no such thing. What she brought then was her own property.

FUENSALIDA (*Beginning to bluster*): It was part of the dowry!

FOX (*Smoothly*): On the contrary, it was her own personal property, her—er—household goods, and, on her husband's death, reverted to his heir, that is, King Henry, although he has kindly allowed Princess Catherine to continue to use it. Are you suggesting that the Princess's dowry should be paid to the King with the King's own goods?

(*Fuensalida stands up and glares at them with his mouth open in furious indignation.*)

FUENSALIDA: But ...

9

Interior. De Puebla's lodgings. Night.

(*De Puebla groans slightly and closes his eyes. Then he opens them and sighs resignedly, like someone treading a well-worn path.*)

DE PUEBLA: They *must* accept the Princess's plate and jewels. It was expressly stated in the marriage treaty. Of course, all depletions will have to be made good. I warned King Ferdinand that the Princess was having to sell her plate, but he took no notice. What I would suggest is that—

(*He pauses, opens his mouth and shuts it again. Fuensalida has evidently gone.*)

10

Interior. Another room in Greenwich. Day.

(*Fuensalida standing by the open window, with an occasional clop-clop from horses being groomed below. Catherine sits in the room, with Maria and Francesca.*)

FUENSALIDA: It is outrageous! Simply outrageous that you should have had to sell your plate! Mind, I'm afraid, your Highness, that you have been guilty of some extravagance.

CATHERINE: Extravagance!

FUENSALIDA (*Indulgently smiling at the little woman*): But there! These are not matters for you to trouble your head with. You have been having to act as your own ambassador, I know, for the past three years, but now I am here to guide you, I will take such things off your shoulders.

(*Catherine nods and smiles, but she is not altogether happy.*)

FRANCESCA (*Under her breath to Maria*): Will he buy us food?

(*Maria frowns at her angrily. Fuensalida hears.*)

FUENSALIDA: Yes, your Highness, if you will forgive my mentioning it, the quality of your purveying leaves much to be desired. The fish that was served at your table at dinner—why, I wouldn't give it to my horse-boy! Your Highness, it was stale!

CATHERINE: Yes, I know.

FUENSALIDA: You *know*?

CATHERINE: If you buy fish in the market which is a day old, it doesn't cost as much.

FUENSALIDA (*Still incredulous*): You mean that you buy stale fish for your table because it is cheaper?

CATHERINE: Of course. It is better than going hungry.

(*Fuensalida stares at her, aghast. A louder clop-clop than usual draws his attention to the window. He sniffs.*)

FUENSALIDA: Are these rooms over the stables?

CATHERINE: I believe so. Yes.

FUENSALIDA: But that is abominable! That you, of all people, should suffer the noise and—and odour of—and in this hot weather, too!

CATHERINE (*Indifferent*): I am used to it. My rooms are usually at the top of the house or over the stables.

FUENSALIDA: It is very plain to see, your Royal Highness, that you have had no one here to maintain your interests since you came to England. You may be sure that I shall complain in the strongest terms both to your father and to King Henry.

CATHERINE (*Beginning to be alarmed*): No! No, don't—

FUENSALIDA: And I noticed that you were not given your correct precedence when you dined with the King yesterday.

CATHERINE (*Impatiently*): Oh, what does that matter? As soon as I am married, I shall have my proper place by right, and all these—these slights and discomforts will be forgotten.

FUENSALIDA (*Swelling*): Not by me! You are a royal Princess of Spain, and I owe it to myself and to my royal master to ensure that you are treated by these English with all due honour and observance! (*He bows.*) Your Royal Highness! (*He goes out.*)

FRANCESCA (*Smiling*): At last it seems that your Highness has found a champion.

CATHERINE: Yes. (*She looks after Fuensalida in dismay, and her eye meets Maria's.*) Yes.

11

Interior. The Council Room. Day.

(*Bishop Fox, Surrey, and the Council sitting facing Fuensalida.*)

FOX (*Glancing at Surrey*): We understand, Ambassador, that you are now prepared to discuss the possibility of King Ferdinand making good the depletions in Princess Catherine's plate and jewels.

FUENSALIDA: I am. Though in fact there would have been no need for any depletions if King Henry had made proper provision for the Princess's maintenance.

(*Swift close up of Fox's face with a surprised twitch of pleasure as he sees that ass Fuensalida giving him an opportunity for pointless wrangling.*)

FOX: I should have thought that it was the duty of a *father* to provide for his unmarried daughter.

FUENSALIDA: Princess Catherine is a widow.

SURREY (*Happily joining in*): But we have always been given to understand that the marriage with Prince Arthur was not consummated, and therefore—

FUENSALIDA: That has nothing to do with it! Princess Catherine is living in England and is betrothed to the Prince of Wales. Your King is notorious for meanness and double-dealing, but I should have thought that even he—

FOX (*Rises violently to his feet*): I refuse to listen to another word! (*He glances at Surrey who, taken by surprise, rather belatedly gets to his feet as well.*) While the Spanish Ambassador sees fit to insult our King, the Council must utterly refuse to meet with him! Let alone discuss the marriage!

(*He glances at the others, who also rise to their feet, and stalks out of the room. Fuensalida, openmouthed, slowly rises to his feet.*)

FUENSALIDA: But—but—how can we discuss the marriage?

(*Surrey to his companion, as he walks out of the room:*)

SURREY: How, indeed? (*He grins and goes on his way.*)

12

Interior. De Puebla's bedroom. Day.

(*De Puebla, weaker and more weary, lying back on his pillows.*)

DE PUEBLA: The English *want* to delay the discussions. King Henry has another marriage in mind for the Prince. He's waiting to see whether King Ferdinand can defeat his enemies before he finally commits himself.

(*Fuensalida somewhat deflated, lurking hopefully by the bed, instead of straddling the room.*)

FUENSALIDA: Then what do you suggest?

DE PUEBLA: I suggest nothing. I am ill. I am ill.

FUENSALIDA (*Uneasily*): The—er—the Princess told me that she had sent you her own physician.

DE PUEBLA (*Smiling a little*): Yes. Her own physician, and—her wishes for my recovery. (*Looking up at Fuensalida.*) King Henry, too, is not well. You know that?

FUENSALIDA: Huh! Well, or ill, he has delayed long enough! You must see him. You must tell him—

DE PUEBLA (*Sitting up, furiously*): *I* must see him? I tell you, I can do no more! I can do no more. (*He lies back and glares up at Fuensalida.*) Do you think you can twist the King of England's ears?

13

Interior. Study/Council Room. Day.

(*Henry VII limps over to the window, and turns wincing slightly. His rheumatism is bad, and his temper increasingly uncertain, but, again, he's making an effort.*)

HENRY VII: I understand that King Ferdinand has now sent enough money to cover the value of the missing plate.

FUENSALIDA (*Standing ready for battle*): He has. And now he expects forthwith the public betrothal of Prince Henry and Princess Catherine.

HENRY VII: I shall need, of course, a paper renouncing in full the dower rights of the Princess.

FUENSALIDA (*Taken by surprise*): Dower—? Er—?

HENRY VII (*Patiently explaining*): The land and property she would hold as Princess Dowager.

FUENSALIDA (*Instantly reacting*): That is out of the question.

HENRY VII (*Outraged*): Out of the—? Do you dare to tell me that—

FUENSALIDA: And it is a suggestion which, in your position, the King of Aragon would have been ashamed to make.

HENRY VII (*Almost speechless*): *Ashamed*? The King of Aragon was not ashamed to allow his daughter to live like a pauper in a foreign country!

FUENSALIDA (*Calm and self-satisfied*): My King does not keep his money locked away in chests. He gives it to his victorious soldiers. You should remember this, and take care how far you provoke him.

(*Henry VII really is speechless this time. He turns away, almost apoplectic. Bangs his knee on a chair, and is in agony for a moment, and then speaks in a stifled voice without turning round.*)

HENRY VII: Go away! Go away!

14

Interior. The gallery in Greenwich. Day.

(*Catherine, attended by Maria and Francesca, is staring aghast, at Fuensalida.*)

CATHERINE: The *dower* rights? But I renounced those on the signing of the marriage treaty! I renounced those six years ago! Do you think I want the title of Princess Dowager? I am the Princess of Wales. I am betrothed to Prince Henry. Shall I need dower rights when I am Queen of England? Go to the King at once, and—

FUENSALIDA: I can't do that.

CATHERINE: Why? Why can't you?

FUENSALIDA (*Slightly aggrieved*): Because the King has said that he refuses to see me again.

(*Catherine stares at him for a moment.*)

CATHERINE: Then if the King will not see you, neither will I. (*She sees a group of people entering the gallery.*) I will not be seen in your company. Leave me!

(*Fuensalida, open-mouthed with indignation, bows and retires.*)

FRANCESCA: Your Highness, it is the Prince!

(*Catherine looks down the gallery. Henry, a tall, broad-shouldered, golden-haired young man, is surrounded by tutors and clerics. He is clean-shaven and very plainly dressed, and carries a book. Catherine in a moment of panic, turns towards the alcove, and then gets command of herself and stands calmly waiting, though with tightly clasped hands. Francesca and Maria glance at each other behind her. The solemn, slow-moving group draws near, a gloomy-faced tutor talking to Henry.*)

HENRY: But then, can we make such a distinction between human and divine learning?

TUTOR: Surely, my Lord—

HENRY: It's true the Bible comes from God, but then God gave man also his mind, and therefore human learning also comes from God.

TUTOR: Doesn't that mean, your Highness, that you are setting up your mind in opposition to God's?

HENRY: No. It means that I want to use all God's gifts to His glory, as best I may.

(*He draws level with Catherine. She curtseys, with the two girls, and as she rises from her curtsey, her eyes meet his. He smiles rather shyly, and bows, and passes on.*)

TUTOR: That would suggest that the mind of a pagan was of the same value as the mind of the Pope.

(*They pass on down the gallery and out of sight. Catherine turns aside into the alcove. Francesca glances at Maria and quickly follows her.*)

FRANCESCA: Your Highness, it is hopeless! We must go back to Spain!

CATHERINE: To Spain? Never!

FRANCESCA: Your Highness, this marriage will never take place. (*Deliberately echoing her.*) Never! (*Catherine stares at her.*) How long is it since Prince Arthur died? More than six years! And your marriage to Prince Henry is further away than ever. Everyone knows it, your Highness. Everyone—except yourself. (*Maria, behind her, makes a gesture of dismay.*) Don Fuensalida knows that it is hopeless. (*She hesitates.*) He is making arrangements to send your dowry out of the country.

CATHERINE (*In a sudden blaze of anger*): Fuensalida is a traitor, and you are a traitor, too, to speak of going back to Spain. Do not ever speak to me of it

35

again! (*Francesca, frightened, turns and runs out of the alcove. Catherine looks defiantly at Maria.*) I suppose you, too, wish to go back to Spain.

MARIA (*Very gently*): Your Highness, wherever you go, I will go.

(*Catherine, broken by the kind tones, bursts into tears. Maria comes quickly to put her arms around her. Catherine raises her head.*)

CATHERINE: I am betrothed to Prince Henry. My mother wished the marriage to take place. I would rather die than go back to Spain unmarried. I would rather die!

(*She breaks down again, and sobs in Maria's arms.*)

MARIA: Oh, your Highness! Your Highness.

(*Fade on her compassionate face.*)

15

Interior. A room at Richmond. Night.

(*A bell heavily and slowly tolling. Close up of Henry VII's pinched, dead face, lying on a rather shabby bed. Henry kneels beside the bed, his hand over his face, crying quietly. He takes his hand away, crosses himself devoutly, stands up and steps back, looking sadly down at his dead father. Fox and Surrey put hands on his shoulders and lead him away.*)

16

Interior. The gallery at Greenwich. Day.

(In the alcove, Catherine sits reading her missal, outside Maria is talking to Lord Willoughby, an attractive young man, very much in love with her.)

WILLOUGHBY: The Council has met twice already. I'm told they were discussing the matter of Prince—of the King's marriage.

MARIA *(Glancing at Catherine)*: His marriage to whom?

WILLOUGHBY: There is one party for a French marriage, to Margaret d'Alençon, and one for the Hapsburg Princess Eleanor.

MARIA: But none for—?

(Willoughby shakes his head.)

WILLOUGHBY: None that I've heard of.

MARIA: What will become of her? If—? What will become of her!

WILLOUGHBY: I am more concerned with what becomes of you.

MARIA *(Quickly)*: Lord Willoughby—*(She checks and smiles.)* The Princess comes first with me. She always will. If she goes back to Spain, I shall go with her.

WILLOUGHBY: Would her father welcome her back in Spain—unmarried?

(Maria looks at him, dismayed.)

MARIA: Perhaps if she could speak to the King . . .

WILLOUGHBY (*Smiling*): What good would that do? I suppose there has never been a young man so protected from the world. He's lived all his life with priests and tutors. One had to pass through the old King's room to reach his bedchamber. He even went out into the garden by a private door. All his life he has done what he was told, and now . . .

MARIA: He will do what the Council tells him. (*Willoughby responds with a sympathetic nod and smile.*) My poor Princess! Madre de Dios! My poor Princess!

(*Willoughby puts his hand on her arm. She covers his hand with hers, and then quickly withdraws it as Surrey comes into the gallery.*)

WILLOUGHBY: The Earl of Surrey.

MARIA: He has always been the bearer of bad news.

(*Surrey comes up.*)

SURREY: I was told that her Royal Highness was in the gallery.

MARIA: Yes, she—

(*Catherine looks up. Surrey glances at Willoughby and Maria, and respectfully takes off his hat and bows low to Catherine.*)

SURREY: Your Royal Highness.

(*Willoughby looks quickly at Maria. She returns his look, puzzled. Catherine crosses herself and closes her book.*)

CATHERINE: My Lord?

SURREY: His Majesty begs to be allowed to wait upon your Highness.

CATHERINE: His-His Majesty? Yes, I... (*Endeavouring to assume her royal dignity.*) I shall be glad to receive the King. When—When will his Majesty...?

SURREY (*Glancing back*): When I left his Majesty, he was already...

CATHERINE (*Standing up*): You mean... He is coming here now?

(*Surrey bows. Willoughby and Maria look at each other in amazement. As Henry comes into the gallery, wearing black and unattended, Catherine tries to brace herself for the encounter. Surrey and Willoughby bow to Henry, and Maria curtseys. Henry sees Catherine and stops short. Surrey, Willoughby and Maria stand aside. Henry and Catherine look at each other for a moment, and then he bows and she curtseys. As they rise again they look at each other gravely, both uncertain and ill-at-ease.*)

HENRY: Your Royal Highness.

CATHERINE: Your Majesty.

HENRY: Thank you for receiving me with—with so little warning.

CATHERINE: May I express the sorrow that I feel for the death of your father? He was like a father to me, too.

HENRY: Thank you. (*He hesitates.*) He expressed a dying wish, which I hope you will help me to fulfil. That's why—that's why I've come to see you.

(*Catherine is terrified, sure that he is going to ask her to renounce their betrothal. She is silent for a moment, and then looks at him directly.*)

CATHERINE: Your Majesty, I will do... (*With a touch of despair.*) I will do whatever *you* wish.

(*Henry hesitates. There is a moment of suspense.*) . . .

HENRY: My father's last request was . . . (*Catherine's hands clasp tightly as Henry hesitates again.*) It was that you and I should be married as soon as possible. (*Catherine looks at him incredulously. He comes a step nearer, takes her hand, and smiles, all his warmth and charm suddenly flowing out towards her.*) And, Catherine, dearest Catherine . . . it is my wish, too!

(*He kisses her hand, and holds it lovingly in both his. She looks up at him, dazed with joy.*)

17

Interior. The Council Room. Day.

(*The table is piled with papers, and there is a general bustle and coming and going between this room and the next one. Fox, Surrey and the others are all busy and happy. Fuensalida sits opposite.*)

FOX: Well, Ambassador, we were surprised not to hear from you before this. His Majesty is anxious that the wedding should take place as soon as possible.

FUENSALIDA: Yes, so I—er—The money. I—er—I cannot immediately—the full sum is not now in England, and . . .

FOX: No doubt there are many merchants in London who, at the request of the Princess, would be glad to furnish you with what you need.

FUENSALIDA (*Startled at the thought*): Oh. Yes. Er—Yes. Then there is the question of the dower rights. I don't know whether Prince Henry . . .

FOX (*Smiling*): The *King*, Ambassador.

FUENSALIDA (*Confused and embarrassed*): Yes. The King . . .

FOX: Is a man very much in love. I think you may safely leave the question of the Princess's dower rights to him!

FUENSALIDA: Yes. Yes. Then—the plate! The—the Princess's plate and jewels.

FOX (*Rising*): Come, come Ambassador, let us not waste time over trifles.

FUENSALIDA: T-trifles? (*He gets dazedly to his feet.*)

FOX: As you see, the Council is busy with many great affairs. The King relies upon you to hasten the settlement of all these details.

FUENSALIDA (*Dazedly*): Details?

(*Fox puts a kindly arm round his shoulder and walks him to the door.*)

FOX: With regard to the marriage settlement, no doubt you will arrange matters as quickly as may be, according to the treaty formerly agreed.

(*He pats him on the shoulder and turns back towards the table where the others are already immersed in business again.*)

FUENSALIDA: Bishop, may I—er—may I see the Princess?

(*Fox turns back into the camera and smiles.*)

FOX: That is for the Princess to say.

FUENSALIDA: I—she—I—

FOX: Write the Princess a letter, Ambassador, and I will ask the King to intercede for you. (*He glances, smiling towards the other room.*) No doubt she will see you—though I must tell you, she is very busy with arrangements for the Coronation. After all, the Princess is now mistress of England.

(*He smiles again, and turns away. Fuensalida stares after him, stunned and confused.*)

18

Exterior. A street in London. Day.

Henry and Catherine in close-up, the background blurred, as they ride along (or indeed could be stationary) surrounded by a deafening roar of cheers and cries. Henry wears white and gold, and Catherine is dressed in white satin decorated with pearls, her red-gold hair down her back, dressed with flowers, a white mantilla on her head. Both look radiant with joy, surrounded by a nimbus of light, all youth and beauty and happiness.

CROWD (*Amidst the universal roar*): God save the King! God save Queen Catherine! God save the Queen!

(*Henry turns to look at Catherine with adoration. She smiles back at him.*)

19

Interior. The Queen's bedchamber. Night.

(*It is not the wedding night, but after the Coronation, when going to bed together might be described as still a novel pleasure, but an assured one. Catherine reclines, smiling, against the pillows, and Henry lies on his side across the foot of the bed, facing her. Both in nightgowns, but it's Summer, so let's pretend they've taken off their nightcaps.)*

HENRY: Not just to have a fine court and wear rich clothes and jewels. I want—

(He pauses.)

CATHERINE: What do you want?

HENRY *(Smiling)*: What do I want, beside you?

(He holds his hand out. She puts hers into it.)

How the people cheered you today!

CATHERINE: The English people have always been kind to me—even when everyone else was unkind.

HENRY: I promise you that no one will ever be unkind to you again—word of a King.

CATHERINE: I would rather have, 'Word of a Henry'.

HENRY: Word of a Henry!

(They both laugh.)

CATHERINE: What is it you want—besides me?

HENRY: I want—*(He sits up clasping his knees. She watches him lovingly.)* When my father came to the throne, England was nothing—a bankrupt country whose rulers had been fighting among themselves for generations. He's given us peace and put money in the Treasury, but—that's not enough. *(Suddenly.)* Did you know your father wants me to take an army into France?

43

(*Catherine knows about it, but doesn't much like the idea.*)

CATHERINE: Oh. Yes. (*Reluctantly doing her duty.*) He—thinks that the power of France is a danger to us all.

HENRY (*In a dream of glory*): I'll fight another Agincourt, and win back all our possessions in Bordeaux and Aquitaine. And while I'm in France, I'll make you Regent. Will you hold England for me against the Scots?

CATHERINE: I'll hold the world for you, against all comers.

(*Henry suddenly laughing flings himself full-length beside her.*)

HENRY: And then we'll bring the Golden Age back to England! That's what I really want—not just to have a rich Court, but a famous one—famous for poets and musicians and painters—famous for scholars!

CATHERINE: Oh yes! Oh yes! You already have friends among the scholars—Erasmus, Colet, Thomas More—

HENRY: They're your friends, too. That's the best of it. This is something else we can share. You're the only woman who would understand and help me. You're so wise, and learned, and—(*Suddenly.*) Catherine! Let's go hawking to-morrow!

CATHERINE: Oh yes! I love it so much.

HENRY: You ride so well.

CATHERINE: Not as well as you, but then I don't take such risks. Henry—

HENRY: And in the afternoon, we'll have a tournament, and I'll wear your favour in my helmet.

CATHERINE: Yes, but Henry, you must be careful—

HENRY: And in the evening, we'll dance. You dance so beautifully.

CATHERINE (*Laughing*): I love dancing, but I get tired before you do!

(*He puts his arm round her waist.*)

HENRY: You're such a little thing. A feather could blow you away.

CATHERINE (*Suddenly sober*): I am strong enough to bear you a son, pray God.

HENRY: Pray God.

19A

Happiness montage.

(*Henry/Catherine dancing, reading together, running through palace etc. Accompanied by happy laughter and music.*

19B

Queen's bedchamber. Night.

(*They fall on to the bed roaring with laughter— Henry becomes suddenly serious—and embraces Catherine.*)

HENRY: I tell you, Catherine, if I were free now, there is not another woman in the whole world whom I would want to marry, except you. Catherine!

(*They kiss passionately.*)

20

Interior. Gallery. Evening.

(*It is a cold day in February. The casement window opens on to a courtyard. Bells ringing joyfully outside. The Earl of Surrey in a furred gown stands by the window with Willoughby.*)

SURREY: My Lord Willoughby—I believe those bells have not stopped ringing since New Year's Day when the child was born.

WILLOUGHBY (*Smiling*): You must admit, they have good cause to ring. A son and heir for the King might keep the bells ringing for a year instead of two months—especially after that first stillborn child.

(*Surrey closes the window.*)

SURREY: The King has become worse than ever now—'Where is the Queen?' 'I must show this to the Queen!' 'The Queen must be the first to know!' Ugh! (*In a response to a surprised glance from Willoughby.*) Matrimonial devotion is a virtue, no doubt, but it can be carried to excess.

WILLOUGHBY: Surely not!

SURREY: You say that because you're about to be married yourself. Your opinion of marriage is about as reliable as that of a condemned murderer upon capital punishment. One can see no harm in it, and the other no good.

WILLOUGHBY (*Laughing*): I'm sure I shall always believe that husband and wife ought to love each other.

SURREY: But a King and Queen aren't husband and wife: they are fluctuating sources of power. While the King feels as he does towards Queen Catherine, this country will be ruled at one remove by that wily old Spanish fox, her father.

WILLOUGHBY: Don't expect me to wish the King less fond. As long as my future wife serves Queen Catherine, the Queen's happiness makes her happy, and her happiness makes me happy.

SURREY: Well, I'll join you in your raptures so far as to rejoice in the Queen's son and heir—though I think that after two months those damned bells have rung for him quite long enough—

(*The bells stop. The two men look at each other and laugh.*)

WILLOUGHBY: My Lord of Surrey, I never knew that you had such power!

(*A single bell begins to toll slowly. They look at each other, startled. Maria comes quickly along the gallery.*)

WILLOUGHBY: Maria—(*he sees her face.*) What is it?

MARIA: A message has just come from Richmond. Prince Henry—

SURREY: Not dead! The child isn't dead?

(*Maria looks at him in silence. All three glance towards the window and the tolling bell. Willoughby takes Maria's hand and presses it in sympathy, as she wipes away tears with the other hand.*)

WILLOUGHBY: How is the Queen?

MARIA: I was with her when she heard the news. Now the King is with her. No one else can comfort her as he can.

21

Interior. The Queen's bedchamber. Night.

(*Catherine and Henry both in warm gowns, she lies on the bed, sobbing, and he kneels beside her, holding her in his arms.*)

HENRY: Don't cry any more. (*Half crying himself.*) Dearest, dearest Catherine, don't cry any more.

CATHERINE: My little boy! My little boy!

HENRY: I know. I know.

CATHERINE: You wanted a son so much. I wanted to give you a son.

HENRY: We're young. We'll have more sons. We will! Nothing matters as long as we love each other!

(*Catherine lifts her head and looks at him with a face full of love and gratitude, and then holds him close and they cry in each other's arms, like children.*)

22

Interior. Anteroom in the Queen's apartments. Day. Sixteen years later.

(*It is an anteroom with chair and window-seats, and with doors leading off into the Queen's closet, bedchamber, wardrobe, etc. The Queen's ladies come and go, carrying linen or dresses or simply idling about. Above the murmur of voices and laughter rises Henry's voice.)*

HENRY (*Off*):
> Pastime with good company
> I love and shall, until I die.

22A

Interior. A room in Greenwich. Day.

(Henry sits playing the lute and singing.)

HENRY:
> Grudge who lust, but none deny.
> So God be pleased, thus live will I.
> For my pastance,
> Hunt, sing and dance,
> My heart is set.

22B

Interior. Anteroom. Day.

HENRY (*off*):
> All goodly sport
> For my comfort
> Who shall me let?

(Zoom up on face of Anne Boleyn, a girl in her twenties, with raven hair unbound and flowing down her back, a swarthy complexion, long neck, small bosom, and brilliant dark eyes. She listens to the song, smiling a little to herself. Nearby sits Inez de Venegas, a Spanish lady-in-waiting, hemming the cuff of a linen shirt.)

INEZ: The song he wrote for the Queen.

ANNE (*Idly*): Did he? Is that for the King?

INEZ (*Proudly*): Yes. One of his new shirts. Of course, I only hem them. The Queen embroiders them herself.

ANNE (*Turning her head away*): It's all she's good for.

(*Inez stitching away, doesn't take this in for a second, but when she does, she looks up horrified.*)

INEZ: Mistress Anne!

(*Anne looks back at her, smiling and raising her eyebrows.*)

ANNE: Mmm? Well, after all—eighteen years of marriage and nothing but a handful of stillborn sons.

INEZ: —And the Princess Mary!

ANNE: If you ask me, it's a judgment of God.

INEZ: On the Queen? How can you say that? There is no one so good or so devout, or who does so much for the poor—

ANNE: Yes. Buying their loyalty. But she couldn't buy a son.

(*She sees Inez's shocked, speechless look, and laughs aloud.*)

ANNE: Well, we all know it's not the *King's* fault!

INEZ: If you mean that boy . . .

ANNE: Henry Fitzroy?

INEZ (*Repressively*): We don't speak of him here.

ANNE (*Anxious to be set right*): Or of his mother Bessie Blount?

INEZ: Certainly not!

(*Anne bursts out laughing again. Inez glares at her, and returns to her sewing in a temper.*)

ANNE: Your stitches are getting very large. (*Inez stops sewing. Anne leans back. She is enjoying baiting Inez, who is fearfully loyal, but awfully dim.*) I was in France when the King made Henry Fitzroy the Duke of Richmond, but I heard that the Queen was furious. Who could wonder at it? 'Duke of Richmond.' That was the title the King's father held, before *he* became King.

INEZ: Henry Fitzroy—(*She pauses, glances round and lowers her voice.*) He would never be made King. Not a—

ANNE: A bastard? (*Carelessly.*) You're probably right. Bessie Blount was a fool.

INEZ (*Satisfied with the first half of the reply*): Princess Mary is the heir to the throne. She will be Queen one day.

ANNE: Unless the King has a legitimate son.

INEZ (*Glancing towards the Queen's closet*): Yes. Anything is possible, by the grace of God.

ANNE (*Glancing in the same direction*): Possible? *That* would need a miracle! When was her last pregnancy? Eight years ago?

INEZ (*Outraged*): Mistress Anne—

ANNE: The King doesn't even go to her bedchamber now.

51

INEZ: He does! He goes every evening, to hear Vespers with her!

ANNE: Vespers? (*This finally does it. Anne bursts into peal after peal of laughter. The other ladies, coming and going, pause, glancing at her and at each other. Maria, now the widowed Countess of Willoughby, has just come in, and pauses in the doorway, dressed in black, with a cloak and hat.*) Vespers! (*She stops laughing, and leans close to the indignant Inez.*) Haven't you heard the rumours about the King's marriage?

INEZ: Rumours? What rumours?

(*Anne gets up, smiling, and walks slowly away, still smiling and glancing back at Inez, who looks after her, frowning and bewildered, and then sees Maria and starts up.*)

INEZ: Maria! Or rather—I should say, Countess!

MARIA (*Coming to meet her*): Inez, how can you be so foolish? It is 'Maria', of course!

(*They kiss.*)

INEZ: I was so sorry to hear of the death of your husband.

MARIA: Thank you. (*She kisses her again.*) Thank you. It seemed such a short time to be happy. But I suppose we were fortunate to have that happiness at all.

INEZ: The Queen will be so pleased to have you with her again.

MARIA: How is she?

INEZ: Not well. She has not been well for so many

years now. But she never complains, and is so cheerful. You know her!

MARIA (*Tenderly*): I know her.

(*Anne laughs again, that laugh which is rather insolently loud for the Queen's apartments, and takes a lute from a young man who has just come in, and sits down to amuse herself with it. Maria looks at her, and at Inez.*)

Who is that?

INEZ (*With meaning*): Anne Boleyn.

MARIA: Oh. (*Looking at her with cold curiosity.*) She was in France when I was last at Court. So that is 'the Lady'!

INEZ: She is just like all the others—only bolder and more knowing.

MARIA: She has every reason to be knowing. No doubt she has learnt from her sister.

(*They smile at each other contemptuously. Maria looks back at Anne, playing an intricate little tune on the lute while the young man gazes at her adoringly.*)

INEZ: They say that this one is different from her sister and from all the others.

MARIA: Oh?

INEZ: They say that she has not yet given the King what he wants.

MARIA: Not—? Impossible! He'd soon lose interest, if she didn't! (*Pause.*) Or perhaps she thinks he'd soon lose interest if she did. But how long can she—delay? (*She gives a little shrug, they both look at Anne again, frowning.*) Does the Queen know about her?

INEZ: Certainly not. (*She meets Maria's eye and smiles wryly.*) The Queen—never knows.

22C

Interior. The Queen's closet. Day.

(*Catherine is praying at her prie-dieu. She is now 42, plump and dumpy, and showing signs of ill-health, but very much the Queen and richly dressed. Her hair is now drawn back behind a jewelled head-dress.*)

23

Interior. The gallery. Day.

(*Cardinal Wolsey is talking to Henry. Wolsey is a heavy-faced man, clever and energetic, now at the height of his power. Henry is now a heavily-built man of thirty-four with a red-gold beard, but still a fine, athletic figure, handsome and glowing with health.*)

WOLSEY: The Queen must be told, your Grace!

HENRY: I know.

WOLSEY: She must be told at once. (*Henry glances at him and away. Wolsey takes a deep, silent breath.*) The ecclesiastical court has found in your favour—

HENRY (*Quickly turning*): Not in my favour!

(*There's just the faint hint of a threat in this, but Wolsey rides it easily.*)

WOLSEY: It found that the marriage was open to question. Now the Pope's dispensation must be annulled. I will see to that. But your Grace must—tell the Queen.

HENRY: Yes, I—(*Turning away again.*) I mean to tell her. But it must be done—gently.

WOLSEY (*Soothingly*): Of course, your Grace. You can simply tell her that you have doubts as to the validity of your marriage, that an ecclesiastical court has confirmed those doubts, and that you are seeking the Pope's assistance. Meanwhile you think it best to separate. (*Henry looks at him and frowns, and then moves away. Wolsey eyes him with some exasperation.*) If you go on living with her after you have—discovered—the illegality of the marriage, you will endanger your marriage with the French Princess.

(*Quick close up of Henry's face with a new secretiveness on it.*)

HENRY: But you think we can obtain a divorce?

WOLSEY: Oh yes. There should be no difficulty about that, with the Queen's consent. And, after all, it is now a marriage in name only, and the terms you offer are very generous. Why should she refuse?

24

Interior. The Queen's closet. Day.

(*Princess Mary sits reading to Catherine, who is embroidering one of the shirts. Mary is eleven, and old for her age, but very slight in build. A round face, like her mother's, with straight red hair drawn back from her face and flowing down her back. Her dress is richly embroidered with jewels. There is a fireplace in the room (empty, because it is Summer) and a table and chairs, and a prie-dieu before a private altar.*)

MARY (*Reading*): 'For they judge it a great point of cruelty, that anybody in their most need of help and comfort, should be cast off and forsaken, and that old age, which both bringeth sickness with it, and is a sickness itself, should unkindly and unfaithfully be dealt withal. But now and then it chanceth, whereas the man and the woman cannot well agree between themselves, both of them finding other, with whom they hope to live more quietly and merrily, that they by the full consent of them both be divorced asunder and married again to other. But that not without the authority of the Council.' (*Catherine has stopped her sewing and listens with a distant, thoughtful look on her face. She glances quickly towards the door as it opens and Henry comes in. She smiles, and Mary jumps up, smiling happily, and curtseys. Henry pauses, dismayed to find Mary there.*)

CATHERINE: My dear Lord! We are so pleased to see you.

(*She holds out her hand to him, and he comes to kiss it. She keeps his hand.*)

HENRY: What are you reading?

CATHERINE: Mary is reading Thomas More's *Utopia*.

HENRY: *Utopia*?

(*He moves towards Mary, making the excuse to release Catherine's hand, and puts his other hand on Mary's head. She smiles adoringly up at him, and he pulls her cap off and runs his hand through her hair.*)

Age, mea filia, eumne comprehendis? (*He takes the book, still open, and smiles at her.*)

MARY: *Plurium vero, mi pater; et ea quae non comprehendo, mater mea mihi explicat.* (*Glancing affectionately towards Catherine.*)

CATHERINE (*Smiling*): I can well explain it, since Thomas More has explained it first to me. He came to supper with us yesterday, and was so pleasant and merry. We were sorry that you could not be with us.

(*Henry gives Mary back her cap, and turns away.*)

HENRY: I had some—business.

(*He glances at Catherine uneasily, but she smiles and nods.*)

CATHERINE: Mary, set a chair for his Grace.

HENRY: I—(*He puts the book down as Mary pulls the chair forward, looking adoringly up at him.*) I would like to speak to you—alone.

(*Catherine glances at him in an infinitesimal flash of alarm, but immediately smiles again.*)

CATHERINE: Of course. Mary, my love, go back to the Countess of Salisbury now.

MARY: Yes, madam. (*She goes to Catherine, who kisses her fondly, and Mary curtseys to Henry, but he holds out his arms and she goes to him. He bends down to hold her close, and kisses her gently on the lips.*)

HENRY (*With unfeigned affection*): My dear little Mary!

(*She goes to the door, curtseys to them both and goes out. They look after her, smiling lovingly, and then look at each other.*)

CATHERINE: Won't you sit down, my Lord?

HENRY: No, I—(*He walks about, getting his courage up. Catherine waits composedly.*) Are Mary's tutors pleased with her?

CATHERINE: Very pleased! I think she loves to learn more than she loves to play. (*Smiling.*) Do you remember what you once said to me?

HENRY (*Rather uneasily*): Said to you?

CATHERINE: About establishing learning in the land. Mary is your daughter in that. One day, she, too, will help to unite all Europe in one noble Christian fellowship of learning.

(*Henry doesn't like this at all. He nearly says what he's come for, but pauses, and postpones it again.*)

HENRY: How is her music? Is she—is she practising as she should?

CATHERINE: Ah yes, she loves it dearly. She knows how much you love it, and she longs to please you. You haven't heard her play for a long time.

HENRY: No. No, I've been—I haven't been able to—I've been—(*He is finally propelled into saying it.*) Catherine—(*In a rush*)—I am greatly troubled in my mind.

CATHERINE (*After a second*): What is it? Can I help?

HENRY: Yes. (*Gratefully.*) Yes. You always help me. (*He comes to sit down, leaning forward eagerly.*) Catherine, someone has shown me—I have seen—There is a text in Leviticus which—

CATHERINE: Leviticus?

(*Henry sees her Bible on the table. He picks it up and quickly finds the place. He know exactly where to look. His face is eager, like a child's. Catherine's eyes are on his face and not on the Bible.*)

HENRY: Chapter 20—there—verse 21. (*He reads it,*

although he has no need.) 'And if a man shall take his brother's wife, it is an unclean thing. They shall be childless.' (*Catherine's eyes widen. She is suddenly still and speechless, as though stunned. Henry feels better now that he has made a start*.) That is the text, and it proves—learned and—and pious men have told me that, because you were first married to my brother, our marriage is unlawful in the sight of God. You and I are—we are living in sin together. That is why we have no son.

(*Catherine flinches a little at this. Henry gets up and walks about again.*)

There is only one answer. Now that we know the truth, we must separate. If you will choose some place—away from Court—and live there in retirement—

(*Catherine slowly stands up, staring at him.*)

You can go anywhere you like, and have anything you want, of course. Anything. Where would you— (*In a little, affectionate burst of goodwill.*)—Where would you like to go?

(*Catherine still stares at him. He looks at her in innocent enquiry.*)

Catherine?

(*Catherine suddenly bursts into an appalling storm of tears, her hands at her side. It is not the innocent grief of the young girl, or of the mother over her dead baby, but a rending, ungraceful, noisy rush of grief and outrage. Henry is aghast.*)

Catherine! Don't cry! Don't—You must understand—It's not that I don't love you. I still—as I always have—And if we could continue to live together, then—I should be so glad. But my conscience—It won't let me—Catherine, don't— **Catherine!**

(*She cries, unheeding, and Henry in a kind of panic, rushes out of the room and through the anteroom and out.*)

25

Interior. The anteroom. Day.

(*Close up of Maria, no longer in outdoor clothes, listening to Catherine's sobs with a look of horror and anguish and then move to find Anne listening too, not smiling or contemptuous, but very grave and intent, as though she watches the first blows of a hard-fought battle.*)

26

Interior. The gallery. Day.

(*Henry pauses, out of breath and distressed. As he stands still, close up of his face slowly setting itself in lines of self-willed obstinacy.*)

27

Interior. The anteroom. Day.

(*Inez comes up to Maria.*)

INEZ (*Glancing towards the closet*): The Queen didn't know?

(*Maria smiles sadly.*)

MARIA: She knew. But she thought that it was just a

plot of Wolsey's. She didn't know that the King himself would be persuaded to . . .

(*She pauses—glances to the closet.*)

27A

Interior. The closet. Day.

(*Catherine sits, crying, more quietly now, but more heartbroken.*)

27B

Interior. The anteroom. Day.

MARIA: She has already written to her nephew, the Emperor, and to the Pope, telling them about Wolsey's plots against her. The Pope will declare that the marriage is valid, and then—(*With a touch of desperation.*)—all this will be over. The Pope will help her—he must!

27C

Interior. A room in Greenwich. Day.

(*Henry confronts Cardinal Lorenzo Campeggio, the Papal Legate, an elderly, scholarly man, a lawyer who was a widower with three children when he came into the church, and is an excellent 'committee man', good at compromises and at getting out from under. Wolsey stands between them.*)

WOLSEY: Cardinal Lorenzo Campeggio, your Grace, the Papal Legate.

See Scarisbn

61

CAMPEGGIO: Your Majesty.

HENRY: Your Eminence.

(*A slightly wary pause. Henry courteously waves Campeggio to a seat. He sits himself as Campeggio painfully takes the few steps to a chair.*)

CAMPEGGIO: I am sorry that my ill-health and the— ah—difficulties of the journey have delayed my arrival.

HENRY: But now that you are here, I hope that we can move with some—speed.

(*Eyeing Campeggio's progress with impatience which turns to a bland smile as Campeggio turns to face him.*)

CAMPEGGIO: Indeed, your Grace. (*He lowers himself into the chair, holding on to the arms. Wolsey quietly sits down at a slight distance.*) His Holiness is most anxious that this unhappy state of affairs between yourself and Queen Catherine should be composed as soon as possible—(*Henry nods in a dignified manner.*) —and that the bonds of marriage between you should be strengthened and purified.

(*Henry's eyes widen.*)

HENRY: The bonds of marriage between us do not exist. That is what you are here to prove.

(*Campeggio looks, startled, at Wolsey, who looks impassive.*)

CAMPEGGIO: That is the question, your Highness, that we are here to *try*.

HENRY: Try it, by all means, but there is only one possible conclusion. The Queen and I have been living in sin, and my conscience won't allow me to continue to do so.

CAMPEGGIO: Such a conclusion would lead to great scandal. (*Henry looks mulish.*) Especially since the Pope's dispensation—

HENRY: —did not meet the case. (*He flicks his fingers at Wolsey, who gets up and gets a copy of a document from a side table and brings it to Henry.*) Among other things, this word, 'forsan'—'perhaps'— implies a doubt in the Pope's mind which makes the dispensation inadequate for the purpose.

(*He points to the word, and Wolsey takes the document to Campeggio, who reads the passage, though he has no need, nods gravely, and Wolsey returns the document to the table.*)

CAMPEGGIO: His Holiness would readily make good any deficiencies which were found in the dispensation.

(*Henry glances at Wolsey, who pauses as he puts the document down, and glances back at Henry.*)

WOLSEY: That would not satisfy the King's conscience.

CAMPEGGIO: But to call the efficacy of the Pope's dispensation into question—(*He looks at Henry, who is mulish again, and at Wolsey who remains impassively standing.*) It would cause scandal and— divisions—and would give much offence to the Emperor, the Queen's nephew, to suggest that— (*Henry regards him steadily.*) His Holiness is most anxious that a reconciliation should be affected. (*Henry stares into the middle distance.*) But if that is impossible, then there might be another way.

(*Henry instantly turns a bright, pleased gaze upon him.*)

28

Interior. The Queen's closet. Day.

(*Campeggio stands a little turned away. Catherine sits behind him, very composed, her hands in her lap.*)

CAMPEGGIO: The Pope feels for you sincerely, but—

CATHERINE: But—?

CAMPEGGIO: He must consider also the welfare of the Church.

CATHERINE: Will the Church be best defended by yielding to an attack on the sanctity of marriage?

CAMPEGGIO: By no means. (*With a touch of irritation which he hastily overcomes.*) Before I left Rome, the Pope impressed upon me his most earnest desire that you and the King should be reconciled.

CATHERINE: The King and I have never quarrelled. We have always loved each other dearly. Wicked men have put doubts into his mind. Once those are resolved—

CAMPEGGIO (*Breaking in*): I have had a long talk with the King. He assures me that those doubts can never be resolved.

CATHERINE (*Quietly obstinate*): The Pope could resolve them.

(*Campeggio is silent for a moment, and then turns to look at her and speaks very reasonably.*)

CAMPEGGIO: Madam, you must understand, this matter could lead to many and great evils—to enmity between the King and the Emperor, divisions within the English Church, scandal throughout Christendom. But there is a way in which all this could be avoided.

(*Catherine gazes steadily back at him.*)

CAMPEGGIO: I would remind you of the saintly wife of King Louis of France, who—

CATHERINE: Who entered a nunnery, so that her husband might marry again.

CAMPEGGIO: Yes. (*He smiles, gratified, and comes to sit beside her.*) I know what a faithful servant of the Church you have always been.

(*Catherine's face doesn't change. She still looks steadily at him.*)

And if it pleases you to enter the religious life—(*With a touch of eagerness.*) King Henry assures me that all your dower rights will be preserved—

CATHERINE (*In sudden, anguished recollection*): Dower rights?

CAMPEGGIO: And the King is very willing to agree that your daughter should be granted the right of succession immediately after his legitimate male heirs—

(*Catherine suddenly stands up.*)

CATHERINE: My daughter is the only legitimate heir to the throne. For my part, I have no calling to the religious life. While my husband lives, I am his wife, his own, true wife. If it were not so, I would have been his whore, and my daughter a bastard, and that I will never say.

(*Campeggio's face hardens. He slowly rises.*)

65

CAMPEGGIO: Then I must warn you that when the matter comes to Court—

CATHERINE: No Court in England has the power to try it. It can only be tried in Rome.

CAMPEGGIO: The King means to bring it to trial here, and that I shall preside—with Cardinal Wolsey. (*Catherine's face responds to Wolsey's name.*) The matter to be tried would be whether or not His Holiness had the right to grant dispensation for the King to marry his brother's wife, and whether the dispensation he granted was legally valid, and this leads us into—

CATHERINE: It was legal, but unnecessary. (*Campeggio looks surprised.*) The marriage between the King's brother and myself was never consummated. I came a virgin to King Henry, as he to me, and therefore I am his lawful wife. If I were torn limb from limb for saying so, I would rise from the dead to say it again.

(*Campeggio's face slowly changes to unwilling admiration. He speaks more gently.*)

CAMPEGGIO: But this is a matter very hard to prove. After so many years, witnesses would be—

CATHERINE (*Smiling*): There is one witness who will speak the truth. I am very sure of that.

(*Fade on her exalted look of triumphant hope.*)

29

Interior. The Court at Blackfriars. Day.

(*Open upon the face of Henry sitting in state, gazing straight before him. Two seats in the middle hold the*

*two Cardinals, Campeggio and Wolsey. Move from
Henry to the seat on the other side, where Catherine
sits, very calm and impassive with folded hands. Find
Norfolk and Suffolk standing talking among the onlookers. Charles Brandon, Duke of Suffolk, is a beefy,
good-looking young man, not too bright and exceed-
ingly insensitive. Norfolk, the third Duke is fifty-six,
much like his father (Surrey, now dead) but, if anything, a little coarser. Warham, Fisher and Bishops
mainly compose the court. Maria and Inez in attendance.)*

SUFFOLK: Well, Norfolk, so the Queen has come into
Court after all.

NORFOLK: Didn't you expect her to?

SUFFOLK: I did hear she said this Court wasn't
qualified to judge her case.

NORFOLK: With the Papal Legate here to preside with
Wolsey?

*(Wolsey speaks aside to Campeggio, who listens with
a hint of reluctance, gazing straight ahead.)*

SUFFOLK: Now she's here, I wonder what she'll do.

NORFOLK *(Irritably)*: Hold her tongue, if she has any
sense, and try to get out of the affair with some
degree of dignity! Anyway, what difference does it
make what she does? Wolsey and the Papal Legate
will manage it all between them.

SUFFOLK *(Heavily sly)*: Much as your niece is now
'managing' the King.

NORFOLK *(Repressively)*: My Lord Suffolk, the Lady
Anne Boleyn has no part in this affair. This is solely
a matter of the King's conscience.

SUFFOLK (*Grinning*): Oh yes. Of course. That's what Wolsey thought at first!

(*Return to Henry, who looks enquiringly at Campeggio. Campeggio nods to the court usher who stands near. The usher bangs on the floor with his staff.*)

USHER: Henry, King of England, come into the Court!

HENRY (*Calmly and courteously*): I am here, my Lords.

USHER: Catherine, Queen of England, come into the court.

(*Silence. A slight rustle. Catherine is expressionless. Henry's eyes move, and then once more stare straight ahead. Campeggio nods to the usher.*)

USHER: Catherine, Queen of England, come into the Court.

(*Catherine slowly rises to her feet. She walks past the Cardinals, turns to face Henry, stands looking at him for a moment, and then falls slowly to her knees.*)

CATHERINE (*In a clear, calm voice*): My Lord, since I can expect no impartial judgment in this court—(*She glances at Wolsey and then back at Henry.*) I appeal to you as the head of all justice in the land. (*Campeggio and Wolsey exchange a quick, dismayed look.*) How have I offended you? I have always been your true and loving wife, and have borne you many children, though it pleased God to take them from me, for no fault of mine. There can be no question but that we are truly married, for when I first came to you, I was a virgin, as you have often said. I put it to your conscience to say whether this is true or no.

(*There is a breathless pause as her eyes meet his, and she waits for his reply. He slightly turns his head away. Catherine's face is momentarily contracted, as though in sudden pain. She still waits for Henry to reply. The whole court is in a state of acute embarrassment and suspended animation. Catherine looks at Henry with a face full of love.*)

I beg of you, my Lord, to spare me this Court. (*Henry gazes straight ahead. Catherine slowly rises.*) But if you will not, I appeal my case to God.

(*She waits another moment, and then turns and walks slowly towards the door. The usher courteously gestures towards the empty chair, but Catherine walks straight past it. The usher looks quickly at Henry, who gestures to him.*)

USHER: Catherine, Queen of England, come into the Court!

MARIA: Madam, they are calling you.

CATHERINE (*Without pausing*): I have nothing to do with this Court.

(*She goes on, and out, followed by her attendants. Henry turns to look at Wolsey, an ominous look, and Wolsey meets it with an apprehension which he attempts to hide. A great shout comes from outside, and Henry turns his head towards it.*)

CROWD (*Off*): God save the Queen! God save Queen Catherine! No Nan Boleyn for us! God save the Queen! (*Close up of Henry's face, with the shouts all about him.*) God save Queen Catherine! God save the Queen!

30

Exterior. Outside Blackfriars. Day.

(*Catherine stands framed in an archway with the shouts all about her.*)

CROWD (*Off*): God save the Queen! God save Queen Catherine! God save the Queen!

31

Interior. The Court at Blackfriars. Day.

(*Close up of Eustache Chapuys, the Imperial Ambassador, a quiet, immensely shrewd, attractive man of about forty-four. He is looking after Catherine and listening to the shouts.*)

CROWD (*Off, fainter*): God save Queen Catherine!

(*A heavy door clangs shut. The shouts stop. There is a general stir and rustle. Draw back to find Norfolk and Suffolk looking at Chapuys who stands beside a Bishop.*)

NORFOLK: Who's that standing beside Fox?

SUFFOLK: Eustache Chapuys.

NORFOLK: Who?

SUFFOLK: The Emperor's new ambassador.

NORFOLK: Really? (*He laughs.*) What a moment to arrive! I wonder what he thinks of his master's aunt now!

CHAPUYS: The power of the King, the Pope, the

English Church and nobles ranged against one woman. Hardly a fair contest, huh, Bishop? (*Close up of his face, with a smile of wry sympathy.*) Hardly a fair contest.

31A

Interior. The Court at Blackfriars. Day.

WOLSEY (*On his feet*): And since it has pleased Queen Catherine wilfully to absent herself from this Court duly and lawfully summoned, the said Queen Catherine is hereby declared contumacious. The court will continue in her absence.

31B

Interior. The Queen's closet. Day.

(*Catherine sits quietly sewing.*)

31C

Interior. The Court at Blackfriars. Day.

(*Henry facing the Court, noble, sincere, and dignified.*)

HENRY: As touching the Queen, if she may be adjudged to be my lawful wife, nothing could be more pleasing to me. For she is a woman of great gentleness, humility, wisdom, and all good qualities, so that I tell you, if I were to marry again, and know that the marriage was lawful in the sight of God, I would surely choose her above all other women.

(*He is immensely convincing—perhaps at this moment even to himself—but a second later his eyes are roaming with a slight challenge along the impassive faces of the Lords and Bishops.*)

31D

Interior. The Queen's closet. Day.

(*Catherine sits quietly sewing.*)

31E

Interior. The Court at Blackfriars. Day.

(*An elderly nobleman is giving evidence.*)

NOBLEMAN: And I well remember Prince Arthur saying next morning, 'Give me to drink, sirs! That was warm work!' (*He looks from the impassive face of Campeggio to Wolsey. Wolsey turns his head very slightly, as though waiting for more.*) And he was given wine, and he drank, and he said, 'Last night, my Lords, I was in Spain!' (*He laughs, or rather, giggles, and then remembers where he is, and uneasily sobers up.*)

WOLSEY (*Very gravely*): What did you take his Royal Highness to mean by that?

NOBLEMAN: Well—er—(*Doubtfully inviting them to share the joke.*)—there was only one thing we could understand by such words spoken by a young bridegroom after his wedding-night.

WOLSEY (*Very patiently*): And what was that?

NOBLEMAN: Why that the—(*Quick glance not quite at Henry.*)—Princess Catherine as she then was—was—no longer a virgin!

(*The last words come out in a rush, and he draws a quick breath of relief and looks for the first time directly at Henry, like a dog expecting a tit-bit.*)

31F

Interior. The Queen's closet. Day.

(*Catherine sewing.*)

31G

Interior. The Court at Blackfriars. Day.

(*Warham, the Archbishop of Canterbury is reading from a document. He is old and timid, but honest.*)

WARHAM: And in addition to these who have subscribed their names to attest the justice of the King's cause, are added the names of Dr John Fisher, Bishop of Rochester—

(*Fisher rises from the Bishop's bench.*)

FISHER: That is not my hand nor seal!

(*Henry sharply turns his head towards him.*)

WARHAM (*Alarmed for Fisher*): My Lord of Rochester—

FISHER: Because, although you asked me, I would not consent.

WARHAM: No—no, but you—you agreed that I should subscribe for you and put a seal to it myself.

FISHER: Under your correction, my Lord Archbishop, nothing could be more untrue. For I held then as I hold now, 'Whom God has joined together, let no man put asunder.'

(*Henry turns his head to look at Wolsey, who looks uneasily back at him.*)

31H

Interior. A room in Greenwich. Night.

(*Henry standing looking out of the window, turns as Wolsey comes in, rather dishevelled, having had to get out of bed to answer Henry's summons.*)

WOLSEY: You sent for me, my Lord.

HENRY: The French army has been defeated in Italy. The Pope is now at liberty to oblige the Emperor— the Queen's nephew. What chance of divorce now? (*He looks steadily at Wolsey, who can't think of anything to say in reply.*) Well—my Lord Cardinal?

WOLSEY: Campeggio may not know of it yet. If we can conclude the case before he hears—

HENRY: You had better go to the Queen. (*Wolsey, slightly startled, looks a question.*) No doubt you will know what to say to her.

(*Wolsey bows and begins to withdraw. As he does so, a movement across the room catches his eye. He meets Anne Boleyn's impudent gaze, and his eyes fall.*)

31J

Interior. Antechamber. Day.

(*Catherine comes out of her closet, accompanied by Maria and Inez and two or three other ladies. She has a skein of white silk round her neck, the end in one hand, and a white silk cloth in the other. She looks in mild surprise at Wolsey, who rather sheepishly confronts her.*)

CATHERINE: My Lord? Forgive this lack of ceremony. I did not expect you here.

WOLSEY: Madam, if we may go into your private room—

CATHERINE (*Instantly*): My Lord, if you have anything to say to me, pray say it openly. There is nothing you can allege against me which all the world cannot hear.

(*Wolsey glances at the women, and clears his throat.*)

WOLSEY: *O Regina nobilissima, huc adveni—*

CATHERINE: I would prefer that you should speak to me in English, though—(*Ironically.*)—I do understand Latin.

WOLSEY (*With a note of desperation*): Madam, I have come to offer my own private counsel, which I would prefer should be in private.

(*Catherine's face loses its hostility and softens slightly. Wolsey suddenly looks old and tired.*)

CATHERINE: I am obliged to you for your solicitude on my behalf, but since truth and justice are on my side, I have no need to ask for mercy.

(*Wolsey takes a breath to answer her, but he has used up all his arguments.*)

CATHERINE (*Gently courteous*): Good day, my Lord Cardinal.

(*Wolsey looks at her steadily for a moment, and then slightly inclines his head and rises and walks away. Catherine watches him as he slowly moves through the room, and her face is calmly sympathetic. She turns away into her closet.*)

31K

Interior. The Court at Blackfriars. Day.

(*The Court in full session with Henry and Wolsey. Campeggio is speaking.*)

CAMPEGGIO: And therefore it has pleased his Holiness the Pope to advoke this case to Rome. The right of this court to try this matter is now withdrawn.

(*Henry slowly turns his deadly gaze towards Wolsey. Wolsey stares straight ahead.*)

32

Interior. The Queen's closet. Night.

(*Catherine, sewing, snips off the thread, and sticks the needle into her pincushion. The camera reveals a pleasant domestic scene, Henry sits in his shirtsleeves, having just finished supper. Catherine sits opposite, stitching some loose pearls back on his doublet. Maria stands by the open lattice window. In the next wing of the palace, opposite, is another lighted win-*

dow, and Anne stands silhouetted behind the lattice. Maria looks at Anne, and glances at Henry and Catherine.)

CATHERINE: You had lost one of these pearls, but I have matched it with one of mine.

(Henry leans back luxuriously, enjoying the peace and quiet.)

HENRY: Mm. No one embroiders as you do. That was a very good supper, too. Your suppers never give me indigestion.

CATHERINE: I only wish you came here—more often.

(He glances at her warily, but decides to let it pass. She smiles at him and puts the doublet down on a stool beside him.)

HENRY: Thank you.

CATHERINE: Will you thank me in another way?

HENRY *(Smiling)*: Mm?

CATHERINE: May I have Mary with me here?

(Henry's face changes instantly. He stops lounging and sits up.)

HENRY: You know where she is. If you want to, you can go to her.

CATHERINE *(After a moment, with gentle dignity)*: My place is with my husband.

HENRY *(Getting up)*: As you please.

(Catherine suddenly loses her temper.)

CATHERINE: You know it is *not* as I please! How can

you treat me like this? I am your wife! I love you, and you have always said that you love me.

HENRY: I *do* love you, but you are not my wife! I can bring a hundred learned men to prove that you are not my wife!

(*Catherine stands up, her Spanish temper finally taking over.*)

CATHERINE: Bring your hundred learned men! I will bring a *thousand* learned men from all over Europe to say that I *am* your wife! I have always been your wife, and I always will be!

(*They stand glaring at each other. Henry suddenly snatches up his doublet, knocking over the stool in the process, and storms out. Catherine stands quite still and closes her eyes.*)

Always!

(*They have both forgotten Maria, who still stands by the window. She turns her head to see Anne's watching silhouette in the window opposite, and then sees Henry join Anne. Their silhouettes move and gesticulate as they argue. Catherine's hand reaches across Maria and draws the curtain across the window. Maria turns into the room.*)

Fetch me those handkerchiefs, Maria, which I was embroidering for the King. I must have them ready for him when he comes again.

33

Interior. Antechamber in the Queen's apartments. Day.

(*To the sound of trumpets, shouts and clatter of*

hooves, Inez stands by the open window, looking down into the courtyard.)

INEZ: There's the King. (*Maria is at a chest, sorting linen.*) He has a new coat. Covered with emeralds.

(*Close up Maria, very firmly not turning her head towards the window.*)

MARIA: Is 'the Lady' with him?

INEZ: Yes, there she is. In cloth of gold! She is wearing cloth-of-gold and emeralds! (*Maria straightens, folding a cloth.*) There's Sir Thomas Boleyn—and her brother—(*Maria turns to look at Inez.*) All the Court is leaving. All, except—

MARIA: Shut the window, Inez.

(*Inez guiltily shuts the window. They look at each other, and then glance towards the door of the Queen's closet.*)

34

Interior. The Queen's closet. Day.

(*Catherine sitting in a tall armchair. Chapuys standing near.*)

CHAPUYS: He is going to Woodstock, with all the Court. (*Catherine slightly inclines her head.*) Did you know?

(*She shakes her head. Pause.*)

CATHERINE: He will send for me.

CHAPUYS: Has he left you before, without saying goodbye?

(*She shakes her head.*)

CATHERINE: But he will send for me. We always appear together in public. Always.

CHAPUYS: You know that Wolsey died on his way to the Tower?

CATHERINE: Yes. So I heard. Poor man.

CHAPUYS: His fate was sealed as soon as Campeggio transferred the trial to Rome. (*Glancing at her.*)

CATHERINE: Yes.

CHAPUYS: And Thomas More has become Lord Chancellor.

CATHERINE: Yes. (*Catherine gets up and moves away. Chapuys stands, watching her.*) I am so afraid for him—for the Bishop of Rochester—for all my friends. If they obey the King, they must go against their conscience. If they disobey him, they may lose their lives. And it is all because of—But what else can I do? (*She returns.*) If only the Pope would declare that our marriage is valid! If only he would do that, and order the King to leave that woman! Why does he delay?

CHAPUYS: He is afraid of losing the King's friendship.

CATHERINE: Doesn't he need the friendship of my nephew, the Emperor?

CHAPUYS (*Wryly*): He needs them both. That is why he prevaricates. The Pope is afraid of losing England to the Lutherans, and he needs the Emperor's help against France.

CATHERINE (*Brokenly*): But my husband is endangering his immortal soul. (*She sits down again, wearily.*)

Doesn't the Pope understand? He is endangering his immortal soul, and the souls of all those who, through fear and—and ambition are supporting him. He still loves me! If he could only be made to leave that woman and come back to me, then I know I could—

CHAPUYS (*Suddenly sitting down and leaning forward*): Madam! (*She looks at him, startled.*) There is a way. The people love you. If you would take it, there is a way.

(*Maria comes in.*)

MARIA: Your Majesty, the Dukes of Norfolk and Suffolk are here, with a message from the King.

CATHERINE: I will come.

(*She gets up and goes slowly out. Chapuys and Maria exchange a troubled glance.*)

35

Interior. The anteroom. Day.

(*Norfolk and Suffolk sternly waiting. The ladies, with Inez ranged near the closet.*)

CATHERINE: My Lords.

(*Norfolk and Suffolk glance at each other and bow slightly.*)

NORFOLK: Madam. The King has left for Woodstock, with his Court.

CATHERINE: I shall be glad to follow his Majesty, at his good pleasure.

NORFOLK: That is not his—pleasure. His orders are that you should go at once to More House in Hertfordshire.

SUFFOLK: Wolsey's old house. He won't be needing it now

CATHERINE (*Loudly*): If I am not to be with the King, I will go to the Tower!

(*Suffolk and Norfolk look at each other quickly.*)

NORFOLK (*Angrily*): The King does not—! (*Restraining himself.*) You are to go to More House.

SUFFOLK: And your household is to be severely reduced.

CATHERINE: My household? Let me have my confessor, my doctor, and two of my women. That will be enough for me. Or, if that is not allowed, I will go out on the streets and beg my bread for the love of God!

(*Suffolk, having got more than he bargained for, takes a step backwards, glancing at Norfolk.*)

NORFOLK: There will be no need for that, madam. The King wishes you to be properly attended, as befits his brother's wife. (*Catherine catches her breath.*) I must tell you also that it is the King's will that you should not appear in public as often as you have done lately.

(*Chapuys speaks softly to Catherine from behind her shoulder.*)

CHAPUYS: Because the people love you. They love *you*, madam!

(*Norfolk can't hear, but glances quickly between*

1. *The young Henry (Keith Michell) and Catherine of Aragon (Annette Crosbie) after the coronation*

2. *Catherine before her marriage to Henry, with Maria de Salinas (Margaret Ford), her Lady-in-Waiting*

3. *Catherine in old age, after Henry's repudiation of their marriage*

them, and stands aside, motioning Chapuys to precede them out of the room.)

NORFOLK: Messire Chapuys.

(Chapuys glances at him, and then comes to kiss Catherine's hand. She hardly seems to notice. He goes out, and Norfolk and Suffolk prepare to follow.)

SUFFOLK: I shall be ready, madam, to attend you to More House tomorrow morning.

(He and Norfolk bow slightly and prepare to depart.)

CATHERINE: Will the Princess Mary be allowed to join me there?

NORFOLK: Princess Mary—*(He pauses and deliberately corrects himself.)* Your daughter has been sent to Richmond.

CATHERINE: When will I see her? *(She takes a step towards him.)* When will I see her?

NORFOLK: At any time.

(A look of joy comes into her face.)

NORFOLK: You can have anything you want—if you will meet the King's wishes.

CATHERINE: You mean, I can see my daughter if I will declare her to be a bastard!

(Norfolk looks at her in silence, glances at Suffolk, and goes out, as Catherine turns away towards the window. Close up of her face as she smiles.)

Word—of a Henry!

36

Interior. The gallery at Greenwich. Day.

(Henry stands near the alcove, talking to Chapuys. It is winter, and a brazier is alight near them.)

CHAPUYS: His Imperial Majesty was greatly distressed to hear of the—pretended divorce—

(Henry throws him a dangerous glance.)

CHAPUYS: —and that his beloved aunt had been declared contumacious.

HENRY *(Mildly)*: She was summoned to the divorce proceedings. She refused to attend. *(He sees Anne lurking and suddenly shouts out in a furious rage.)* And I wish the Emperor would cease to meddle in my affairs! The Princess Catherine is not my wife, and anyone who wishes me to remain with her is my enemy, whether it is the Emperor or his puppet, the Pope!

(Chapuys looks at him in amazement, and then sees the curtain of the alcove move, and catches sight of Anne behind it. He decides to reply in kind.)

CHAPUYS: Be careful, my Lord, how far you provoke the Emperor. When I tell what you say, he may meddle in your affairs with more than words! He has an army raised and in the field!

(Henry after another alarmed glance towards the alcove, hastily takes Chapuys' arm and propels him along the gallery. He speaks mildly, but gestures furiously with the other hand.)

HENRY: I don't want to have the Emperor as my enemy. He needs my friendship as I wish for his.

(*He stands still, far enough away from the alcove to feel safe. He stops gesticulating, and looks at Chapuys with the shrewd, calculating look of a King who's learned the true business of international diplomacy.*)

HENRY: The Emperor won't take the field against me in this cause. You know that. And when you next write to the Princess Catherine, you can tell her so as well.

(*Chapuys looks at him in silence, and then bows.*)

CHAPUYS: Your Majesty.

(*As he begins to move away, Henry suddenly shouts after him.*)

HENRY: The Emperor will never go to war with me!

(*Chapuys glances back at him, hesitates, and then goes out. Anne comes up behind Henry. She is richly dressed, but looks thin and hollow-eyed and constantly under strain.*)

HENRY (*Without turning round*): But Catherine might.

(*He turns and suddenly is close to her, his eyes looking into hers.*)

36A

Interior. Queen's room. Kimbolton. Day.

(*Catherine suddenly turns into camera.*)

36B

Interior. Gallery. Day.

(*Resume Henry / Anne.*)

HENRY: My dearest love—(*It isn't an endearment, but a hungry snap.*) Catherine might. (*He turns away. Anne closes her eyes for a moment. She lives constantly on the edge of acute danger and difficulty and is almost exhausted.*) If she took the field against me, she could cut the country in two!

37

Interior. The Queen's room at Kimbolton. Day.

(*It is a bare, poor-looking room, with a prie-dieu, brazier and chairs, and a bed with a chest beside it. Catherine's dress is nearly as shabby as it was when we saw her first, and she wears no jewels except a couple of rings. She sits in an armchair and Chapuys stands near.*)

CATHERINE: No! (*He takes a breath to speak.*) No.

CHAPUYS: I tell you, half the nobility of England would rise in your defence, and all the common people. They hate Norfolk and all the Boleyn crew as much as they hated Wolsey. If you would only put yourself at their head—no, not even that. Only say the word, and Princess Mary will be rescued to ride with the army. Only say the word!

CATHERINE: No. I have brought England little good. I don't want to bring her harm.

CHAPUYS: It is your only hope, madam!

CATHERINE : No. I still hope—the King still loves me. Surely the Pope will order the King, on pain of excommunication to leave that woman, and then—

CHAPUYS : Madam. The whore is pregnant.

(*Catherine slowly stands up.*)

CATHERINE : Pregnant?

(*It is a fearful blow.*)

CHAPUYS : Last Christmas. And since then, they have been secretly married.

(*Close up of Catherine, stunned by this second blow. We hear the cheers of her coronation as we mix to . . .*)

38

Exterior. A street in London. Day.

(*Anne riding in a deathly silence, dressed in white her hair flowing down her back, and a circlet of gold and diamonds round her head. She endeavours to smile graciously, but her eyes go from side to side.*)

39

Interior. The Queen's room at Kimbolton. Evening.

(*Catherine, fully dressed, but with her foot bandaged, lies on the bed. She is feeling ill and has a cough. Norfolk and Suffolk, in riding dress, stand before her, Norfolk holding an official-looking document, and a clerk beside them carrying other papers. Maria and Inez stand beside the bed.*)

CATHERINE: I am sorry that I cannot rise to greet you. I have pricked my foot and it is painful to stand. What is this—message—you have for us?

NORFOLK (*Reading from the paper*): 'It is hereby declared to the Princess Dowager—'

CATHERINE: Why do you read this to me? There is no such person here.

NORFOLK (*Furiously*): Madam, this will do you no— (*He stops, glares at her, looks at Suffolk, gestures to the clerk, and goes on reading. The clerk diligently writes on a piece of paper.*) 'That the Princess Dowager's marriage to his Majesty being declared invalid, and his Majesty having contracted a true marriage with the most illustrious lady, Anne Boleyn, the said Lady Anne is the only Queen of England, and the heirs of her body are the only true heirs to the said Majesty, King Henry the Eighth.' (*He rolls up the paper.*) From henceforth, Madam, you will style yourself Princess Dowager.

(*Catherine coughs, takes time to recover, and then looks at him calmly.*)

CATHERINE: My title is Queen, and that it will be until I die.

NORFOLK (*Threateningly*): Your death may not be so far away. Do you know that Sir Thomas More and John Fisher have gone to the Tower, only for refusing to recognize the King's marriage?

CATHERINE: I am very sorry for it. They are both good men. But I would die a hundred deaths before I would damn my husband's soul, or mine.

SUFFOLK: His Majesty has been lenient with you until now, but—

CATHERINE: If I am to be put to death, then all I ask is that it may be a public execution.

(*Norfolk and Suffolk exchange a nervous glance. There is nothing anyone wants less than a public execution of Catherine. Catherine coughs again. Maria steps forward.*)

MARIA: Her Majesty (*With only slight emphasis.*)—is not well. This house is on the marshes and the damp and the constant mists are destroying her Majesty's health. We must ask you . . .

NORFOLK: We have only two more slight matters of business with the Princess Dowager, when she has signed this account of our interview.

(*He snaps his fingers and the Clerk gives him paper and pen, which he offers to Catherine, pointing to the foot of the paper. Catherine takes the paper and swiftly glances up and down the writing.*)

CATHERINE: What is this? 'The Princess Dowager said—'? (*She seizes the pen and strikes the words through, and writes firmly above them.*) 'The Queen.' 'The Queen said'. 'The Queen replied' Now I will sign it. Catherine—the— Queen. (*She gives the paper back to Norfolk.*) What other business?

NORFOLK: I have summoned a meeting of the members of your household. They will be required to sign a paper promising to address you henceforth only as Princess Dowager. (*Maria takes another step forward, eyes blazing. Norfolk gives her a sardonic grin.*) Before you speak, Countess—(*To Catherine.*)— perhaps I should mention that in no circumstances will the Countess of Willoughby be allowed to stay with you.

(*Catherine looks at Maria, and Maria looks back, both determined to show no dismay in front of Norfolk.*)

CATHERINE: And—the other business?

NORFOLK (*Moving towards the door*): I will leave Suffolk to deal with that. Good-day, madam.

(*Suffolk looks horrified and goes after him to the door. He has to fall back to let the clerk out first and then grabs Norfolk by the sleeve. Maria whispers to Catherine.*)

MARIA (*Whisper*): Inez had better sign. You must have someone you can trust.

CATHERINE: No! I won't be served by—(*Suddenly.*) Maria, as soon as he has gone, send Inez and two others up here—you'll know who. We'll stay in here and bolt the door. They won't dare to break it down.

MARIA: Let me stay.

CATHERINE: No. Not against the King's express command.

SUFFOLK: Why should I have to do it?

NORFOLK: Oh, do it and be done with it!

(*He goes out. Suffolk turns towards Catherine, bracing himself. She lies back and closes her eyes, thinking they have gone. Suffolk clears his throat aggressively. She opens her eyes and looks at him in surprise, cold and regal.*)

CATHERINE: Are you still here, my Lord? What further business have you with the Queen?

SUFFOLK: My errand is to the Princess Dowager.

CATHERINE: There is no such person here.

SUFFOLK (*Exasperated*): These fits and starts will do you no good at all! You do not understand your position!

CATHERINE: I understand my position perfectly, and the place in life to which it has pleased God to call me. It is you, my Lord Suffolk, who do not perfectly understand *yours*.

SUFFOLK: I am a servant of the King—

CATHERINE (*Quick as a flash*): And I am his wife! (*Suffolk glares at her, silenced.*) Well, my Lord, what is your—errand? (*She makes the word sound very insulting.*)

SUFFOLK: The King requests—commands—will you be so good as to convey to me—(*He stops.*)

CATHERINE: What? (*With contempt.*) What have you come for this time? It cannot be my jewels. They were stolen from me—let me see, when was it?—ah yes, (*With a healthy touch of viciousness*)—they were stolen from me *last Christmas*!

(*Maria bites her lip, glancing with a touch of nervousness between Catherine and Suffolk.*)

SUFFOLK (*Losing his scruples*): The King commands that you shall deliver to me the christening robe!

CATHERINE: The—?

SUFFOLK: The christening robe, which—You are to deliver to me the christening robe.

(*Catherine looks at him in silence, her eyes very large. Then she looks down and speaks calmly.*)

CATHERINE: I absolutely refuse.

SUFFOLK (*Beginning to bluster, as usual*): I have instructions to find the robe, if I have to search your room.

CATHERINE: You shall not search it.

SUFFOLK: I have orders to search it, if need be!

(*He moves towards the chest beside the bed. Catherine suddenly gets up and stands in front of the chest, wincing as she puts her foot to the ground.*)

Stand aside!

CATHERINE: You will not touch that chest unless you first throw me to the ground!

(*Suffolk takes a step towards her, and then pauses and backs away.*)

SUFFOLK: I shall tell the King what you—I shall tell the King!

(*Maria comes quickly round to support Catherine, who still stares defiantly at Suffolk.*)

CATHERINE: Tell him what you please!

(*Suffolk goes out. Catherine falls on her knees by the chest, opens it, with Maria's help, and takes out a heavily embroidered christening robe: she breaks down and puts her face in the robe.*)

Our son wore it!

MARIA (*Kneeling with her arms round her*): It's not the King. It's that—it's that woman. I hope the whore miscarries!

CATHERINE: Oh no!

MARIA: They say the King is tired of her already. They spend all their time quarrelling.

(*Catherine lifts her head, suddenly calm.*)

CATHERINE: Poor creature! She is as little to be envied as I am.

40

Interior. Gallery. Day.

(*A door from which Henry's laughter is heard. Camera finds the hair of Anne Boleyn in foreground. Henry comes out, looks quickly at Anne, then goes. Anne clutches herself as the baby within her, kicks.*)

41

Interior. The Queen's room. Night.

(*Catherine, very shabby now, sits with folded hands. Inez is warming soup on a brazier, with another lady, they exchange glances.*)

INEZ: The news came today, madam. It was a girl.

CATHERINE (*Very calmly*): A girl.

(*Inez glances at the other lady again, nervously.*)

INEZ: They—they have called the little bastard Elizabeth. It's said—(*Hesitating.*)—it's said that they asked Princess Mary to wait on her, but she refused.

CATHERINE: My poor daughter! My poor Mary!

42

Interior. The gallery at Greenwich. Day.

(*Henry moving restlessly about. Chapuys, a letter in his hand, speaking urgently.*)

CHAPUYS : Sir, the Princess Mary—

HENRY: Lady Mary!

CHAPUYS (*With emphasis*): *Your daughter* is ill. She is surrounded by those who wish her dead—

HENRY (*Flaring up*): She is with the Queen's aunt, Lady Shelton! (*He looks round. Chapuys meets his eye, calmly accusing.*) I—will send her my own physician.

CHAPUYS: Read this letter from her mother, I beg of you. (*He gives the letter to Henry. Henry reads it, and tears come into his eyes.*) Let her be nursed by her mother. Let her go to her mother, or let her mother go to her.

HENRY: If Catherine will acknowledge the title of Princess Dowager, she may go where she likes and do what she pleases.

CHAPUYS (*Very gently*): Declare herself to be a whore and her daughter a bastard? Do you think she will ever do that—knowing her as you do?

(*Henry stands with his hands at his sides, crying quietly.*)

HENRY: She must! She must! I shall have a son next time. A son and heir!

43

Interior. The Queen's Room. Night.

(*Catherine in bed, coughing, with Inez sitting beside her, and a doctor in black robes just moving away from the bed. He purses his lips and shakes his head. Inez looks alarmed. Catherine turns her head to look at her.*)

CATHERINE: You said, she is pregnant again?

INEZ: Yes. But they say the King hardly ever sees her. There's—(*She eagerly, hopes to please her.*)— there's talk of divorce!

CATHERINE: Oh no. Not while I am alive. The King knows that if he should be divorced from her, he would still be married to me. (*She smiles at dear, stupid old Inez, and puts a hand on hers.*) No, Inez. While I am alive, Mistress Anne is safe.

44

Interior. Study/Council Room. Day.

(*Henry sits working at papers. Chapuys stands over him.*)

HENRY (*In high good spirits*): What do you think of this affair in Italy, hey? The King of France means to attack your Emperor.

CHAPUYS: My Lord, I hear from her physician that she is very ill. May I be allowed to go and see her?

HENRY: If the Emperor wants Milan, he is going to need my friendship, don't you think?

CHAPUYS: My Lord, the—the Princess Catherine has no money! She is glad of the food which the poor people, out of their love for her, bring to her door!

(*Henry leans back in his chair.*)

HENRY: Oh, that's no affair of mine. You had better talk to Cromwell about it.

CHAPUYS: My Lord—

HENRY (*Getting up*): Of course, I might join France against the Emperor, if he continues to meddle in my affairs. And if the Pope excommunicates me, I'll declare the Pope a heretic! (*He catches the flash of shock in Chapuys' eyes and smiles.*) After all, I'm already Supreme Head of the Church, so what can he excommunicate me from? (*Chapuys keeps his face carefully expressionless. Henry smiles again.*) You see, I know my own power now. I must be grateful to the Princess Dowager for teaching me how to use it.

CHAPUYS: My Lord, the Princess is ill. I beg that I may be allowed to go and see her.

(*Henry walks to the door.*)

HENRY (*Carelessly*): Go to her when you like. They tell me she won't live long. (*He turns to look at Chapuys, and smiles with the new, cruel look.*) When the old harridan is dead, then all my troubles will be over.

45

Interior. The Queen's room. Night.

(*Catherine is very ill and wasted. She has just been vomiting, and Inez has given the basin to another lady and is clumsily wiping her forehead. Catherine moves her head impatiently.)*

INEZ: How do you feel, madam?

CATHERINE: I feel—(*She turns her head away.*) —so alone!

46

Interior. The hall at Kimbolton. Night.

(Only a stout door need be seen, with the foot of a staircase. A heavy knocking at the door. A servant partly opens it.)

SERVANT: Who's there?

MARIA (*Off*): Let me in! This is the Countess of Willoughby.

SERVANT: No one's allowed to come—

(Maria pushes the door open and comes in. She wears riding habit and cloak, muddy and wet.)

MARIA: Nonsense! My horse fell in the marsh, and I am soaked to the skin. I must come in and dry myself.

(Sir Edmund Bedingfield, ostensibly governor of the Queen's household but actually her warder, comes up carrying a candle.)

BEDINGFIELD: What's that? Who's there?

MARIA: I must see the Queen.

BEDINGFIELD: No one sees the Qu—the Princess Dowager, without written permission from the King.

MARIA: I will show you the documents when I have changed my dress.

(*She hurries past him to the staircase*.)

BEDINGFIELD: Countess! (*He takes a horrified step after her*.) Countess!

47

Interior. The Queen's bedroom. Night.

(*Inez is just opening the door. Maria slips inside*.)

MARIA: Bolt it, Inez, quickly.

(*She goes to the bed. Catherine opens her eyes*.)

CATHERINE: Maria!

(*Inez bolts the door. There is a heavy hammering at it*.)

BEDINGFIELD (*Off*): Countess! Come out at once!

CATHERINE: Don't leave me.

MARIA (*Holding her in her arms*): Never! Never!

(*Catherine closes her eyes again, smiling. Maria kneels by the bed, still holding her in her arms*.)

48

Interior. The hall at Kimbolton. Day.

(*Bedingfield stands examining a document which Chapuys has just given to him*.)

CHAPUYS: That admits me to the Queen, I believe.

BEDINGFIELD (*Sharply*): It says you may see the Princess Dowager!

CHAPUYS (*Kindly*): My good Sir Edmund, do you think I would have ridden all these miles through the January snows to see a Princess Dowager?

(*He goes towards the staircase.*)

BEDINGFIELD (*Shouting after him*): She will be buried as Princess Dowager! The King has already given orders for that!

(*He turns away, just in time to see the servant crossing himself. He glares at him, and the servant hurries away.*)

49

Interior. The Queen's bedroom. Day.

(*Catherine is smiling and animated, though still very ill. Chapuys sits by her bed, and Maria stands the other side.*)

CATHERINE: Eustache, my dearest friend, it is so good to see you! Tell me the news—all the news!

CHAPUYS: Most important—the Pope has declared Anne Boleyn's marriage invalid. He commands the King to return to you on pain of excommunication.

CATHERINE: If only he would have done that nine years ago! But it will help Mary. How is she? Is she better? Tell me how she is!

(*Chapuys hesitates, glancing at Maria, who looks anxious.*)

CHAPUYS: Much better—and happy. The King—the King has sent for her to be with him.

CATHERINE (*Overcome with joy*): Oh, I knew he would! He still loves me. I know he still loves me.

(*Chapuys glad to speak the truth.*)

CHAPUYS: Certainly he loves you. He always has. That is why, at times, he has behaved as though he hated you. He was a prisoner of his love for you and you know that prisoners hate even the kindest gaoler.

CATHERINE: Is that why he has been so cruel? Because he loved me? The monks he tortured and killed—his friends, like More and Fisher—the monasteries he despoiled, the religion he destroyed—he who was once Defender of the Faith! Was this because of me? Have I made him cruel?

(*Chapuys cannot answer Catherine has a violent coughing fit, then she gazes at Chapuys. Maria has moved away to a side table, where she is preparing medicine, and listening.*)

Eustache, my dear friend, was I wrong?

CHAPUYS: No! No! You followed your conscience when no one else did.

CATHERINE: Conscience and love. That can't be wrong—can it? (*She looks at him in a moment of profound doubt and alarm.*) Can it?

(*Chapuys hesitates, and then puts his hand on hers.*)

CHAPUYS: Never. Never!

(*She leans back and closes her eyes, satisfied.*

Chapuys gets up and Maria goes with him to the door and hands him a letter.)

MARIA: She has written a letter—to the King—to be given to him on her death.

(They both look at Catherine, sleeping peacefully.)

MARIA: Was it true? Has the King sent for Princess Mary? *(Chapuys shakes his head.)* And the other? Was that a lie, too?

CHAPUYS: The other?

MARIA: Was she wrong?

CHAPUYS: My dear Countess—

MARIA: Maria. Maria is my Spanish name. Speak to that.

(Chapuys sits down on a stool by the door, suddenly tired.)

CHAPUYS: When her Highness first came to England I have heard that there were great storms all the way. The ship was nearly lost.

MARIA *(With a shudder)*: Yes. I was with her.

CHAPUYS: When a storm strikes, it sometimes happens that everyone on board runs about from side to side, trying to save themselves. There is no hand at the wheel. The ship yaws to and fro with every gust and every wave. And then some hand, more determined than the others, grips the wheel and turns the ship into the wind, and holds it there. Perhaps this course upon which it is set drives it upon the rocks, but rocks can be scrambled upon, and though the ship may be broken, some fragments of it remain.

101

Left to itself, wallowing unpiloted in the waves, it would founder without trace. Our Princess—(*He looks up at Maria and smiles and shakes his head.*) Our—Queen—when danger threatened, turned her ship's head into the wind, and drove it upon the only course she knew, the course of truth. It struck upon the rocks of passion and circumstances, and all aboard perished—herself, the King she loved, her friends, the other woman, the Church—even Spain, perhaps—all perished. But they did not vanish without trace as they might otherwise have done. Some spars and timbers of that ship remain, to show—

MARIA: To show?

CHAPUYS: That there were human beings there, and that they cared profoundly about the terms on which they lived and died. (*He stands up. They look at Catherine. She sighs in her sleep and turns her head on the pillow. Chapuys smiles.*) Europe sundered, a kingdom nearly plunged in revolution, the power of the Catholic Church weakened forever—and yet it was such a little thing. She wouldn't say that she was not married, when she was. She would—not—say it.

(*Close up of Catherine's round obstinate sleeping face.*)

50

Interior. The gallery. Day.

(*Henry stands reading the letter. Catherine's voice over.*)

CATHERINE (*Off*): Lastly, I make this vow, that mine eyes desire you above all things.

(Henry crumples up the letter and throws it down, striding straight into camera, looming huge and threatening, like the Holbein portrait, or like the tyrant of history.)

(Fade out.)

Anne Boleyn

NICK McCARTY

Anne Boleyn was first presented by BBC Television on 8 January 1970 with the following cast:

ANNE BOLEYN	*Dorothy Tutin*
HENRY VIII	*Keith Michell*
MARK SMEATON	*Michael Osborne*
LADY ROCHFORD	*Sheila Burrell*
LADY BOLEYN	*Hilary Mason*
GEORGE VISCOUNT ROCHFORD	
	Jonathan Newth
THOMAS CROMWELL	*Wolfe Morris*
ARCHBISHOP CRANMER	*Bernard Hepton*
DUKE OF NORFOLK	*Patrick Troughton*
SIR HENRY NORREYS	*Christopher Hancock*
EARL OF SURREY	*Christopher Beeching*
ARMOURER	*Arnold Peters*
JANE SEYMOUR	*Anne Stallybrass*
SIR WILLIAM KINGSTON	*Robert Cawdron*
LADY KINGSTON	*Patricia Heneghan*
SIR CHRISTOPHER HALES	*Peter Cellier*

Produced by Ronald Travers and Mark Shivas
Directed by Naomi Capon
Designed by Peter Seddon

Characters

HENRY VIII

ANNE BOLEYN

THOMAS CROMWELL

THE DUKE OF NORFOLK

THOMAS CRANMER, *Archbishop of Canterbury*

GEORGE ROCHFORD

LADY ROCHFORD

LADY BOLEYN

SIR WILLIAM KINGSTON

SIR CHRISTOPHER HALES

LADY KINGSTON

MARK SMEATON

HENRY NORREYS

GAOLER/EXECUTIONER

JANE SEYMOUR

Dancers

EARL OF SURREY

SIR FRANCIS WESTON

WILLIAM BRERETON

COURT LADIES

Sets

Interiors:

The Great Hall at Hampton Court
Anne's bedchamber
A gallery at Hampton Court
The King's bedchamber
The Queen's bedchamber at Greenwich
The Council Room
Anne's room in the Tower
A room in the Palace at Greenwich
A hall in the Tower
A corridor in the Tower

Exteriors:

The garden at Hampton Court
A field
Traitor's Gate at the Tower
Execution site at the Tower

1

Interior. Hall. Day. September

(*In the middle of the great hall at Hampton Court is a stone hearth on which smoulders a completely open fire. Anne sits by the fire and Henry stands near her. Closer to Anne are Lady Rochford and Lady Boleyn.*)

SMEATON (*Sings*): 'As the holly groweth green and never change the hue, So am I—ever hath been—unto my lady true.'

ANNE: The King writes a fine song. And you play it rarely.

SMEATON (*Bows*): Madam!

ANNE: Constancy is a goodly virtue, Mark. Remember it. (*Turning to Henry.*) What d'you think, your Grace.

HENRY: Aye. He plays well enough.

SMEATON: I thank your Grace.

ANNE: The sentiment was a fine choice. We turn with such ease from love to hate, do we not? (*Quietly.*) Leave us, ladies. Mark, you may withdraw a little.

(*The ladies rise and go. Mark moves off along the gallery and we only hear him playing very quietly through this scene. Anne goes to Henry. Both Anne and Henry are ill at ease with each other. Desperate to make the meeting work at least superficially.*)

Your Grace.

HENRY: Aye, madam?

111

ANNE: They have carved our arms, the royal and those of Anne Boleyn.

HENRY: They do well. Their work pleases me.

ANNE: And I. I owe you many thanks for giving me this. (*She indicates the hall.*)

HENRY: No need for thanks. (*He turns away.*) Wolsey could build well, madam.

ANNE: And die fortunately.

HENRY (*Subdued*): Aye. He was a proud man.

ANNE (*Going to him*): You did right, your Grace.

HENRY: I know.

ANNE (*Suddenly smiling*): No more talk of dying—that's the way to sadness. (*Taking his hand.*) Please. (*Simply.*) I love you when you laugh.

HENRY: And when I do not?

ANNE: I love you.

HENRY (*Smiles despite himself*): You are a child, Anne.

ANNE: And a woman—as you know well enough. (*She is brazen enough about her meaning.*) You remember those times—in the country? We'd no fears, no evil tongues to come between us. And now . . .

HENRY (*Interrupting*): And now we are older, Anne, and you are less a child.

ANNE: You made me what I am.

HENRY: No.

ANNE: Constant to you, my good Lord. (*She puts a finger on the worry lines across Henry's forehead.*) I would smooth the care from your face. (*Henry takes her hand. Anne kisses the hand that holds her. She looks up at him over their joined hands.*) Our hands are interlocked as are our arms.

(*She kisses his hand again as he raises her head and looks at her.*)

HENRY: There was a time, Nan, when we were younger. Do you remember?

ANNE (*Softly, looks up*): You called me Nan.

HENRY: Not while he plays here. (*Indicating Smeaton.*)

ANNE: I'll send him away, your Grace. Or we could go.

HENRY (*Breaks from her*): No.

(*Change of mood on his move.*)

ANNE (*Hurt*): I no longer please you?

HENRY: You please me well enough.

ANNE: And yet you'll not bed with me.

HENRY: I have other matters, madam.

ANNE: Other women!

HENRY (*Cold*): And if I have?

ANNE: I am your Queen. Your wife.

HENRY: And I am your King.

ANNE (*Softly*): And husband.

(*Henry nods.*)

HENRY: I've told you. No.

ANNE: Those other women. Do you love them? Can they give you an heir?

HENRY: Can you?

ANNE: Our daughter, Elizabeth.

HENRY: A girl!

ANNE (*Angry*): You were pleased enough at her birth.

HENRY: Aye. But a woman is no fit heir.

ANNE: They are fit only for your bed, it seems.

HENRY (*Shaking head*): There are no other women, Anne.

ANNE: I don't believe it.

HENRY: It's the truth.

ANNE: No.

HENRY (*To her*): You ask too much of me. I speak truth. Believe me.

(*He takes her hand and she snatches it away.*)

ANNE (*Sharp*): Soft words. Soft words. You do not love me.

HENRY: I'll not be miscalled by any woman. Queen or no.

(*He turns to go.*)

ANNE: Please, Henry stay.

4. *Anne Boleyn* (*Dorothy Tutin*) *with Henry*

5. *Henry and Anne banqueting with Norfolk* (*Patrick Troughton*), *Cromwell* (*Wolfe Morris*), *Smeaton* (*Michael Osborne*) *and Cranmer* (*Bernard Hepton*)

6. *Henry and Anne Boleyn dancing with their court*

7. *Lady Rochford (Sheila Burrell) and Thomas Cromwell (Wolfe Morris) plotting Anne's downfall*

HENRY: My name, madam.

ANNE: Husband.

HENRY: You give me the lie, madam. Name me whoremaster. I'll leave you till your temper's cooled.

ANNE (*Crying now*): Please, your Grace.

HENRY (*Embarrassed by her tears*): Don't use your tears, with me. I'll have no more of them.

ANNE (*Quietly*): I am to bear your son ...

HENRY (*Interrupting*): Madam, I've told you ... (*It sinks in.*) My son? (*She nods.*) No. I'll not believe it.

ANNE: Believe me.

HENRY: My father had three sons. Three chances of an heir and I have none save bastards.

ANNE: I'm to bear you a son, sir. Your Grace's heir. (*She has moved close to him.*) And yet, I have heard some say I am not your rightful wife.

HENRY: Who? Who dares say it?

ANNE: We have been strangers since we made this that pumps up my belly, and I would see those who say I am not your Queen gutted on Tower Hill. I would have them scattered like offal when my son is born.

HENRY (*Quietly*): So they shall be. Should you bear me a son.

(*He turns from her.*)

ANNE (*Round him*): Your Grace, can we dance this night that all may see we're right together.

115

HENRY: Tonight? Aye, Nan . . . we shall dance.

ANNE: My Lord, then all the world may rejoice with us in our son. We'll dance and share all our joy.

(*She reaches out both hands for him to take her hands. Her face is smiling at the mouth and the worry by her eyes is only minimal. Henry doesn't touch her hands.*)

HENRY: Pray for a son.

(*He goes. Anne walks slowly down the hall to Smeaton who is still playing. Lady Rochford has come into the doorway of the hall and watches.*)

ANNE: Mark, play for me again. Come to my room and play me something gentle.

(*She gives Mark a coin. Lady Rochford slips away.*)

2

Interior. Anne's bedchamber. Day.

(*Lord Rochford alone in the room for the moment. He is at the window. A handsome young man. Very close to his sister, Anne, and utterly estranged from his wife. Lady Rochford comes in and shuts the door without seeing him. He watches her for a moment and she then registers his presence.*)

LADY ROCHFORD: Husband.

ROCHFORD (*Gently sarcastic*): Madam.

LADY ROCHFORD: You wish to speak with your sister and not with your wife, I think.

ROCHFORD : I think so. Yes.

LADY ROCHFORD : And I may go hang?

ROCHFORD (*Coldly*) : As you will, madam.

LADY ROCHFORD : Could you but see beyond her eyes, which bedazzle you, you would not love her and fawn upon her as you do.

ROCHFORD (*Blaze of anger*) : Mind your tongue, madam.

LADY ROCHFORD (*Contempt*) : No spirit in you. No manhood. I've married a jelly.

ROCHFORD : And I a tight-lipped bitch.

LADY ROCHFORD : You knew, sir, when we married.

ROCHFORD (*Shaking head; genuinely*) : No. I did not.

LADY ROCHFORD (*Laughs*) : You wanted love, my Lord? You confound me.

ROCHFORD : Maybe.

LADY ROCHFORD : I could never love a jelly.

LORD ROCHFORD : The French whores are better spoken than you will ever learn to be. (*Lady Rochford is near him and goes to strike him. He catches her hand, as it rises.*) It would be folly, madam.

(*Smeaton has opened the door. And Anne has come in, as this is going on. She is followed by Lady Boleyn whom she dismisses at a gesture. She faces the two of them, as Smeaton shuts the door.*)

ANNE : It is folly.

ROCHFORD (*Crossing to her*): My sweet sister.

(*He kneels to her. She leaves him kneeling, and goes to Lady Rochford.*)

ANNE: Brawling, madam?

LADY ROCHFORD (*Sarcastic*): It was love play, my Lady.

ANNE: Do not juggle words with me.

LADY ROCHFORD (*Apologizing*): Madam.

ANNE: I would speak with my brother. (*Lady Rochford goes. Lord Rochford is still on his knees. Anne goes to him and looks down at him.*) They say I am overbearing, brother. D'you think it?

ROCHFORD: No. Proud maybe. And you are Queen, so that is well.

ANNE: George. You should not kneel to me.

ROCHFORD: You're the Queen.

ANNE: And your sister.

(*They kiss. A greeting? Rochford breaks away from Anne, who stands by a mirror. She preens a little.*)

You have never loved her, have you, brother? (*Rochford says nothing.*) And yet she is a strong woman and rich enough. (*Turns to him.*) She does not take your fancy?

(*He turns away a little.*)

ROCHFORD: I would not talk of it.

ANNE: I would you did!

ROCHFORD (*To her*): She is a tight-lipped ...

ANNE (*Completing it*): Bitch. Aye. And she is jealous.

ROCHFORD: How can you know of that?

ANNE: I watch her. And I am a woman. She is jealous.

ROCHFORD (*Nods*): Aye.

ANNE: With cause?

ROCHFORD: If you can be accounted a cause. Yes.

(*Anne looks at him and laughs.*)

ANNE: I? She is a fool. Any sister loves her brother. She is a fool. What of the ladies in France? (*Rochford smiles and says nothing.*) You liked them well this time? (*He nods a touch.*) And your wife is jealous of your sister?

(*She laughs again.*)

ROCHFORD: She and I have never loved, Anne.

ANNE (*Gently*): That is sad, I am sorry.

ROCHFORD: Aye.

ANNE: Truly. To love a man and to be loved is a most ... complete experience.

ROCHFORD: Would I could know it.

(*Anne goes to him and very close:*)

ANNE: That is so sad, brother. The King and I do love each other so.

ROCHFORD (*Shaking head*): Loved, Anne, it is not so now, I think.

ANNE: And, George, it will be so. (*She indicates her belly. He is delighted.*)

ROCHFORD: Anne.

ANNE: Yes, it will be a son.

3

Interior. Hall. Night. September.

(*A ball is in progress. The masked courtiers turn and dance their figures and leading them are Anne and Henry. Across the hall, Cranmer stands and watches. He disapproves of it all and does not wear a mask. A masked figure sidles to him.*)

CROMWELL (*The masked figure*): Times run well for you, Master Cranmer.

(*Cromwell is laughing at Cranmer, who is worried about this person whom he can hardly see in the candle-light.*)

CRANMER: Master Cromwell?

CROMWELL: Aye. You are in favour?

CRANMER: Times are topsy turvy, Cromwell, and men should watch their heads.

CROMWELL: Aye. Some more than others I am warned. (*He smiles.*)

(*Henry and Anne move closer in the dance.*)

HENRY: You must take care, madam.

ANNE: Not yet, your Grace.

HENRY: That son of mine shall not be early born as was the last.

ANNE: You should forgive me that.

HENRY: This son of yours, (*Pats her belly.*) will forgive all things. Believe me. (*He laughs and she stays silent.*) You are weary?

ANNE: Afraid.

HENRY: Of what?

ANNE: Men. I told you, sir.

HENRY (*Alert, angry*): What men? Show me them that frighten you. You shall not fear, for the sake of him in you.

ANNE (*In his ear*): There are some who still refuse to believe me Queen. They are guilty of treason, your Grace. For they will lead others to think the same and would make your son a bastard.

(*Henry nods shortly.*)

HENRY: We will dance, my Lady, and it may be that such men will dance to another tune. I'll talk with Cromwell.

(*He whisks her into the dance. The best dancer in Europe at the time. Cranmer watches. Lady Boleyn watches. We see a glimpse of others. Lord Norfolk watching Brereton dancing. The dance progresses and Anne is whisked away from Henry. For the moment Henry is not in the figure. Anne is dancing with Norreys. George Rochford is with the King watching the figure.*)

121

LORD ROCHFORD (*Referring to Norreys*): A handsome man, your Grace.

HENRY (*Scornful*): Henry Norreys?—He dances like a horse, Rochford.

LORD ROCHFORD: But handsome, you'd agree your Grace?

HENRY: Aye, handsome enough. Were I not a better man I might be jealous. (*He laughs. Rochford does not.*) You're not jealous, Rochford, are you?

LORD ROCHFORD: She is a sweet sister, your Grace.

HENRY: With a sharp tongue, on occasion.

ROCHFORD: You'll kerb her, no doubt.

(*He is still watching Anne and Norreys. Anne is laughing and happy with Norreys.*)

4

Interior. Gallery. Night.

(*Shadows and deep dark corners. Arches stretch away into the distance. Vaguely we can see in the nook of one of these arches a figure, a masked man. A woman enters quickly and slightly scared. She looks around and then joins the figure in the archway.*)

CROMWELL (*Impatient*): Well?

LADY ROCHFORD: She shows favour to two or three over all others.

CROMWELL: I need names, woman.

LADY ROCHFORD: Mark Smeaton.

122

CROMWELL (*Surprised*): A musician?

LADY ROCHFORD: It is true. I heard her talk with him and she bade him come to her chamber and play to her.

CROMWELL: Music?

LADY ROCHFORD: She paid him overwell for a strum of his lute. Of that I'm sure.

CROMWELL (*Cold*): How well?

LADY ROCHFORD: Gold.

CROMWELL: Smeaton. What others?

LADY ROCHFORD: Sir Francis Weston and Master Norreys she favours. I have heard her talking with Norreys of the time when our Lord King be dead.

CROMWELL (*All ears*): Go on.

LADY ROCHFORD: She did ask him who would be her husband then. And Norreys seemed to feel he fitted her bill.

CROMWELL: Aye?

LADY ROCHFORD: They played with words but there was meaning behind it.

CROMWELL: Would you say they plotted for King Henry's death?

LADY ROCHFORD: I could not say they didn't.

(*Cromwell sighs. He has the start of a case now.*)
There are others. Lord Rochford.

123

(*Cromwell is quite still.*)

CROMWELL (*Very quietly*): He is her brother. D'you know what you say, my Lady?

LADY ROCHFORD: Aye.

CROMWELL: Lady Rochford, remember what I know and remember I will use it. Against you if I must. Listen and watch and wait your time. Goodnight.

(*She goes. A smile appears under the mask that Cromwell is wearing.*)

5

Interior. Hall. Night.

(*The ball is on. Henry and Anne are dancing.*)

6

Exterior. Garden. Day. October.

(*Henry practising archery. There are two arrows in target. Anne is watching from a litter.*)

7

Exterior. Fields. Day.

(*Henry using falcons for hunting. A bird smacks into his gauntlet. Anne is watching, delighted, from a litter.*)

Cut to:

8

Interior. Hall. Night. December.

(*A banquet with Anne at Henry's right side. They are eating and drinking heartily. Henry leans across the table to her.*)

HENRY (*Almost in her lap*): I would come to you tonight, Nan.

ANNE: My Lord—

HENRY: We will ride a few furlongs together, eh?

(*He belches in her ear.*)

ANNE (*Touching her belly*): Would it be so wise, my Lord? We must protect your son.

(*Henry belches again and takes a drink. Smeaton is watching from a distance. Lord Rochford watches too. Henry runs his hand lovingly over her stomach.*)

HENRY: I'd mount you now, Anne. Son or no son.

ANNE (*Laughing but nervous*): Before your Archbishop?

(*Cranmer is watching them.*)

HENRY: Before all. We'll go, madam.

ANNE: You must not take pleasure of me now, my Lord.

HENRY (*Angry*): Then I'll take it elsewhere. (*He goes.*)

(*Anne watches him go. She is livid—no one speaks.*)

9

Interior. Anne's bedchamber. Morning.

(*Anne is combing her hair. It is morning and the clean light shafts into the room, warming the linenfold wooden panels of the walls.*)

ANNE: I will not endure it.

ROCHFORD: You can do little else. He is your King.

ANNE: He is my husband. I will not let him whore.

(*Rochford takes comb from her.*)

ROCHFORD: Anne, take care your tongue doesn't loosen your head. What he does, he does. There is no help for it—for it is in his nature. But when that son of yours is born—then you can demand his faith— maybe.

(*He is combing her hair, as he speaks. Wrenching her head away from the comb, Anne says:*)

ANNE: Take care. That hurts. (*Looks round at him.*) I can't endure my hair pulled.

ROCHFORD: There is much you 'can't endure'. And there is much you must learn to endure, sister.

ANNE: He will not whore further.

ROCHFORD (*Round to her*): Anne ... (*He is close now.*) The King will love you for your son. But don't, please don't demand or order his Majesty or you will reap a bitter harvest. Let it lie.

ANNE: I have my honour.

(*Rochford who has heard enough, says:*)

ROCHFORD: Your honour . . .

ANNE (*Warning*): I am Queen, George.

ROCHFORD (*Bored with her tantrums*): Let us forget it. And by the Mass, leave your husband to his own devices at this time.

(*Anne gets up and leaves. Her hair is still flowing in disarray down her back. George Rochford sighs and puts the comb down.*)

10

Interior. King's bedchamber. Same day.

(*Henry is being fitted with his armour. It has been made specially of course and the main reason is that Henry is putting on weight. He is pretty evil-tempered with the people fussing around him. We do not see who he is talking to at first.*)

HENRY: I cannot breathe out you fool. I'm locked in this like one pressed. I cannot breathe.

ARMOURER: It was made as measured . . . your Grace.

HENRY: Don't . . . don't . . . dare to say I lie.

(*The armourer hangs his head. He knows he can do nothing with Henry in this mood. Henry removes helmet. Anne comes in past a dissenting courtier. Henry is raging on.*)

Well . . . do we lie?

ARMOURER: No, your Majesty. It is my foolishness.

HENRY: It is. (*Henry turns and sees Anne.*) What d'you want, woman. I told them to admit no one.

ANNE: I am the Queen, your Grace.

HENRY: Well?

ARMOURER: Will you try the armpiece, your Grace?

HENRY: The devil choke you. Get me out of this before I die for lack of air. (*To Anne.*) What d'you want?

ANNE: To speak with your Grace.

HENRY: I would rather not. (*To armourer.*) Go with this and make me something that will fit.

ANNE: Will you hear me?

HENRY: I am weary of that too. You, Cromwell, Cranmer. All of you sounding in my ears. (*To armourer.*) Leave us! I would talk with my wife. Leave us! (*He aims a kick at the cringing man.*)

(*Armourer goes. Anne is smiling.*)

ANNE: Now, will you hear me?

HENRY: I tell you I am weary of it. (*Quoting.*) 'Your Majesty would do well to consider the French offer.' ... 'The Emperor Charles desires ...' Talk, talk, talk. 'You never come near me'—I hear enough.

ANNE: Why do you never come near me, and talk to me?

HENRY (*Crossly*): I do not wish to see you so.

ANNE: Yet you desire what causes my state. You want our son.

HENRY: Aye.

ANNE: But you cannot take a minute from your whores and take that minute with your wife.

HENRY (*Quite deliberately*): D'you know what some still call you, madam? (*She does, but won't admit it.*) The great whore. (*Goes to her.*) Is it mine? That, in there?

ANNE (*Angered*): That is your son. You got him. No one else. You use me as a whore—I cannot endure it.

HENRY: You will endure all, Anne. I rule here.

ANNE: I shall leave.

HENRY: You will stay, Anne, until I give you leave. And then you will—go.

ANNE: No. You mock me. To other women and to men in my court. You keep people by you who hate me. You dare say that your son was sired by another man. (*Shouting now.*) You're not fit to be father to my son.

(*Henry white with anger at this, says*:)

HENRY: My Lady, remember with whom you speak. I have the power to humble you more than I have raised you. Remember that before you speak again.

ANNE: Threaten me. Strike me if you will. But my Lord, for pity's sake, do not humble me as you do. That I cannot endure. The ladies that you bed I hear of it, my Lord. My ladies delight to tell me. They see me suffer as they tell me and they say it is well for you to go to other women as I am in this state. But you are my husband and no whoremonger.

HENRY (*Coldly*): If this offend you, shut your eyes, as your betters have done. All you have to do is give me a son. Then I shall love you as is fitting. Just a son. (*Shouts.*) Armourer!

(We see the fear start in Anne. She leaves and returns to her own room. Armourer returns.)

11

Interior. Anne's bedchamber. Day.

(Rochford is setting out chess men. Lady Boleyn and Lady Rochford are in the background. Lady Rochford watches intently as Anne enters; she sits and begins the game of chess. It is clearly one of their habits. They play silently for a while.)

ANNE *(Playing a piece)*: Jane Seymour, I have heard it said.

ROCHFORD: Who says it?

ANNE: Your wife told me.

ROCHFORD *(Harsh)*: Aye. She would delight to tell you.

ANNE: It was her duty, she said.

ROCHFORD: I will not believe it.

ANNE: I need you near me, George. *(Puts her hand on his.)*

ROCHFORD: I can do little.

ANNE: I am far from all who love me. It has ever been so.

ROCHFORD: No.

ANNE: Aye. You remember you were sent away . . . when I was crowned.

ROCHFORD: You needed none then.

ANNE: They whispered down the streets as I passed them. I needed you by me, George. They whispered 'the Great Whore' as I passed them.

(*Rochford moves a piece.*)

ROCHFORD: It's your move. Those people are nothing.

ANNE: And yet they loved Catherine and I would be loved by them as much.

ROCHFORD: Madam, you are Queen. What matters that they should whisper down a street. They are but common folk and you are Queen. Though she be in danger as I see it. (*Referring to Chess board.*)

(*Anne taking his piece with her Queen.*)

ANNE: Jane will be sorry that I heard of her. For when I have my son she shall feel my power. As others have.

ROCHFORD: And the King will give you the honour due to you.

ANNE (*Snapping out of gloom*): Aye, Aye, so he will when this, (*She pats her belly.*) is born. (*A tight laugh.*) We shall win back the King from the Seymours.

(*We see Lady Rochford's angry face.*)

12

Interior. King's bedchamber. Day. January.

(*The King has his leg up on a stool. He has hurt it in a fall from his horse. Cromwell is with him.*)

131

CROMWELL: She is well hated, your Majesty.

HENRY: Aye, I believe it.

CROMWELL: You have seen it. The women on your progress north with the Queen a year ago: they spat at her, your Majesty. You remember that.

HENRY: I remember. (*Cromwell tentative, wanting to find out.*)

CROMWELL: And your Grace loves Mistress Seymour.

HENRY: Now, Crum, I love no one. Least of all mares. Mine threw me this afternoon and I have done riding for a time.

CROMWELL: I have talked with Cranmer as your Majesty would have me.

HENRY: I would have you?

CROMWELL: Very wisely. Very wisely.

HENRY: And what said Cranmer?

CROMWELL: He was of my opinion your Majesty. That your Grace knows where your duty lies and we know where ours is.

HENRY (*Blustering*): The truth.

CROMWELL: Your Grace is blamed by many for the death of the Princess Dowager Catherine. And for the fate of men like More and Fisher. You are blamed for the indiscretions of your Queen.

HENRY: Cromwell. Tread softly.

CROMWELL: I tread as my duty directs me, your Majesty. I tread for your interest. The Queen, barren, or with a daughter, is nothing for you. She can be seen to be guilty of so much that you are blamed for. Master Cranmer and I both think your Grace did well.

HENRY (*Surprised*): Did well?

CROMWELL: We have found means to release you from her.

HENRY: What cause?

CROMWELL (*Shaking his head*): No cause, your Majesty. But means. England needs your heir or we'll have the bloody wars of York and Lancaster again.

HENRY: You think of your neck, eh?

CROMWELL: We think of our duty to your Grace.

HENRY (*Laughs*): I'm not a fool, Thomas. Ask friend Cranmer to start to pray for you and to pray that the Queen has no son. For by God, if she does I'll take you. Be assured. You have ways you say to remove her. And you've gathered causes I've no doubt. But should she mother an heir she must be above suspicion and you will be silenced. Good day Thomas, and ask friend Cranmer to start his prayers.

(*Cromwell goes.*)

13

Interior. Anne's bedchamber. Day. January.

(*We start in on Cranmer praying in silence before a Crucifix and lamp on the wall. As we pull out we see that the room has a bed in it and that on the bed Anne lies. She is crying. Cranmer crosses himself. He rises. Goes over to Anne who is still crying. Just lying staring up at the ceiling and crying.)*

CRANMER: ... Madam. (*Anne moves to look at him.*) ... Madam.

ANNE: I am frightened.

CRANMER: Pray, madam, for the safety of your child.

ANNE: I am so afraid. They leave me ...

CRANMER: No.

ANNE: I am alone, Cranmer.

CRANMER: Not true.

ANNE (*Almost shouts*): How can you ... my Lord. I'm sorry.

CRANMER: Please. Pray, my Lady.

ANNE: For what? Forgiveness? Should I pray for that? They blame me. Point the finger and accuse me, should I pray for their forgiveness? Catherine, her daughter, Mary ... should I pray that they will forgive ... Cranmer they all turn against me.

CRANMER: My Lady you must try to ...

ANNE (*Interrupts*): I dreamed last night.

CRANMER (*Quietly*): Aye, madam.

ANNE: A room, hung with rich crimson cloth, a box of pearls and fine gowns, they were for me ... (*The memory of the dream is too much for a moment. Her voice breaks with the horror of it.*) Cranmer, I am afraid. In my dream I saw this room through what seemed a gauze. I pushed against it and was held.

Held fast. The gauze that spread across the room—it was a web, Cranmer and I was held fast in it. (*Anne has become more and more fearful as she has gone on. She sobs out.*) I am in great fear. And I am alone, Cranmer, I am left alone.

CRANMER: Madam, this is not true. You must pray to God to give you peace.

ANNE: I must pray to God to give me a son. The King would have a son and I would give him one. But—(*Very quietly.*) I am afraid.

CRANMER (*Lying*): There is no need.

ANNE (*Despairing*): What would you know of fear? It sinks itself in me and roots there. Have you held something beautiful. Something you could not endure to lose. Have you? (*He doesn't answer.*) A jewel, a flower, a woman? (*No answer.*) I saw the King weep for me once. I'd left him for one day only and he wept. A single tear now would be so precious. It would be our love, Cranmer. It goes. It rots into a canker as I watch it. And I would have a son to make it bloom again. (*Anne grabs her belly. Cranmer steps towards her.*) A son, Cranmer. Get help. Get me help. (*He goes as she sinks on to the bed. Anne is crying still and winces once. Her long hair frames her swollen and none too attractive face.*)

14

Exterior. Garden. Day.

(*Early morning. Henry and Jane are walking in the cold Winter sunshine. They are so obviously happy together. The sun glistens on them and across the formal garden. Henry Norreys comes rushing to them. He reaches Henry. Jane watches with apprehension.*)

HENRY NORREYS: Your Majesty, a message. The Queen is delivered of her child, your Majesty. Before the time.

HENRY (*Excited*): Well?

NORREYS: A boy ...

HENRY (*A cry of triumph*): A boy! Jane. A boy!

(*Henry whirls and races off across the garden leaving Norreys standing with Jane.*)

NORREYS (*Calling*): Your Majesty ... there is more to ...

(*But Henry is out of earshot and Norreys cannot deliver his full message. Jane stands alone under the gleaming sun. A puff of breath hangs in the cold air. The light shimmers on a dew spangled spider's web.*)

14A

Interior. Gallery.

HENRY: Out of my way. Out of my way. Where is he? Where is my son?

15

Interior. Anne's bedchamber at Greenwich. Morning.

(*Subdued light and subdued helpers around Anne. Anne is weeping in the bed. Henry bursts through the door and rushes in. Anne is still weeping.*)

HENRY: Where is he? (*Henry slowly gets the message.*

Something is wrong. He swings on Lady Boleyn who is behind him. Lady Boleyn doesn't answer him. He goes to the bed. Roughly.) Well, madam. My son?

ANNE: It was before the time, your Grace. Too soon.

HENRY: Where is he?

ANNE: Forgive me.

HENRY: Forgive . . . ? What . . . What have you done to my son?

ANNE: I have been so afraid, he came too soon.

(*Henry whirling on the women.*)

HENRY: Where is he?

(*Anne reaches for his hand.*)

ANNE: Our son was born dead, sir. It was too soon. I hadn't gone my time. There can be no blame for that. Our son is dead.

(*Henry looks at her. Wrenches his hand away and turns to the people there. Very quietly.*)

HENRY: No.

(*They drift out very quietly. Henry turns back to Anne who is lying looking up at him. She has no tears now.*)

ANNE: God's will, your Grace.

HENRY: No.

(*He shakes his head.*)

ANNE: Aye. We've had ill luck, but it will change.

HENRY: You had him—dead, madam. (*He shakes his head again.*) I cannot weep for you. Not now.

ANNE: You will, my Lord. Weeping and love are close.

HENRY: And I am empty. I hear one thing only. Pounding at my brain.

ANNE: Sir.

HENRY (*Very quietly*): The Great Whore. (*She turns away as if he's hit her.*) You killed him. You killed my son.

(*She turns to look up at him.*)

ANNE: No.

HENRY: You killed my son.

ANNE: Our son.

HENRY: My son. You killed him. You bewitched him as you bewitched me these last years. You are a foul thing. You shall have no more by me.

(*He turns to go. She kneels up in the bed and takes his hand. Anne kissing the hand.*)

ANNE: Don't leave me. We can try again. I am young enough and you have the power, your Grace. Don't leave me to them.

(*She kisses his hand as she speaks. He strikes her once across the face. She lets the hand go and Henry leaves. Anne stays kneeling in her bed. Hand to her face. Sobbing in great wracking heaves and with no tears.*)

16

Interior. A room in the Palace. Day.

HENRY: Three months you've had.

CROMWELL: It takes time, your Grace. We have all we need now. The Queen has been unfaithful.

HENRY: As I thought.

CROMWELL: Her musician, Smeaton, will be accused.

HENRY: Her musician . . .?

CROMWELL: There is worse, your Grace. Norreys, Brereton, Francis Weston and still worse.

17

Exterior. Tourney. Day.

(*We hear the sound of a crowd of people. Anne and Henry are at the balcony of a marquee. George Rochford is beneath the balcony on his horse talking to Anne who is leaning out of the balcony. Henry is talking (unheard) to the Captain of the Guard. On the balcony, Anne is very tense. George pulls away a second and looks at her. Then very quietly.*)

ROCHFORD: My dear sister it is no time for fear. His Grace has come with you. You are forgiven.

ANNE (*Forcing a smile*): Maybe, brother, I hope . . .

(*She bites on the smile and stops her lip from trembling. Then she turns away from Rochford.*) The jousting is a brave sight, your Grace. (*Henry grunts in reply.*) And yet you are displeased.

HENRY: No.

ANNE: Did you see my brother? He is a fine sight.

HENRY: Rochford? You love him, madam?

ANNE: My brother? (*Laughs.*) Yes, indeed, sir. (*Henry grunts and turns away. He takes a goblet of wine and drinks. He has had rather too much anyway. He watches as Anne gives a handkerchief to a lady and sends her away. Anne comes to Henry. Gently.*) Your Grace rarely smiles upon me now.

HENRY (*Quietly, almost sadly*): There is rarely cause for me to smile, madam.

ANNE: We're seldom joyous together and I would make you happy.

HENRY (*Laughs*): Or a cuckold.

ANNE (*Shocked*): What?

HENRY: That kerchief?

ANNE: Aye?

HENRY: I gave it you.

ANNE: No, your Grace.

HENRY: Who then?

ANNE: I made it, sir.

HENRY (*Snorts*): Made it!

ANNE: It is true.

HENRY: And where does it go? Where now?

ANNE (*Confused*): I do not know what you would say.

HENRY: 'Tis clear I think.

(*A shout from the tourney.*)

ANNE: I gave it to my knight, your Grace. A favour.

HENRY: To your knight—a favour. A handkerchief?

ANNE: Aye.

HENRY: Which knight, madam?

ANNE: Norreys. Henry Norreys.

(*Henry slowly turns from pouring wine into his goblet. He is not pouring straight now and it pours onto the wooden floor in a rich red stream.*)

HENRY: You give favours to Henry Norreys? (*To a guard.*) Tell Norreys we would see him.

ANNE: The wine. (*She points.*)

HENRY: Curse the wine. (*He turns to the men about him.*) We leave.

(*He steps away from Anne who looks at him in dismay.*)

ANNE: Your Grace. Not yet. I pray you. (*She starts to move to him. He strides away across the balcony and away from Anne.*) Sir!

(*He looks back at her a moment and then spins away and on to the steps. Henry Norreys stands in armour, on one of the steps about to mount to Henry.*)

THE SIX WIVES OF HENRY VIII

HENRY (*Standing above him*): Norreys, do you love our Queen?

NORREYS: As we should all love our Queen, your Majesty.

HENRY (*Louder*): Cross no words with me, sirrah.

(*Anne is watching and can do nothing nor say a thing.*)

NORREYS (*Shattered*): Your Majesty I did not mean to cross words . . .

HENRY (*Close to Norreys*): It was meant. Do you admit you love the Queen and that she is more to you than she should be? Admit it, and we could find an easy way for you. Deny it and you know what you will suffer.

NORREYS: I do deny it, your Majesty. She is a sweet kind lady.

HENRY: Aye, all that and she does give you favours.

(*Henry steps past Norreys and Henry's men close after him. Two grab Norreys. Anne watches in silent horror.*)

18

Interior. Council Room. Night.

(*Cromwell is seated at a table. There are two men with him and seated in a chair opposite him is Mark Smeaton. His face is puffed and a trickle of blood has dried on his face.*)

CROMWELL: We have Norreys too, Smeaton. He will tell us what we have to know should you deny us.

SMEATON: This is madness, sir. I know nothing.

CROMWELL (*Quietly*): You lie.

SMEATON: No.

CROMWELL (*Picking up a paper*): We have it here. Written and attested on oath. (*He reads.*) That the Queen, on the 12th day of April in the twenty-sixth year of the reign of Henry eight procured and incited Mark Smeaton esq., one of the musicians of the King's chamber to have illicit intercourse with her and that the act was committed at Westminster on the 26th day of that month. (*He looks up.*) It's all here, d'you see?

(*He might be talking to a simpleton from the tone he takes.*)

CROMWELL: You were favoured by the Queen.

SMEATON: I do not deny it.

CROMWELL: She paid you money.

SMEATON: Aye.

CROMWELL: How much?

SMEATON (*Confused*): I . . . I do not recall it.

CROMWELL: She paid you in gold coins Master Smeaton, didn't she?

SMEATON: Sometimes. Yes.

CROMWELL: Gold for a musician, Master Smeaton.

SMEATON: She is kind.

CROMWELL: To those she favours.

(*He laughs a moment, and the other two men laugh with him.*)

SMEATON : Those are lies on that paper, sir. I swear it.

(*Cromwell leans across the table.*)

CROMWELL : You had best swear they are the truth.

SMEATON : I don't . . . I cannot.

CROMWELL : 'Twould be to your advantage.

SMEATON : They are lies.

CROMWELL : But they will be your death, Master Smeaton. Believe me. For to know the Queen is an act of high treason.

SMEATON : I have never known the Queen.

CROMWELL : And yet she pays you gold. Not for songs alone. You cannot expect me to believe a song is worth gold. Or are you Orpheus in your playing? (*Harshly.*) And the Queen, Euridyce?

SMEATON (*Shaking his head*) : I have been guilty of nothing. I will swear to it.

(*Torturer goes close to him and catches the man's hair and pulls his head back. Fast, brutal and vicious.*)

CROMWELL : And I tell you it were best to admit your faults as written. For if you do you may escape. You understand me?

SMEATON : You seek charges against the Queen.

CROMWELL (*Tapping the sheet of paper*) : I have the charges, Smeaton. And I will have the admissions. I offered you an easy way to freedom.

144

SMEATON: Nor worth a spit. You know it. I am a friend to the Queen.

CROMWELL: Ah! A friend. We know that, Master Smeaton. From this paper we know what sort of friend. Admit it. It will be easier.

SMEATON: No.

(*Cromwell looks at him for a moment more. He goes to the table again and takes up from it a piece of rope. There are three knots in the rope. He dangles it from his hand.*)

CROMWELL: You know what this is?

(*Smeaton is horrified at the sight of it.*)

SMEATON: No.

CROMWELL: When we put this round your head and start to twist, these little knots will push your eyes out. Pop! Like chestnuts in the fire.

SMEATON: No. You cannot.

CROMWELL (*Gently*): Admit your guilt! It will suffice.

(*Smeaton shakes his head. They advance on Smeaton who waits for them. They place the cord about his face and one stands behind him, the other in front to hold him in the chair. Smeaton is moaning with fear.*)

(*Gently.*) Admit the charges Smeaton. Just say 'I am guilty' and we shall not need to twist the rope.

SMEATON (*Croaks*): I cannot.

CROMWELL: As you wish.

(*He signals to the man behind the chair who starts to*

twist a bar through the rope. He starts to turn the bar thus tightening the rope around Smeaton's head. We cut to Cromwell's face. Quite calm. To the man twisting the rope who is finding the going harder now. To the foot of the chair where Smeaton's foot taps and shudders on the floor. He groans.)

(*Sharply.*) Enough. (*Gently.*) Now, Mark. You will tell me you were guilty? (*Smeaton stays silent.*) Say 'guilty', and 'twill be done. (*Smeaton stays silent. Just moaning a little.*) So. I trust a blind man may play the lute. For you will be blinded very soon, Mark.

(*Cromwell sits at his table still smiling. The two men go on and suddenly Mark Smeaton screams. One sharp piercing scream across the room. The two men go on. Mark screams again. It is as if he's trying to say something.*)

Enough. (*He goes close to Mark and masks his face for us.*) Well? Do you confess?

(*Smeaton croaks once and then one word.*)

SMEATON: Guilty.

(*Cromwell stands up well pleased. He is quietly satisfied with things. He turns to the two men.*)

CROMWELL: You shall be rewarded. Take that offal out.

SMEATON: You promised . . .

CROMWELL: I promised nothing to a traitor. You shall not burn perhaps. But you shall die for sure.

(*He gestures to the men to remove Smeaton. They rush the broken man out as we cut to :*)

146

19

Interior. Anne's bedchamber. Night.

LADY BOLEYN: The Tower, madam. I heard it from one of Cromwell's household.

ANNE: Poor Norreys.

LADY ROCHFORD: What does it mean, madam?

ANNE: It means we have very little time before we are taken too. (*She turns to Lady Boleyn.*) And Smeaton? What of him? I have not seen him today.

(*Lady Rochford is enjoying it.*)

LADY BOLEYN: Taken. Did I not tell you, madam? Cromwell took him also.

ANNE (*Quietly*): Poor Mark. (*Lady Rochford sighs a fake sigh.*) I think you play act, madam. That sigh is not meant.

LADY ROCHFORD (*Shrugs*): I cannot say it was. He is but a musician. Nothing.

ANNE: And Norrey's too. They are men at least. And good men.

LADY ROCHFORD: As was Sir Thomas More, madam.

ANNE: How dare you ... Leave us. We would have no more of you. And take care, for the King shall love me yet and you shall go—wife to my brother or no. (*Pause.*) And yet Aunt, she was right on one score. (*Lady Boleyn looks her question.*) Thomas More was a man for all that. And he died.

LADY BOLEYN (*Bitterly*): Aye. He did.

ANNE: Poor Mark and Henry Norreys. They will die. If his Grace takes men so silently and leaves them to Cromwell then you may be sure of that. There is little we can do. (*She is helpless.*) I would only know of what they have been accused.

LADY BOLEYN: I do not know, Anne.

ANNE: Nor I.

(*And she means it.*)

20

Interior. Council Room. Night.

(*A large jug of ale is near Norfolk and he swigs deep every so often. Cromwell drinks nothing.*)

CROMWELL: Brereton. Norreys, Weston, Rochford and Smeaton. They shall all be taken in their turn. Is it clear?

NORFOLK: Aye. 'Tis clear enough.

CROMWELL: And my Lord of Norfolk, his Majesty would have you act as Commissioner of the first hearings.

NORFOLK: You'll learn nothing from those men.

CROMWELL: I have one confession. From Smeaton. For the rest, you may be right. At least they are gentlemen.

NORFOLK: They would rather be torn in pieces than admit aught under torture.

CROMWELL: You've read the charges through?

148

NORFOLK: Aye. A broad batch they are too.

CROMWELL: The net must hold. And you must pull it in. The King wishes it.

NORFOLK: Shall I hear the Queen?

CROMWELL: Aye.

NORFOLK: My niece shall have no joy of her uncle, of that you may be sure. She's a proud shrew. (*Drinks.*)

CROMWELL: She must not speak. She has cunning words. Else how did she bewitch our King?

NORFOLK: She'll not bewitch me, Master Cromwell. But the form of justice must be done.

CROMWELL: It will be. You will read the charges. She'll plead not guilty. You will tell her there is a man confessed and she shall be held in the Tower for questioning.

NORFOLK: Will he have her killed?

CROWELL: The King?

(*Cromwell nods.*)

NORFOLK: The Tower then. She'll find it cold. (*He goes.*)

21

Exterior. Tower. Traitor's Gate. Night.

(*The evening is very quiet. There is the occasional chink as water drips in the background. Light from the flare in the wall casts shadows in the archways.*

There is the sound of a group of people approaching the gate. A guard steps from the shadows and takes the flare from the wall. The group comes close to him and stops. They are lit in the flickering flame. Norfolk, Cromwell, Lord Audley (Lord Chancellor) are there. A number of guards range themselves in the dark patches beside the main group. Anne Boleyn and her attendant, Lady Boleyn. Anne is white under the flare's light. Norfolk and the guard talk a moment and a door opens. We close in now. Sir William Kingston, the Constable of the Tower, comes over to Norfolk.)

NORFOLK: Kingston. We have your prisoner.

KINGSTON: We await her.

NORFOLK: Her lady is to accompany her. And we thought my Lady Kingston . . .?

KINGSTON: Aye.

(Cromwell has been watching this exchange and he now moves to them.)

CROMWELL: She is to be kept close. You understand, Kingston?

(Kingston doesn't like Cromwell.)

KINGSTON: Prisoners in the Tower, Master Cromwell, are rarely kept anything but close.

CROMWELL: See to it.

KINGSTON *(To Anne)*: Madam, I'll not welcome you. It would not be fit.

ANNE *(Quietly)*: Hardly. Yet you should have bid me welcome the last time I was lodged here. Before my Coronation.

150

KINGSTON: You shall have that same chamber, madam.

ANNE: A witty man. But don't fear for me, sir, for I shall soon be free.

KINGSTON (*To Norfolk*): Your business is done then, my Lord.

NORFOLK: For the moment. We'll speak later you and I.

KINGSTON: No doubt. (*To Anne.*) We'll go in then, madam.

(*Anne is only just beginning to understand fully.*)

ANNE: In?

(*Kingston nods. Anne looks at Lady Boleyn. She looks up at the flaring shadow over the arch that seems to press down upon her. A guard's face leers at her in the sudden revelation of the flames from the torch. Cromwell looks at her deadpan. Norfolk says nothing. Anne takes a decision and moves a step closer to the door in the archway. At the door, Anne stops and turns to the group.*)

I am truly afraid of this place.

(*Cromwell is still cold. Norfolk doesn't like the business now. Lady Boleyn is quite still. Anne kneels suddenly before the Lords.*)

Dear Jesus, help me. Before you I am innocent. You know I am innocent of the crimes I am accused of. Help me, my dear Lord Jesus, at this my time of need.(*She waits a moment and crosses herself. Anne then looks up at the Lords.*) And you gentlemen, I beg you, beseech my gentle Lord, King Henry, to be good to me that love him.

(*She goes up the steps and the gate clangs shut behind her. Mix to a crucifix.*)

151

22

Interior. Anne's room in the Tower. Day....

(*Anne is kneeling before a prie dieu. Her hair is now neatly brushed. She looks much calmer as she prays. The room is that from which Anne left the tower to be crowned only two and a half years ago. Behind Anne, the Lady Kingston is sewing at a simple dark grey dress. It has a very low collar. We shall see more of this dress as Anne was executed in it. Lady Boleyn comes in. Anne crosses herself and stands up. Throughout this scene Anne is nervous. Near hysteria. Laughter and giggles that are the prelude to breakdown twitter through her lips at the wrong times. She is physically very nervy, picking at imaginary threads on her clothes. Holding her hands together. Not too much but she is obviously under huge strain and she is beginning to show the signs. After all her friends are being eliminated and she knows deep inside that she has little hope of leaving the tower in one piece.*)

ANNE: Are you wearied ladies? Eleven days seems nigh on eleven months to me. (*She is pacing around the room, too. The window to the fireplace, around chairs and table and back to the window again.*) Yet there is time for thinking, such as we've never had before. Which may be no evil.

LADY BOLEYN: I have some news for you, madam.

ANNE: Bad news by your face, aunt.

LADY BOLEYN: Aye. Bad news.

ANNE: Well, let's hear it.

LADY BOLEYN: It is of Sir Francis Weston, Brereton, Master Norreys and Mark Smeaton . . .

ANNE (*Quite still by the window*): Well?

LADY BOLEYN: They are found guilty of the charges, madam. Your father was at their trial. He too proclaimed them guilty. (*A long pause.*) They will die, madam.

ANNE (*A sharp laugh*): Oh indeed!

LADY KINGSTON: And in finding them guilty . . .

ANNE: They will find me guilty too.

(*Anne laughs more. Not a healthy laugh. Strained.*)

LADY BOLEYN: Anne . . . Anne. No more. No more.

ANNE (*Still laughing*): They will find me guilty also. They will try me. A trial for the Queen of England. (*She stops laughing abruptly.*) They would never dare. The King would not have it so. (*She is desperately trying to persuade herself. Her ladies can offer no help. The talk gets wilder and wilder as she goes on and on and finally she is talking through tears.*) I grieve for Mark and for the others. But the King will never have me tried. They will free me. And should they wish to keep me from the world I'll go to a nunnery. That will suffice. I'll write to him and make that offer. A nunnery would answer it. It would answer? It would? (*To the ladies who say nothing.*) The King would not put me away. I am his wife and Queen of England. He would not try me. (*She turns to the ladies.*) He wouldn't try me. There are no men who can judge me. Save only my Lord, the King. Once, I made him weep, did you know that. When we were younger I left him. Aye. It's true. And he begged me on his knees to come back to him. He wept before my father and brother and begged them to get me back. He is a handsome fool. (*Gently.*) And now his tears are worth nothing for he weeps so often. He will make no trial for me? (*Lady Boleyn*

153

looks at her flatly.) And the charge against my dear brother. I and my brother bedded together. The King cannot press it. (*Certain.*) We shall go free. I know it. I know it. I know it.

LADY KINGSTON: Madam, sit and rest for a little. You are weary. Overwrought.

ANNE: Did you know that three years but a few days and I lay dreaming of a coronation. Today—shall I sleep, think you? Shall I sleep again? (*Lady Kingston is near her. She gets up.*) I must pray, I must find forgiveness. I've ill treated the Lady Mary, Catherine's child, been jealous, proud. And I would be quiet in my mind. I shall pray ladies. Do you likewise.

23

Interior. A room in the Palace. Early evening.

(*Henry and Cromwell. Henry is drinking again. Heavily. Henry is pleased with life and couldn't give a damn about anything but Jane and living the good life. He is trying on some new garment.*)

CROMWELL: She will be found guilty, your Majesty.

HENRY (*Offhanded*): Yes, I'm sure of it. I'm sure of it. (*He nods.*) D'you like this colour, Cromwell?

CROMWELL: Your Majesty, I've ascertained from France . . .

HENRY: D'you think a lady would like the colour, eh?

CROMWELL: . . . and from the Emperor's ambassador . . .

HENRY: It suits me well, Cromwell.

CROMWELL: ... that they will be pleased to salute a new Queen.

HENRY: Jane should please them all. Though me above the rest. Eh? (*He laughs.*)

CROMWELL: They must think they have some advantage through the death of the Queen.

HENRY: Death? (*It shocks him.*)

CROMWELL: She will be tried, found guilty of treason and will die. It is the law.

HENRY (*Goes to the window*): It is too fair an evening to talk of death, Cromwell. Do you see to it.

CROMWELL (*Bows*): Your Grace.

HENRY (*Suddenly sharp*): What of the Lady Elizabeth? Well?

CROMWELL: We await your Grace's orders, your Majesty.

HENRY: She will be a threat to my heirs when Jane gives us sons. She shall be a bastard.

CROMWELL: Aye.

HENRY: See you to it. The trial is tomorrow, make sure that Cranmer divorces us before she is ... He should find it a simple matter. He got us married to the whore. Now he can unmarry us.

CROMWELL: Then it is in my hands?

HENRY: And Norfolk's. Be sure he knows his duty, Cromwell. I'll get a fitting heir to our throne. Perhaps this noon. Or tomorrow. Don't let that whore bewitch your court, Cromwell. And tell me when she's finished.

24

Interior. The Tower. Hall. Day.

(*The sun shines brightly through the windows and picks out the Yeomen of the Guard with axes and halberds. A scaffold has been set up in the hall. Norfolk stands and the hall becomes quiet.*)

NORFOLK (*In a firm and strong voice*): Gentleman gaoler of the Tower, bring in your prisoner.

(*The doors are thrown open and standing there is Sir William Kingston, bearing an axe with the edge turned away. He steps into the hall and after him comes the Queen. She walks steadily and utterly composed past the crowds of men. Slowly the court rises to her and men begin to bare their heads. By the time she has reached the chair set for her every man has bared his head. Anne is followed by Lady Boleyn and Lady Kingston plus Sir Edward Walsingham. Anne looks across at Cromwell and at Sir Christopher Hales. Then at the Jury of Lords. They bow at her. She inclines her head to them and sits. The Court sits and Norfolk motions to Hales.*)

Be seated, madam. Sir Christopher Hales will read the indictment so that all are clear as to the charges.

SIR CHRISTOPHER: My Lord. (*He bows.*) 'In the 28th year of the reign of our most gracious King Henry the Eighth, here in the Tower, be it known. That the lady Anne, formerly Anne Boleyn, now Queen of England, is charged on the following counts ... Under the Statute of Treasons, that being seduced and instigated by the devil, she has traitorously committed adultery. (*See Anne's face. Utterly impassive and calm. And mix through as Sir Christopher goes on.*) Also under the Statute of Treasons she is charged with compassing and imagining the King's death.

(*Anne stands and turns to Sir Christopher and Cromwell and directs her questions directly at Cromwell. Ignoring Hales.*)

ANNE: You have no right to try me. I am the Queen and you are not my equals. You cannot try me.

CROMWELL: But the fact is that we are, madam.

(*He laughs and others laugh too.*)

ANNE: But your verdict is written already by my uncle. (*Pointing at Norfolk.*) Why d'you hate me, Master Cromwell? (*He sits quite still.*) No answer. (*She smiles.*) Then I will tell you. You hate me because I know you as a liar and a self-seeker. And if you know the truth at all you know that to be so.

CROMWELL: My Lord, must I take such words from . . .

ANNE (*Interrupting*): The Queen. (*She waits. He subsides.*) My Lords, I love my husband and honour him as I am bound to do. It is his enemies who bring me here. It is his enemies who would bring me to my death. You are tools of the enemies of the King. You will be used by them.

(*There is a buzz of conversation from the Lords. Cromwell is openly smiling as we cut to him. He leans across to Sir Christopher.*)

NORFOLK: Quiet in this court. (*A rise in buzz of conversation, and it then stops. Leaning forward.*) Sir Christopher, we shall hear the attorney general.

(*Sir Christopher rises again and looks across the court at Anne who has sat down.*)

SIR CHRISTOPHER: My Lords, this is a simple matter simply disposed of. It is idle to believe that we would accuse a Queen of treason, or of Crimes against God it were not so. (The Queen as you have heard, has committed acts of fornication and of treason, and in so doing, by our laws is still guilty of crimes against our Sovereign Lord, King Henry.) You, my Lords have only to listen to the facts as we present them to see the monstrous nature of those crimes and to see also that our case rests on truth. It rests on confession freely given and on evidence of witnesses also freely given. I do but present you with the facts and from hearing them it will be your duty to agree the fate of that lady. You will find your duty unpleasant, my Lords, but you will be steadfast in your application of our law of the just punishment she so richly deserves.

ANNE (*Quietly to Norfolk*): I do protest, my Lord. I am found guilty before I am tried.

NORFOLK: You shall have your turn, madam, Sir Christopher . . .

SIR CHRISTOPHER: It is a fact that the lady did procure one Henry Norreys Esquire, on the 6th October, 1533, to have illicit intercourse with her. And that act was committed at Westminster on the 25th October in that year. It is a fact that she committed the same acts with William Brereton, Francis Weston and even, my Lords, with a musician, Mark Smeaton. We have dates and places set out and admissions, madam. It is a fact that this lady was jealous of those aforementioned and also of her brother George, Lord Rochford. So jealous that she would allow them no familiarity with other women. It is a fact that she gave them gifts to entice them to her will. But, mark this, she is guilty of worse and greater evils. It is a fact that she and the said traitors did, several times, compass and imagine the King's death. And she did promise to wed one or other of them when that should be accomplished.

ANNE (*Sweetly*): A lie, Sir Christopher. How could I when I love my husband?

CROMWELL (*To Norfolk*): My Lord, I do protest. The lady shall have her chance. The Attorney General must speak first.

NORFOLK: Aye. Be silent madam.

(*Anne sits. Cromwell grins at Sir Christopher.*)

SIR CHRISTOPHER: The lady did say, often, that they would deprive the King of an heir and they practised to compass this. We have testimony of this from witnesses who came freely to us that the truth could be known. My Lords, this is no matter for debate. This be fact. That lady is guilty and you will find her so I have no doubt.

(*He sits down. Cromwell pats his arm. He's done a good job. The Lords chatter a moment and Anne rises. The chatter stops instantly.*)

ANNE (*Sweetly*): Do I have my chance, now, my Lord? (*Norfolk nods.*) They say they have proofs. I would hear those proofs.

(*Cromwell is up in a flash with papers in his hand.*)

CROMWELL: These papers. These are proof enough. These are confessions. Signed by those who made them. Freely. (*Anne shakes her head and smiles.*) You may smile, madam. Listen and remember. 'I, Mark Smeaton, musician, do hereby admit to knowledge of Anne the Queen. She did beg me and promise me many rewards should I agree. She did give me gifts both before and after our intercourse.' When I asked

159

him when he was procured he told me the 12th April, 1534. It is here, in this paper. He knew her at Westminster on the 26th of that month. It is in this paper.

(*Sir Christopher Hales is up immediately. Sir Christopher another paper in hand.*)

SIR CHRISTOPHER: The truth is here too. In this paper. Freely signed. A serving woman of the Queen's declared that she had seen at different times, Norreys, Weston and Brereton in my Lady's privy chamber.

ANNE: Is she here? Will she say to us what you say is in those papers?

NORFOLK: We have no swearing of witnesses into this court, my Lady. You answer to us and no other.

ANNE: Can she be found? This serving woman?

CROMWELL: That is not material.

NORFOLK: Agreed.

ANNE: Where is she?

SIR CHRISTOPHER: She is dead.

(*The Lords on the jury look at each other.*)

CROMWELL (*Quickly*): You were heard with Henry Norreys plotting who should marry you when the King was dead.

ANNE (*Smiles*): No.

CROMWELL: We have more proof.

ANNE: More paper!

CROMWELL: One of your ladies.

ANNE: Mine?

CROMWELL: My Lady Rochford.

ANNE: My Lady Rochford. Aye, that rings true.

CROMWELL: You admit it then? You planned to kill the King.

ANNE (*Simply*): My husband.

SIR CHRISTOPHER: You should answer.

ANNE: You will answer, Sir Christopher. Before God.

CROMWELL: You dare not prate of God, madam.

ANNE: I dare. (*Gently.*) I am closer to him than you will ever be, I think.

CROMWELL (*Trump card*): You knew your brother, carnally. (*Anne's reaction. Jury and court reaction of horror.*) And you say you are close to God. You have sold yourself to the devil rather.

ANNE (*Very calmly*): I loved my brother.

CROMWELL (*Closer*): Ah. You loved your brother.

ANNE: Aye. (*She turns to the Lords.*) My Lords, I am accused of knowledge of my brother. Can you believe that? Can anyone? I love my brother, aye. I love my brother. Would any of you that have brothers deny that you love them? It is your duty before God. It is also my inclination, my Lord, for we were children of the same parents. We played together, ran free in fields together, rode together. I watched him as he learned to hunt, to shoot, to dance. I watched him at his learning and watched him in the closeness of our

161

family. He is my friend, my Lords, as much as my brother and I do love him for that.

(*There is a very favourable reaction from the court as a whole, and from the jury in particular. Cromwell leans close to Hales. There is a look between Cromwell and Sir Christopher.*)

SIR CHRISTOPHER: He stayed overlong in your bedroom many times.

CROMWELL (*Interrupting*): You loved him overwell it seems.

ANNE: I loved him, Cromwell, as any sister loves a brother.

SIR CHRISTOPHER: And how did he love you.

ANNE: We talk of love. I would hardly think that master Cromwell understands us. For he has never known it I fear.

CROMWELL (*Interrupting*): My Lord, this assault on my good name is hardly . . .

(*Anne laughs aloud. Anne to Norfolk.*)

ANNE: Forgive me, Uncle.

CROMWELL: You do not deny you kissed your brother.

SIR CHRISTOPHER: On the lips.

ANNE: I kissed my brother.

SIR CHRISTOPHER: Before he kissed his wife many times.

ANNE: She has charged that we did commit incest together?

162

SIR CHRISTOPHER: Aye.

ANNE: Then judge you how she loved him.

(*Jury reacts.*)

CROMWELL: You had no heir for the King. Your last child was still-born.

ANNE: My Lord—

CROMWELL: Aye. You did not even want a son fr his Grace's sake. You practised not to have one. You used forbidden knowledge to prevent it. You and those other traitors planned for the death of our King that you might take his place. (*Anne laughs. Cromwell to the Lords. He holds up papers.*) My Lords, think on this. She laughs when I talk of death for our King. And yet she says she loves him.

SIR CHRISTOPHER: You and my Lord Rochford spoke often of the problem of getting an heir.

ANNE: Yes, I was afraid that the King would not be content until he had a son.

SIR CHRISTOPHER: But you did say to Rochford that the King was not capable of begetting a son.

ANNE: No.

CROMWELL: Or any child.

SIR CHRISTOPHER: He could not be a father, you said. And yet you were brought to bed of children.

CROMWELL: Whose, madam?

SIR CHRISTOPHER: Whose?

ANNE: You malign me Cromwell. And you are safe to

do it now. It has taken you so long to bring me here and you must savour it.

CROMWELL (*To the Lords*): I am here because I love his Grace.

ANNE: You accuse me of bearing the children of others when I am married to the King.

CROMWELL: You cannot deny it.

ANNE: Tell me, am I proud?

SIR CHRISTOPHER: Overproud, madam.

ANNE: And if I am proud would I descend to have lowborn children by lowborn men?

(*The Lords look favourable again. Cromwell asides to Sir Christopher.*)

SIR CHRISTOPHER: And yet you took the traitors to your bed.

ANNE: Those? I had sooner take the king's dog.

CROMWELL (*Very bland*): Aye madam?

SIR CHRISTOPHER: We hold confessions and statements that alone condemn you.

ANNE: And how did you get them? (*There is a buzz around the court.*) Well?

(*Cromwell after a moment, walks to the jury benches.*)

CROMWELL: My Lords, a man confessed before two witnesses. That man was condemned with the other traitors of these crimes. Those men are guilty and so is she. The Great Whore she is called by the people and the great whore she is. One Smeaton, musician, confessed his guilt.

ANNE: Then I would see Mark Smeaton who freely confessed to things he'd never dreamed on, nor yet performed.

CROMWELL: He is condemned.

ANNE: And therefore ...?

SIR CHRISTOPHER: Cannot testify here. It seems a foolishness to ask for a condemned traitor to appear for you in defence.

CROMWELL: But note my Lords, she defends herself through a traitor.

SIR CHRISTOPHER (*To Norfolk*): I said we had no need of debate, my Lord. I require a verdict on this lady. The case is clear.

NORFOLK: Madam.

ANNE: It is sure that I am innocent, my Lord. And I am a victim. That, too, is sure. This whole mockery is unworthy of you, Uncle. It is unwrthy of you as representative of my gentle husband. This trial is no trial but a signature on the document. The poorest subject has justice that I am denied. I am the Queen, and entitled to better than you have given me. Accusations, paper and lies are easy means of denying the truth before a court of men. The truth shall be known before that court which shall judge us all in time. (*To Cromwell.*) I am sorry for you for in condemning me in this court you condemn yourself elsewhere. Give your verdict gentlemen and remember that I am your Queen.

(*She sits down and Sir Christopher sits also. Anne is quiet and composed again. Cromwell stands and looks at her and at the Lords. Cromwell very gently.*)

CROMWELL: My Lords, your Queen denies your right to hear her. She denies the honesty of each and every one of you. She denies that you are unbiased. She denies that you are gentlemen. She threatens you with the wrath of that court we shall all face in time. She dares to deny your justice. She dares to threaten you with the wrath of a God whom she has forsaken in her sinning. She calls you panders and liars and unworthy. She may be the Queen but she is a traitor and as such is judged by all of you. And I believe you honest men.

(*He sits down. The speech has made a good impression on the Lords.*)

NORFOLK: My Lords, consider your verdict. This lady is brought to us charged with abominable crimes. Adultery, incest and treason. You have heard her prosecution. You know of the confessions and of the accounts from witnesses. Your verdict, my Lords.

(*They move closer and start to chatter. They are subdued. Norfolk sits back. Anne is quiet. Cromwell sits and a soft smile lingers. Sir Christopher is still. He leans forward.*)

SIR CHRISTOPHER: There will be no dissension?

(*Cromwell shrugs and smiles a touch. The people in the court are quiet.*)

NORFOLK: My Lords, have you reached your verdict? (*There is general assent.*) We would hear it.

SURREY (*Standing*): Guilty upon my honour.

NORFOLK: Do you speak for all?

PEERS (*Chorus*): Aye!

(*Pause. Anne rises.*)

NORFOLK: Because you have offended against our Sovereign the King's Grace, in committing treason against his person, the law of the realm is this, that you have deserved death, and your judgment is this: that you shall be burnt here, within the Tower on the Green. (*See Anne's horrified face. A murmur from the people.*) Or you will have your head smitten off, as the King's pleasure shall be further known.

(*Anne's face. She looks across at Cromwell who is quite still. She turns after a moment and steps through those grouped behind her. Kingston and the rest. The Lords stand and the people watch her slow and stately march out in absolute silence. The door booms open and she steps from the Court. Cut to:*)

25

Interior. Tower corridor. Day.

(*The low arches of a corridor from the hall where the trial has taken place. A number of soldiers are about the place. Through the large doors at the end, Anne, Lady Boleyn, Lady Kingston, Sir William Kingston and a number of other men appear. Anne is absolutely upright. Proud, calm and dignified. She sweeps ahead of the others. Soldiers straighten up as she passes them. A group of soldiers appear along the corridor. In the middle of them is Lord Rochford. The two groups approach each other. Anne steps through the soldiers and to her brother as we close on them.*)

ROCHFORD: It's a sorry end.

ANNE: A beginning perhaps. (*Rochford is grabbed by one of the soldiers. Anne reaches up and kisses him again. He is ripped away from her.*)

KINGSTON: Come, madam. Come.

(*Anne looks at him very coolly and nods. She smiles at him.*)

ANNE: Master Kingston, I do love my brother.

(*She sweeps off down the corridor. They go with her and out of our sight. Mix to:*)

26

Interior. A room in the Palace. Evening.

(*Henry and Jane are eating dinner.*)

27

Interior. Anne's Tower room. Evening.

(*Anne and Kingston, Lady Boleyn and Lady Kingston. They are eating dinner.*)

ANNE: More wine, Master Kingston? (*Kingston shakes his head.*) You have a tickle stomach, sir. It is I who should be careful now.

KINGSTON: I have little appetite, my Lady, for this sort of work.

ANNE: Yet you do hate me. And you did love your other Queen, I am told.

KINGSTON: I did love Queen Catherine. Aye.

ANNE: And you hate me?

KINGSTON: I cannot, madam, I could not eat at table with one I hated.

ANNE: There are many, sir, who would not feel so. It pleases me that you cannot hate me now.

KINGSTON: Aye.

ANNE: Master Kingston, will you grant me one favour.

KINGSTON: If I can, I will.

ANNE: Should the King allow them to execute me, which I doubt. Though your long face would have it so. Can you ask the King to make it quick? I am frightened of the fire, Master Kingston, and would rather die by quicker means.

KINGSTON: I will try, madam.

ANNE: It is a fearful slow death by flame. I have watched and know it.

(*Cut to:*)

28

Interior. A room in the Palace. Evening.

(*Henry and Cromwell. Lady Jane is still eating.*)

HENRY: Burned or beheaded, there is no jot of difference.

CROMWELL: Unless one is the victim your Majesty.

HENRY: This is not fit talk for a lady, Cromwell. I will have it finished.

CROMWELL: Then is she to die slowly?

HENRY: Fire is slower I grant you. I shall be merciful. Should she divorce me, admit her guilt, I shall be merciful. She shall die the quicker way. Tell Cranmer he must move quickly.

CROMWELL: I dared your Majesty to ask Master Cranmer to come here tonight.

HENRY: We shall not see him. Tell him he has no time for thinking. He must act on this. I want that witch divorced from me. I would marry again. Come Jane. (*They go out. Cranmer enters.*)

CRANMER: I've sat and waited. You ask me to come down and now the King will not see me. You shame me.

CROMWELL: Sit down. Some wine, Master Cranmer.

CRANMER: Soft words are of no use. I . . .

CROMWELL: Sit down. (*Cranmer sits on the order.*) Now a word in your ear. His Majesty wants his divorce and quickly. We do not concern ourselves with how you obtain it. But obtain it you must. For he would bastardize Elizabeth and shame Queen Anne before she dies.

CRANMER: I dislike this matter.

CROMWELL: Like it or not, it will be expedient for you to manage it. Else you will be tied with the Boleyns and that could mean another death. You understand me.

CRANMER: I follow.

CROMWELL: Get her confession. It will be easiest. Offer her freedom. Anything. But get her confession and have it written down.

CRANMER: Freedom?

CROMWELL: Offer it, Cranmer, if needs be. She will die whatever you offer. We want that divorce and she can confess and provide it. His Majesty would sleep easy in his bed. Now and after she is dead. (*He looks across his goblet at Cranmer.*) Goodnight, Archbishop.

29

Interior. Anne's room in Tower. Day. 16 May 1536.

(*Anne is sitting combing her hair. She is looking from the window. In the distance can be heard the faint echo of men's laughter and the sound of hammering. Lady Boleyn is with her.*)

ANNE (*Of the laughter*): They are merry. (*Lady Boleyn takes the comb and starts to comb out Anne's long hair.*) That sound, that hammering, Aunt. It is a scaffold they are building?

(*Lady Boleyn is about to answer when there is a rattle at the door. Anne smiles at Lady Boleyn who goes to the door and opens it to admit Cranmer, who hurries across the room. He almost forgets to make the customary salute in his hurry.*)

CRANMER: Good day, madam.

ANNE: My Lord.

CRANMER: I have little time. I would speak alone with you.

ANNE (*Edge*): My aunt hears all that passes. We have nothing to hide. Have you, my Lord? (*She smiles at him. Cranmer looks squarely at her and doesn't respond.*) I see. Go. (*She gestures to Lady Boleyn to leave them. A burst of laughter from outside the window.*) Now, save for those men we are alone. And what you say will not concern such common men. Will it?

CRANMER: I come to remind you of your duty.

ANNE: I think on it at all times.

CRANMER: Do not mince words with me, madam. (*He is angry now.*) I have no time for play.

ANNE: But I have. All the time.

CRANMER: Less than you think. Unless you act to save your head.

ANNE: How? Act?

CRANMER: I can offer one hope for you, madam. But one hope and that a slender one.

ANNE: The King has sent you?

CRANMER: I can offer one hope to you.

ANNE: Of freedom?

CRANMER (*Not wishing to specify*): Hope. Surely that is something. (*Finality.*) I cannot offer more.

ANNE: You could offer freedom, my Lord. And then I would know that you were lying. What do you want of me?

CRANMER: An admission. (*Anne looks at him and laughs. Short and sharp.*) It could save you, madam.

ANNE (*Pointed*): It could save you, my Lord.

CRANMER: You agree that your duty is to your King?

ANNE (*Bored*): My duty is to my husband, yes. I will not admit to anything.

CRANMER: We have the proofs.

ANNE: Those papers you showed at my trial? (*She is sad and smiling now.*) You cannot believe in those 'proofs'. You had no witnesses.

CRANMER (*Interrupting*): That trial was not in my hands. I had no part in that.

ANNE: You, my Lord? No. Indeed you had no part in any trial. You run with the times, it is true.

CRANMER: I serve the King. And my Lord Jesus.

ANNE (*Sarcastic*): And I am a stewed whore.

CRANMER (*Missing the sarcasm for a moment*): You admit . . .

ANNE (*Shaking her head*): Nothing.

CRANMER: Your duty . . .

ANNE (*Interrupting*): Is to me, my Lord. It is to me.

CRANMER: If you confess you will be given life.

ANNE: You lie.

CRANMER: You dare . . . ?

ANNE (*Standing. Angry*): I dare because I am the Queen, Cranmer. You offer me my life for the confession I suppose, that I have been guilty of adultery with those poor men, and that I have been guilty of incest with my brother, George. You offer me life for

173

confessions which you know to be untrue. The world is topsy turvy, Cranmer, when a lie would save an honest woman and the truth will strike her dead. They offered life to Smeaton? (*Cranmer doesn't respond.*) I cannot blame him, my Lord. You cannot trap me with offers of life, my Lord.

CRANMER: Then of salvation, maybe?

ANNE: You cannot offer me that.

CRANMER: Indeed I can.

ANNE: Not for lies.

(*Cranmer gets up and walks over to the window and looks into the courtyard beyond. The sound of hammering in the distance. Almost wistfully.*)

How is my Lord, the King?

CRANMER: Angry.

ANNE: I see.

CRANMER: He would marry again.

ANNE: Jane? (*And the one word has no malice. Just a word hanging between them. He nods.*) I shall soon be no impediment, my Lord.

CRANMER: You have been that impediment since you first entrapped him. He has seen you shame him. For that he is angry. He has been ensnared by your craft and now he wants to break your web, that is all. Let him go free.

ANNE (*Determined*): I cannot swear to things he knows to be untrue. I love him. I have never charmed him with any craft. You know that. You have been my confessor since I was a girl. You know I would talk of that to be the truth.

CRANMER (*Nods and pauses*): The Lady Elizabeth?

(*Anne is suddenly wary. She has been awaiting the real approach. This she knows is the key to the matter. Cranmer is fiddling with Anne's comb.*)

ANNE (*Holding out her hand*): My comb. (*He hadn't expected that reply. Doesn't know what she's talking about. Then realizes he has her comb. He gives it to her. She starts to comb her hair.*) If I used witch craft to entice the King then Cranmer, both you and my Uncle who condemned me, were my familiars. You know that.

CRANMER: Norfolk. No, madam. It is false.

ANNE: He is my uncle and has been known to use his power. And you my good Archbishop, you know as well as I how you were advantaged by being chaplain to the Boleyns. You know enough to make you powerful and it made you so. My familiars. He wants to divorce me?

CRANMER: Aye. He does.

ANNE: I cannot.

CRANMER: Yet you were found guilty of those charges.

ANNE: Which poor Henry knows to be false.

CRANMER: Your peers judged you.

ANNE: My equals did not. I am the Queen. (*Cranmer is stumped again. Gently.*) You may tell my husband that I cannot, even to ease his conscience admit to incest and whoring. If he feels guilt at marrying Jane, then I am sorry for her. For she will suffer as I have. Maybe if I refuse to clear his conscience he will be angry and forget his conscience. He may be fortunate enough.

175

CRANMER: There must be no impediment to the marriage. Or to the inheritance.

ANNE: Elizabeth?

CRANMER: Shall be a bastard. Whether you admit or not. I shall pronounce your marriage null and void tomorrow. Be assured I shall.

ANNE (*Contempt*): You are a creature, Cranmer. Run with the times. Run with the times. But I am not your creature. Nor, now am I his. You may pronounce as you will tomorrow, I will admit nothing. I shall accuse you of nothing. But you will have to answer when you make my child a bastard. For she will remember. She's a Boleyn as much as a Tudor and she is no bastard.

CRANMER (*Sighs*): You make matters hard for me.

ANNE: I deal with truth. Is that hard for you? I am not mad my Lord. If need be I would say much of my innocence. I could make public the reasons and the truths of these matters. I would not harm my daughter Elizabeth. If my child is threatened I will lay it before the people. And your head will feel unsure upon these shoulders.

CRANMER: You threaten the King?

ANNE: I threaten no one. I fight, Cranmer. For that is what I am made of. Fighting. I will say nothing to harm my daughter Elizabeth.

CRANMER: But you will say nothing to harm . . .?

ANNE: You? Norfolk? The King? I will say little.

CRANMER: Nothing.

ANNE: Come, my Lord. Let's have no long faces. They

may build that scaffold for no one. No one will come
and there will be nothing to watch tomorrow.

CRANMER: You are cool, my Lady Anne.

ANNE: I am afraid.

CRANMER: Of death?

ANNE: The manner of it. I have seen men writhe in
flames. That slow stench as they melt into the fire.

CRANMER: Madam, you said you would be silent.
Would offer no public comment or blame. (*She nods.*)
You shall not be burned.

(*Anne kneels and murmurs a prayer. Cranmer stands
a moment embarrassed. We hear the murmur of a
Hail Mary and Cranmer turns from the window and
starts for the door. Anne doesn't get up or look
round.*)

ANNE: What news of my brother, my Lord?

(*Cranmer stops.*)

CRANMER: No news.

(*Anne turns to him still on her knees.*)

ANNE: I ask you, my Lord. On my knees.

CRANMER: Incest is a capital crime.

ANNE: When does he die?

CRANMER: Tomorrow. All those found guilty.

ANNE: I shall pray for them. (*He turns to go.*) Will
you, my Lord? (*He stops to look at her a moment
and then turns and goes. Quickly. Anne stays on her*

*knees a moment longer and Lady Boleyn comes
through with Lady Kingston. Anne crosses herself
and gets up.)*

You did not tell me they were to die tomorrow?

LADY BOLEYN: We thought it best . . .

(She kneels by the lighted candle and starts to pray.)

30

Exterior. Tower executions. Day.

*(Through this scene don't lose sight of Anne. We see
it all through her mind and eyes. Mark Smeaton
being carried to the platform for execution. Cut
to: Mark Smeaton's face. It is a puffed mess. His ears
are tatters. His lips blubber and nose bloody. Mix
to:)*

31

Interior. Anne's Tower room. Day.

(Close up of Anne's face as she prays and mix to.)

32

Exterior. Tower executions. Day. Wind.

*(Close up Norreys, Brereton, Weston and Rochford
on raised platform. We hear the hum of a large
crowd.)*

ROCHFORD *(To the crowd)*: Masters all, I come here

not to preach and make a sermon, but to die. As the law has found me so to that law I submit me. I would ask you all, and especially those who are members of the Court to trust in God and not in the vanities of the world.

(*Mix to: Anne's face. She is smiling through her tears.*)

For if I had so done I think I had been alive as ye be now.

(*Mix to Rochford.*)

As for mine offences, it will do no good to hear them for which I die here, but I beseech God that I may be an example to you all and that you all may beware by me. And I heartily require you all to pray for me and to forgive me if I have offended you, and I forgive you all. (*The executioner.*) And God save the King.

(*He kneels and puts his neck on to the slippery block. The drum throbs quietly as the axe arches from the sky and we cut to:*)

33

Interior. Anne's Tower room. Evening.

(*Lady Kingston, Lady Boleyn and Anne.*)

LADY BOLEYN: The King will remember what you are to him.

ANNE: They have not built that scaffold out there for nothing.

LADY BOLEYN: I'm sure he will remember. (*Anne goes to kiss her aunt. Lady Boleyn pulls away.*)

179

ANNE: I am dead for him already, I know my husband. He has sported and now he would kill. It is his nature. And I am the prey. (*She stands and goes to take a drink from the table near the back wall.*) Ladies, would you drink with me?

LADY KINGSTON: Madam! No!

(*They both move to stop her waiting on them.*)

ANNE: No. Soon I shall have no crown. You shall see. My Lady Boleyn. My Lady Kingston. (*She smiles and brings two goblets over to the women. She goes back for her drink.*) You are both most kind. (*They drink.*) I would make my confession. Can it be arranged for me? I would confess to Cranmer. He shall bear that burden. He shall know my innocence. See to it ladies.

34

Interior. Room in Palace. Day.

(*Jane Seymour sitting near a window. She is sewing.*)

35

Interior. Council Room. Day.
(*Cranmer is there with Cromwell. A message is in Cranmer's hand.*)

CRANMER (*Having read it*): No, I cannot do this.

CROMWELL: You have been their chaplain for many years. A duty may be.

(*Cromwell smiles. He is enjoying Cranmer's discomfort in the situation. A smooth man this. Two smooth men together.*)

CRANMER: No. She asks too much.

CROMWELL: Hear her confession. You divorce her from his Grace tomorrow. You may find a few pearls to improve our case against her.

CRANMER (*Genuinely horrified*): From the confessional?

CROMWELL: My good Archbishop. (*He laughs and takes an apple from a bowl.*) You'll go to Heaven with a clear conscience. (*He stops polishing the apple on his gown.*) You have no conscience have you?

CRANMER: I cannot do this.

(*He throws the message on to the table.*)

CROMWELL: She has played you well. Are you afraid that the truth she tells in her confession will be more than you can bear, Cranmer?

CRANMER: She was found guilty by her peers.

CROMWELL: And so, by the law of the land, is guilty. (*He looks at Cranmer sharply:*) And before God? (*Cranmer looks up at him and away.*) You will know that. Through confession and the taking of the Host. You will know if she is guilty. Or innocent. Before God. And you can say nothing, Cranmer. Take care that you say nothing. (*Harder.*) Go and hear her confess. Better it were you than some priest with a conscience.

36

Interior. Anne's Tower room. Day.

(*Anne is finishing her penance while Cranmer prays beside her. We hear the end of a Hail Mary and she*

181

*crosses herself and stands. Her Rosary in her hand.
Cranmer goes on praying, he seems intensely moved.
He crosses himself. We hear the hammering outside
and the laughter of the men at work in the distance.
Cranmer stands. He moves to the window and looks
out. Anne watches him quietly. She's had her moment
with him.)*

ANNE (*Quietly*): So mild a penance. (*Cranmer nods.*)
And you have nothing to say, my Lord Archbishop.
(*He turns to her. She moves to him.*) Often you have
so much to say to me. Have my little sins shocked
you into silence?

(*He still says nothing. He is very upset. Anne is calm
as she moves yet closer.*)

CRANMER (*Broken*): Why did you bid me come,
madam?

ANNE: Someone had to hear my last confession.
Someone had to listen to those fearful sins.

CRANMER: Why me?

ANNE: You have a conscience, my lord. I wanted you
to hear and to lock away my sins. (*A thought.*) They
are locked away? You will say nothing of what
happened today?

CRANMER: I can say nothing.

ANNE (*Brightly*): And you know my innocence. For
what it is.

CRANMER (*Nods*): I would to God I'd never known.
You shame us all. (*Pause.*) Tomorrow . . .

ANNE: Shhh. Enough of that—tomorrow. A priest
will come?

CRANMER: Yes.

ANNE: Early?

CRANMER: Aye. Early, madam.

ANNE: I thank you then. You stand as if you carry my sins heavily. You grow old before us. Tomorrow is soon enough for sorrow. After the axe . . .

CRANMER (*Without thinking*): There is to be no axe.

ANNE (*Sudden panic*): You promised. An axe. You said my Lord King had been merciful. No fire you promised. No fire.

CRANMER: Be calm. They have sent to France. A swordsman.

ANNE (*Quietly*): Is that swift? (*Cranmer nods.*) Then the King is merciful. Thank him for me when next you see him.

(*Cranmer turns away. This is too much for him. He slowly moves to the door. She watches him go. He stops and turns to her.*)

CRANMER: Madam . . . one word. Set your ladies to see to your hair. The swordsman is quick I am told. Very quick. Towards noon.

(*Anne just looks at him. A fractional nod. Cranmer opens the door and slowly goes out. Anne sits quietly. She starts to plait her hair that tumbles over her shoulders.*)

37

Interior. Anne's Tower room. Early morning.

(*The flickering light of candles. Outside a crisp May morning makes the candles useless but no one has*

183

thought to put them out. In the background a priest prays. Sir William Kingston stands by the window. Lady Boleyn and Lady Kingston have just finished doing Anne's long hair. They put in the final pins or combs that hold it piled up on top of her head. It is in vast coils like a simple crown. The priest is still praying in his corner by the prie dieu.)

ANNE: It's high enough, ladies. I'd not impede the Frenchman's work and make it longer. (*Anne smiles at her ladies.*) We may start a new fashion as I did with those gloves in France. Master Kingston, I hear I shall not die afore noon and I am sorry therefore, for I had hoped to be dead and past my pain by this time. Even my Lord King has deserted me. It is a lonely world I live in now.

SIR WILLIAM: The pain is little, madam. And quick.

ANNE (*A laugh*): And I be dead. (*The others don't react at her little joke.*) I heard say the executioner was very skilful. (*Sir William nods. Anne measures her throat with her hands and shows the span to him.*) And I have but a little neck. You see? (*She smiles at him. The light is streaming into the room now. Nods at the candles.*) Snuff them ladies. It is waste.

(*The sound of heavy tramping feet and a muffled command to halt outside. Sir William stiffens. The ladies stare at the door in fear. Anne sits coldly. To Sir William.*)

It is time?

SIR WILLIAM: They are ready, madam.

ANNE: Early. I shall be ready in a moment, Master Kingston. You have been kind.

(*She goes to the priest and kneels with him. She prays as the door is hammered by a mailed fist.*)

38

Exterior. The Tower. Executions. Day.

(*Start on a drum and the muffled beating. Pull out to reveal the scaffold and on it the French executioner with his sword. Around the scaffold sit: The Lord Chancellor, the Dukes of Richmond and of Suffolk, members of the King's Council, Earls and Nobles of the land. Those who found Anne guilty at her trial. The Mayor of London and Aldermen plus the Sheriffs and craftsmen of London. A buzz of chatter and indecent spurts of laughter and then chatter again. All the while the drum throbs its mournful muffled note. The executioner still as a rock. The chatter dies away as a group appears beyond the green. Anne is walking with the priest in the middle of the group. In charge of the group is Kingston. Anne's ladies are close to her. She is quite steady as she walks beside the priest who is praying as he walks. She looks neither to right nor left and the sun flashes on her piled hair. It could be a crown and for this moment Anne is utterly Queen. She walks to the scaffold steps and Kingston offers his hand. She refuses it and mounts the steps to face the executioner. A trembling smile as she takes in his sword. At the platform Kingston stops and Sheriffs take over. Her ladies join her on the platform. Her point of view: the assembled men who are staring at her silently. Anne has a moment of panic and she turns to Kingston. He starts a smile of encouragement and she catches hold of herself. She turns back to look at the assembled men.*)

ANNE (*Clearly and gently*): Masters, I here humbly submit me to the law as the law has judged me, and as for my offences, I here accuse no man, God knoweth them. I remit them to God, beseeching him to have mercy on my soul. (*She gathers strength for a moment.*) I beseech Jesu, save my sovereign and master, the King, the most godly, noble and gentle

185

prince that is, and long to reign over you. (*She stops. Not a word can be heard. She takes off her head-dress that holds her hair more firmly in place. She hands the head-dress to a lady. She turns to the executioner.*) My hair—(*She gestures at it*) will not be in your way? (*The executioner shakes his head—once. Anne steps from her gown and stands in her simple low grey dress. See the faces of the Mayor, Duke of Suffolk, Richmond. Eager anticipation in their faces. Blood lust. The ladies kneel and pray. Anne kneels and one of her ladies places a kerchief over her eyes and binds it at the back. The swordsman takes a good grip on his sword.*)

To Jesu Christ I commend my soul.

(*Swordsman raises sword as we zoom into close-up of Anne's face. Repeating:*)

To Jesu Christ I commend my soul. To Jesu Christ I commend my soul.

(*She flings her arms out and the sword swings. Cut to black. A drum pulses.*)

Jane Seymour

Winner of the Prix d'Italia for 1970

IAN THORNE

For Raymond Whitehouse
of the Canadian Broadcasting Corporation

Jane Seymour was first presented by BBC Television on 15 January 1970 with the following cast:

JANE SEYMOUR	*Anne Stallybrass*
EDWARD SEYMOUR	*Daniel Moynihan*
DOROTHY SEYMOUR	*Gillian Bailey*
LADY MARGARET SEYMOUR	*Dorothy Black*
THOMAS SEYMOUR	*John Ronane*
SIR JOHN SEYMOUR	*Howard Lang*
HENRY VIII	*Keith Michell*
SIR FRANCIS BRYAN	*William Abney*
SIR NICHOLAS CAREW	*Louis Haslar*
ANNE STANHOPE	*Jo Kendall*
THOMAS CRANMER	*Bernard Hepton*
LADY ROCHFORD	*Sheila Burrell*
THOMAS CROMWELL	*Wolfe Morris*
DUKE OF NORFOLK	*Patrick Troughton*
BISHOP GARDINER	*Basil Dignam*
LADY EXETER	*Marion Methie*
PRINCESS MARY	*Alison Frazer*

Produced by Ronald Travers and Mark Shivas
Directed by John Glenister
Designed by Peter Seddon

Characters

JANE SEYMOUR
HENRY, *The King*
EDWARD SEYMOUR
THOMAS SEYMOUR
SIR JOHN SEYMOUR
MARGARET SEYMOUR
DOROTHY SEYMOUR
SIR FRANCIS BRYAN
SIR NICOLAS CAREW
LADY ROCHFORD
ANNE SEYMOUR, *Edward's Wife*
CROMWELL
DUKE OF NORFOLK
ARCHBISHOP CRANMER
LADY EXETER
BISHOP GARDINER
PRINCESS MARY
GARTER KING-AT-ARMS

Sets

Interior:

The Queen's chamber at Hampton Court, which
connects by staircase to:
The chapel at Hampton Court
Chamber of Presence, Hampton Court
Wolf Hall, the great chamber
A Room of State in Greenwich Palace, which con-
nects by passage to:
The apartment at Greenwich
Dining area in Sir Nicholas Carew's House

Exterior:

Wolf Hall exteriors
A bridle path at Greenwich
Garden fragment, Hampton Court

*The action takes place between September 1535 and
October 1537.*

1

Interior. Queen's bedchamber. Hampton Court. Day.

(The hand of Jane Seymour, ringed. It moves nervous on the royal bed, clutches the sheet. Women's hands come and disengage it, lift back the sheet. All from Jane's point of view. The lifting of her from bed to state pallet. All this in silence or with a drum like a heartbeat, the two tones alternate. Decoration at back of pallet, the Crown and Arms of England. Sound of trumpet call. The placing of a mantle of crimson velvet furred with ermine. Pillows etc. on Jane's pallet.)

2

Interior. Staircase. Hampton Court. Day.

(The flare of torches. Walls. Ceiling. Stairway. Angles. The heartbeat, for this is really a movement of the imagination. Beside entry to Chapel, the Royal Arms carved in the stone.)

3

Interior. Chapel. Hampton Court. Day.

(Hit with Te Deum.

Chapel preparatory to baptism.

Bishop Gardiner and priests near the font. Peers in attendance. But strange angles again, and the candles and torches throw long dream-like shadows.

The music distorts, pounding and racking the head. Images distort.

Clarify as procession comes from the traverse.

The infant Edward is carried by Lady Exeter under a canopy.

As Edward Seymour carrying the young Princess Elizabeth comes level with his brother Thomas near the font—move in on them and then as music and picture distort with pain: Dissolve to:

Telecine over which the titles are superimposed.

The humming of bees. A beehive on the estate of Wolf Hall, the Seymour home in Wiltshire.

Open to Jane Seymour, hatted and masked against the bees with a comb of honey.

There is a distant shout. She turns.

Longshot of the manor and drive with a horsed figure—Edward—and two others near him—Tom and Dorothy.

Jane waves and starts toward them, removing the mask.

Cut to the group in the driveway as Margaret, Lady Seymour, comes from the house and a groom approaches to take the horse.)

DOROTHY (*Touching saddlebag*): He's brought presents!

MARGARET: Edward! (*Margaret goes to him as he dismounts, embraces him.*) My dear boy, welcome home.

(*Jane comes into the circle and also embraces him.*)

EDWARD: Jane.

THOMAS: The King's on his road here.

MARGARET: Oh—you should have warned us . . .

EDWARD: I only knew this morning, Mother, between salt and grace. I had to dissuade him from fetching the whole court on you.

MARGARET: But how many?

EDWARD: Carew, Francis Bryan, about thirty men with him.

MARGARET: God's life!

(*Groom hands Edward saddlebag and starts to lead horse off.*)

EDWARD: Stuff for you, my dear, and for Jane. Bruges satin.

(*They smile with pleasure.*)

EDWARD: Give him a good rub down, Mark, and a bottle of hay!

GROOM: Yes, Master Edward. Welcome home, sir.

DOROTHY: You haven't brought it.

EDWARD: Haven't I?

(*He feels in saddlebag, brings out small caged bird.*)

EDWARD: Here you are, kitten. Straight from a seaman who'd been in the south islands.

DOROTHY: Oh, Edward—thank you!

EDWARD: You'll have to make a bigger cage.

DOROTHY: Oh, yes, he must have a very grand yellow one—

THOMAS: Gold, I think, with a silver bell.

MARGARET: Bells and cages! When his Grace will be here at any moment expecting a banquet . . .

(*Margaret starts for house.*)

EDWARD: Now nothing elaborate, Mother.

JANE (*Also starting for the house*): I'll order fresh rushes.

MARGARET: Yes, and herbs.

EDWARD: And that musk scent, Jane, for the King.

MARGARET: And fresh flowers, Jane.

(*Jane is hurrying off with her as Sir John comes out from the house. They stop. Sir John stops as he and Edward regard each other. There is a moment of complete stillness and then Edward brings something out of the saddlebag and comes to him.*)

EDWARD: Sir, this is for you.

(*Gives him small clock.*)

SIR JOHN: That's a beautiful thing.

EDWARD: It's yours, Father.

SIR JOHN (*Nods, moved*): We had your letter. So you're to marry again.

EDWARD: Yes.

SIR JOHN: I'm glad of it.

EDWARD (*After a moment, turns*): You know her, Jane. Anne Stanhope. You were at court together.

JANE: Mistress Stanhope, yes. She'll suit you, Edward. (*Warmly.*) Oh, I hope you'll be happy.

(*And then the others are adding their congratulations all together.*)

EDWARD: Thank you. All of you.

SIR JOHN: Come then, you'll want a bath and change of clothing.

(*Edward turns back to him.*)

SIR JOHN (*Low*): It's forgotten then?

EDWARD: Long ago, Father.

DOROTHY: Do you think his Grace will like the yellow bird?

(*Dissolve from the birdcage to*:)

4

Interior. Great chamber. Wolf Hall.

(*Period cards on table.*)

BRYAN (*Voice off*): The nine, your Grace.

HENRY (*Voice off*): Aha, I have a Cromwell. (*Knave played on to nine. Open first to Henry at table, then Bryan, Carew, Edward, Thomas, Sir John. Some Venetian glasses or goblets. Henry speaking off to other side of room, expansive, radiant, his most charming.*) Yes, that's undoubtedly where your bird comes from, my dear, the Canary Islands.

(*Cut to Dorothy and Jane in bay window seat across the great chamber. They are embroidering cushions* (*sacrifice of Isaac and Orpheus charming the animals*). *The canary cage, still the small one, is beside Dorothy. Rain outside window.*)

DOROTHY (*A quick curtsey*): Thank you, your Grace.

(*Cut to the table, servants refilling glasses from sideboard.*)

HENRY: No, no, don't tell us the total, Francis. He's won so much from me on this progress I shall have to pawn the jewels. You're a wicked man, as bad as de Longueville. You two were only boys then but that Frenchman, between the tennis court and the card table, practically paid his ransom.

EDWARD (*The diplomat*): One cannot imagine your Grace being bettered at tennis.

HENRY: Ah but de Longueville was a *very* clever player. You remember how we took the Duke, Sir John?

SIR JOHN: The Day of the Spurs—they ran like hares, your Grace.

HENRY: Didn't they!

BRYAN: I always thought de Longueville may have let himself be taken.

HENRY: What? No, too clever. (*With sudden suspicion.*) Of course he *was* French. Oh, but didn't they run! That was chivalry, before all this gunpowder.

THOMAS: Yes, it's sad, the bowman's passing.

(*Edward throws him a warning look, too late.*)

HENRY: The bowman is *not* passing, Master Seymour.

EDWARD: I think what my brother intended, your Grace...

(*Perhaps it is fortunate that Lady Margaret enters at this moment.*)

HENRY: Ah, Lady Margaret—a splendid dinner. Now if only this pelting weather would abate...

MARGARET: Your Grace will forgive me but there is a monstrous fellow outside, speaking of bolts and bars. He says he is in your Grace's service.

BRYAN (*Rising and going to her*): Dear Lady Margaret, if you will be kind enough to have the man shown to the King's chamber. He is a locksmith. Don't be alarmed. His Grace sleeps nowhere nowadays without these precautions.

(*Sir John has risen and come to them.*)

SIR JOHN: I'll see it done.

BRYAN: *Merci*, Sir John.

(*Sir John goes out.*) *At the table Carew has been shuffling the cards and he now deals.*)

HENRY: You've been at sea, Master Thomas, or you'd know better. Artillery has its uses certainly but the longbow will never be superseded. Never.

CAREW: There is a wide belief in the West country, your Grace, that in a few years English bowmen could conquer the whole of Africa.

(*Cut to Jane and Dorothy at the window. Table talk still audible across the room.* NOTE: *The following two speeches are spoken simultaneously.*)

199

DOROTHY: There's no more pink. Do you think Orpheus would mind being done in blue? (*Looks to table, low.*) It's funny, with *him* here the room seems so small.

HENRY: It's true. And it's the countryman who constitutes the defence of the kingdom. I don't give tuppence for the townsman. He's soft. He's no stomach for a fight.

(*Jane smiles, Dorothy returns to embroidery. Cut to table.*)

HENRY: And all these beggars we've been seeing on the roads will drift into town unless they're found employment. (*Plays card.*) My point, Seymour. *We stand in grave danger of invasion, gentlemen.* It's for you landowners to train these men in the use of arms . . .

(*Cut to gallery where Lady Margaret and Bryan are walking or to fireplace with roaring fire at furthest part of room. Table talk now only a murmur in background.*)

MARGARET (*A little worried*): In danger of invasion?

BRYAN: Not this evening, Lady Margaret.

MARGARET: Ah. You were speaking of the Dormers . . . As you will understand, Sir Francis, we are most anxious to see Jane well mated, now that she and Dorothy are the last of our girls left single.

BRYAN: Yes, I think we may have a match there. I have represented my niece in glowing terms to Sir Robert Dormer and his wife. Naturally the boy is anxious to meet with Jane but I think the only question will be one of dowry.

MARGARET: Of course Sir John and I are prepared to be generous.

BRYAN (*Not disinterested*): Of course. (*Looks towards the window.*) Poor Jane! If only she had something to say for herself. Not a lot, but something. (*See Jane and Dorothy in window.*) And so pale. You really must keep her out of doors more.

MARGARET: But it's her natural colour, Sir Francis.

(*Cut to Jane and Dorothy. Table talk again audible across room. Jane looking towards table. Dorothy looks up at her.* NOTE: *The following speeches are spoken simultaneously.*)

DOROTHY (*Low*): Do you like him, Jane?

HENRY: There are statutes. My statutes.

JANE (*Low*): He is the King.

DOROTHY (*Pause, then lower*): But do you like him?

CAREW: It's the example set by the landowners, sir. You can't expect the others not to follow them.

JANE (*Very low*): I wish someone could help him.

DOROTHY: The King!

JANE: Ssh.

HENRY: I will not have the laws broken by baron or commoner. If they're using more sheepruns, then they're acting contrary to statute.

(*Cut to the table.*)

EDWARD: Of course most of Wiltshire is still champion land, sir.

HENRY: Then these men should be employed on the roads. I've never seen so many potholes.

201

THOMAS: Your Grace, I think it's the brickmakers, they come out at night digging for clay and gravel.

HENRY: Well, Aristotle said there are some jobs in which it is impossible for a man to be virtuous. You shall catch them for me. Eh, Master Thomas? With your artillery? (*Laughs. General laughter.*) Come, a round game. Bryan, Lady Margaret. And the girls, all of you. Do you know Pope July?

DOROTHY (*Already there, eagerly*): No, your Grace.

HENRY: Sit down then. It's a splendid game Sir Francis invented for us and no one can say it isn't topical. Carew, make room for Mistress Seymour. Sit beside me, my dear, and I'll teach it to you. (*It is Jane he means and she comes shyly and sits beside him as the others take their places.*) The points are matrimony, intrigue, pope and the stops.

(*Music enters, of the lute. Jane's head remains down, whether from her natural reserve or out of allegiance to Henry's first wife we don't know. Dissolve to:*)

5

Interior. Great chamber. Wolf Hall. Night.

(*Night scene. The same table. Goblets. The cards to one side. It is late, the shank of the evening. Henry and Sir John sitting at the table, opposite each other. Carew near at hand with Edward. Servant at sideboard. The lute continues off in the gallery.*)

HENRY: Still raining, is it?

CAREW: Yes, your Grace.

HENRY: Goodnight then, Sir Nicholas. You too,

Edward. And send the lute away. (*They retire, the music stops presently*.) Are you tired, Sir John?

SIR JOHN: Me? No, your Grace.

HENRY: It's the simple life, I envy you. Girls and huntings. (*Glances at servant*.)

SIR JOHN: Will your Grace require more wine?

HENRY: No.

SIR JOHN: You can go to bed, Stephen. (*The man retires, they are alone*.)

HENRY: Girls and huntings! The girls at Lille ran out to us with garlands in their hands. Remember? So long ago. You had a redhead, didn't you?

SIR JOHN: Yes, what a woman—how she danced!

HENRY: I hear you've danced again, old man.

SIR JOHN: Your Grace?

HENRY: With Edward's wife, your son's wife.

SIR JOHN: Your Grace shames me.

HENRY: But it was her doing?

SIR JOHN: And mine. (*In deep distress*.) And mine, sir.

HENRY: I heard that you were not to blame. But you find them dark, do you, these women?

SIR JOHN: Yes, sir.

HENRY (*Nods slowly, then*): Was the harvest poor here too?

SIR JOHN: Yes.

HENRY: They say it's rained ever since More and Fisher . . . lost their heads.

SIR JOHN: Superstition, sir. Fisher and Sir Thomas were traitors.

HENRY: These last weeks in the Marches, some of them didn't know me in plain dress. They blamed the King for their crops—or the Queen, or the Queen's bastard. They hated me. My people. (*Rises to the window, rain.*) An old man in Gloucester spoke of the birth of monsters—and said it was God's wrath at England's wickedness. (*Comes behind Sir John.*) All my sons put away by stealth, in darkness, like things accursed of God! (*His hands on Sir John's shoulders, on his back.*) What is your flesh that can get *living sons*? Am I not a man? Am I not a man like you?

SIR JOHN: You have a son, your Grace.

HENRY: Oh, Richmond! Weak. Sickly. Not like yours. Not proper issue. I need a son to succeed me. I have prayed for him. Made pilgrimages. But I think God does not mean me to have sons.

SIR JOHN: Queen Anne may yet be blessed, your Grace.

HENRY: You're a good man, Sir John, but you know nothing. There, the rain's stopping. We can go out tomorrow.

SIR JOHN (*Relieved at this subject*): There's some fine boar in Middle Wood.

HENRY: We'll ride out early. Sleep first. No dreams. They say—they say that the Bishop—that Fisher's head grows younger on London Bridge. But that's not possible.

(Dissolve from Henry's eyes to Telecine:

The boar hunt. Dissolve to the gallop home. Jumping of stream. The hooves. Dissolve to the fields by Wolf Hall. Henry and Sir John riding in, the others following. Henry sees Jane across the field, waves others on and wheels towards her. Cut to Jane beside fruit tree with basket. She turns as Henry rides up. Mounted, he picks an apple and bites into it.)

HENRY: We caught three boars. Big ones. Your father's a lucky man.

(Jane is reserved, passive, but not nervous.)

JANE *(Low)*: Your Grace.

HENRY *(Finding it difficult)*: Very lucky.

(Henry pulls horse from tree.)

Greedy devil. Stand. I remember you at court, Mistress Seymour—but before that—were you ever in a convent?

JANE: Yes, sir.

HENRY: I knew it! It has left its mark. Humility and duty.

JANE: God giveth grace to the humble.

HENRY: And you are not without grace, mistress.

(Jane frowns at his meaning.)

HENRY: Why do you always look away?

JANE: I was told your Grace was averse to being stared at.

HENRY: Honest too. You were maid-in-waiting. Why did you leave Court?

JANE: Why, sir, when Queen Catherine, that is, when the Princess Dowager retired—

HENRY: Yes, of course.

(*A religious chant, roughly sung, has been growing louder.*)

HENRY: Is there a shrine near here?

JANE: No, sir, the people use that lane on their way into Gloucestershire and the Abbey of Hailes, to seek absolution from the Blood of Christ.

HENRY: You have been there?

JANE: Yes, sir.

HENRY: And seen the Blood?

JANE: Yes.

HENRY (*Shyly*): I have a phial of Our Lord's Tears. It once saved me from the plague, you know.

JANE: I am very afraid of the plague, sir.

HENRY: You are right to be. So am I. I always feel better in the country.

(*They have a common bond. Jane looks up at Henry now, he at her. The chant grows louder.*)

JANE: They are crowding to Hailes now since they hear it is to be visited by the Commission. They are afraid for the abbeys, sir, for their souls.

(*Henry is at once on the defence or rather the attack.*)

HENRY: My Commissioners are only anxious to report abuses. They are as good catholics as you or I, Mistress Jane.

JANE (*Withdrawing into herself*): I meant no criticism, sir. Forgive me.

HENRY (*Smiles*): I know your meaning. Ours is to reform, not to destroy.

(*Bryan rides up to the King and whispers to him.*)

HENRY: Alas, my stay is ended. The French envoy is in London and I too have my duty. Farewell, little nun.

(*Jane curtseys as Henry rides off across the field with Bryan. Cut to centre of field as Henry wheels and pulls up, looking back at Jane. Bryan stops level with him.*)

You once asked that Mistress Seymour be returned to Court.

BRYAN: Yes, sir, but a match has now been arranged between her and William Dormer.

HENRY: Break it.

(*As he wheels away, the field revolves wheeling out to:*)

6

Interior. Room of State. Greenwich. Day.

(*Music of the Court. And the glitter of Court dress as Jane, newly arrived at Greenwich, comes down gallery to greet her brother Edward and Anne Stanhope who is beside him.*)

7

Interior. Room of State. Greenwich. Day.

(*A corner of the Room of State in Greenwich Palace with suitable furniture. Jane stands across table from Thomas Cranmer. Take out Court music.*)

CRANMER: We are pleased to see you returned to Greenwich, mistress. You are made comfortable?

JANE: Thank you, your Grace.

CRANMER: You have not previously taken the Oath of Allegiance?

JANE: I was not required, sir.

CRANMER: It is his Majesty's wish that all who serve at Court now do so.

(*Track back to Henry, watching, unseen by Jane.*)

JANE: I understand, sir.

CRANMER: I Thomas Cranmer, Archbishop of Canterbury and Chaplain of the Royal House, do hereby require you, Jane Seymour, to answer me upon oath. (*Cut back to Cranmer and Jane.*) Do you acknowledge Our Gracious Sovereign Supreme Head on earth of the Church of England?

JANE: I do, sir.

CRANMER: Do you allow the Bishop of Rome or his servants to have any authority over you?

JANE: No, sir.

CRANMER: Do you acknowledge the legality of Our Sovereign's marriage with Queen Anne?

JANE: I do.

CRANMER: Do you acknowledge the annulment of Our Sovereign's former union with the Lady Catherine and the illegitimacy of its issue? (*Silence.*) Mistress?

JANE: The Lady Mary?

CRANMER: The Lady Mary.

JANE: I cannot think but she is the King's true daughter, sir.

(*Cut to Henry, his startled reaction. Then watch them from his point of view.*)

CRANMER: Do you know what you are saying?

JANE: Your Grace.

CRANMER: You stand on oath and in grave danger, mistress. Are these your words or another's?

JANE: I speak my own heart, sir.

(*Cut back to Cranmer and Jane. He is biting his lip.*)

CRANMER: Who succeeds his Majesty to the throne?

JANE: The Queen's child.

CRANMER: Name her.

JANE: The Princess Elizabeth.

CRANMER: Then you admit the King's union with the Lady Catherine invalid and the Lady Mary to be no true issue? (*Silence.*) To deny this is to allow the supremacy of the Pope. To deny this is treason, mistress.

209

JANE: I do not deny the union invalid, sir.

CRANMER: Then how can there be true issue?

JANE: At the Lady Mary's birth there was true issue, sir.

CRANMER: Mistress Jane—

(*Henry comes out to them. Jane sinks into a deep curtsey.*)

HENRY: Enough, Thomas. Don't you see she is in ignorance? Stand up, little nun. Now then, you are loyal to your old mistress and her girl. I like that. But can you not be loyal to me too?

JANE (*Strongly for her*): I am, your Grace. (*They hold a look.*) I am, sir.

HENRY: We are distantly related, you and I—did you know that, Mistress Jane?

JANE: I believe so, sir.

HENRY: Through your mother who is partly descended from the blood royal of Edward the Third. The College of Arms looked it up for me. Raise your head. You cannot be loyal to me and to the Lady Mary. She is a wilful, disobedient girl. (*In the silence Cranmer starts to speak but Henry stops him.*) We are beset by enemies, France, the Empire. The Pope has charged them to invade us—in the name of Mary and her mother. In their title. To support their cause is to support the enemies of the realm. My enemies. Do you understand me now?

JANE: Yes, sir.

CRANMER: And will you now acknowledge the Lady Mary to be no true issue? (*Jane nods slowly.*) Swear.

(*Henry motions to Cranmer who leaves by a near door. Jane sways. Henry holds her.*)

HENRY: It's done, over. Sit here. Oh, Jane—Jane—

JANE: Your Grace—I beg your respect—(*Sits.*)

HENRY: But I have plain feelings. How can I speak to you in a cold frost? When you were taking the oath, I wanted to wrap you in my arms.

JANE: You cannot, sir. I am to marry Master Dormer.

HENRY: Do you fancy him? That boy?

JANE: I never met him.

HENRY: No, you have not.

JANE: But in honesty your Grace should not see me alone . . .

HENRY: Don't be afraid. I shan't harm you. (*His hands touch her neck.*) So warm, gentle. I could never harm you. (*His hand opens to reveal a stone on a chain and he now fastens it round her neck.*) This is a token of our esteem. Wear it in loyalty.

(*The jewel and the room revolve and spin out to :*)

8

Interior. Room of State. Greenwich. Day.

(*Jane's head and shoulders in a different dress. She is struggling for possession of the stone at her neck. The hand of Anne Boleyn, gloved and ringed, opens the jewel, then grips the delicate chain holding the stone*

211

and pulls it violently, breaking it. Jane stifles a cry of pain, as stone and chain are thrown down. Steps recede. Cut to the Queen's shadow passing below the archway. Near the arch hidden but watching, stands a tall thin-faced woman, who now emerges from the shadows and enters this Room of State in Greenwich Palace. Cut to Jane biting back tears. She picks up the Jewel as Lady Rochford comes to her.)

LADY ROCHFORD : Less than wise.

JANE : I beg you . . .

LADY ROCHFORD : A little less than prudent.

JANE : My lady . . .

LADY ROCHFORD : But then we must endure hard justice and bitter blows, mistress. (*Taking the stone.*) Wearing the King's image . . .

JANE : He gave it to me.

LADY ROCHFORD : So we must wear it.

JANE : No one knew of it.

LADY ROCHFORD : She knew.

JANE : How could she?

LADY ROCHFORD : Oh, she sees within the stone, beneath the shadow. Her marriage night there was an azure cross against the moon. Poor lady. Your neck.

(*Touches it.*)

JANE : I was startled, madam.

LADY ROCHFORD : Startled, yes. Will you forgive me if I offer you advice, my dear? I think you need it. Go back to Wiltshire. Now. This is no time for you. The Queen's temper, the Queen's jealousy could mean your ruin. You know how the wind lies. The King is waiting. If the child's a boy, she will ride the world again. If not, you may return.

(*Anne Stanhope, now Anne Seymour, enters to them.*)

ANNE SEYMOUR: Mistress Jane, are you . . .?

LADY ROCHFORD: She is unhurt, madam. And her Grace must be attended. Her Grace will be violent—and will have to be controlled. Remember what I said, my dear.

(*They watch Lady Rochford go. Then to Anne's look, Jane says.*)

JANE: She said leave Court, for my own good, go back to Wolf Hall. I want to, Anne. I miss them. I need to do ordinary things, weigh wool, choose flowers, feel the new bread.

ANNE SEYMOUR: Be patient.

JANE: I was wrong to come again, wrong to stay here now.

ANNE SEYMOUR: You were commanded.

JANE: And William Dormer?

ANNE SEYMOUR: He will wait for you.

JANE: Whatever I do here . . .

ANNE SEYMOUR: We will ask Edward. He will know the right course.

JANE: Yes. Shall I ever find such happiness as you two have?

ANNE SEYMOUR: Dear Jane, I hope so: For the present, make no decisions, accept no further gifts. As for my Lady Rochford, remember she is still the Queen's sister-in-law and her intimate.

(*Sound of Jane's heartbeat as*:)

9

Interior. Chapel. Hampton Court. Day.

(*The chapel at Hampton Court, the baptism. The service has now reached the point of the Benediction of the Salt.*)

BISHOP GARDINER: *Exorcizo te per Deum vivum* (*Sign of the cross*), *per Deum verum* (*Sign of the cross*), *per Deum sanctum* (*Sign of the cross*), *per Deum*... (*Mix to the Bishop giving the salt to the infant.*) *Eduarde, accipe sal sapientiae—*

(*Cut to Cromwell, watching.*)

(*Voice over.*) *Propitiatio sit tibi in vitam aeternam.*

ALL: *Amen.*

BISHOP GARDINER (*Voice over*): *Pax tectum.*

ALL: *Et cum spiritu tuo.*

(*But the Vicar-general does not speak the responses. Instead the sound distorts, the images distort to:*

10

Interior. Chamber of Presence, Hampton Court, March 1536, Day.

CROMWELL (*Addressing the King*): We are doing everything in our power, your Grace. My Lord of Canterbury has most ingeniously proved that all passages in Scripture concerning the Antichrist refer to the Pope . . .

HENRY: The Bishop of Rome.

CROMWELL: The Bishop of Rome. And we have shown the people that secularization of the monasteries will relieve their taxation.

HENRY: Are you mad, Cromwell?

(*Camera now opened. Henry, Cromwell, Cranmer, Norfolk.*)

CROMWELL: A portion, of course. There are close to four hundred abbeys which will yield your Grace an annual revenue of over 30,000 pounds in addition to plate, jewels, bells and lead.

HENRY: Yes, yes, but when shall we see all this?

CROMWELL: As soon as the due process of the law . . .

NORFOLK (*Chortles*): The Bill's stuck in the Commons.

HENRY: Has it?

CROMWELL: Temporarily. A few minor objections, legal quibbles.

HENRY: I'll have that Bill or some of their heads.

They've heard the Commission's report, that record of corruption. What's their quibble? Once and for all the monasteries must be put down.

CROMWELL: It's merely a question of precedence, your Grace, the degree of guilt, the size of establishment . . .

(*As Cromwell is speaking cut or mix back to*:)

Telecine: Exterior. Orchard. Day.

(*Jane in the orchard. This time entirely from Henry's point of view.*)

JANE: They are crowding to Hailes now since they hear it is to be visited by the Commission. They are afraid for the abbeys, sir, for their souls.

HENRY: My Commissioners are only anxious to report abuses. They are as good catholics as you or I, mistress Jane.

JANE: I meant no criticism, sir. Forgive me.

HENRY: I know your meaning. Ours is to reform, not to destroy.

11

Interior. The Chamber of Presence. Hampton Court. Day.

(*Henry's point of view.*)

CRANMER (*Voice over*): . . . the revenue from monastic property, your Grace.

HENRY: What's that?

CRANMER: I said your Grace will remember his promise for the endowment of Colleges and Seminaries?

HENRY: Yes, yes, my curate, but Dover first, eh, our defences first. Now where is Carew? Why isn't he back from Greenwich? Are we finished for today, gentlemen? This leg of mine—

NORFOLK: Take the footstool. (*Gives it to him.*)

HENRY: Thank you, Howard.

NORFOLK: Still that fall?

HENRY: No, the other thing. Buttes thinks it may be an ulcer now.

CRANMER: Your Grace must take greater care of his health. Our prayers can only do so much.

HENRY: There's nothing the matter with me, Archbishop, that a little healthy exercise cannot cure. I'm out of condition, that's all.

NORFOLK: The King's right. A few days' hunting—

HENRY (*Cutting him short*): Are we finished?

CROMWELL: Your Grace, the French envoy has been asked permission to visit the Lady Mary again.

HENRY: Let him do so. Let him make the journey, she shall be locked up during his visit. (*Suddenly furious.*) I will no longer live in this fear and suspicion of my own daughter! She shall write to me, not to the Emperor!

CROMWELL: Sir, she—

HENRY: She has, she's been writing to Charles. I know what goes on behind my back. And these damned Papists trying to spirit her out of the country! Well, she shall be sent to the Tower and tried and sentenced as any other subject who is guilty of treason. Make out the order and I will sign it.

CRANMER: Your Highness, I beg you to consider the consequences.

HENRY: There's nothing to cry about. I will not have another Catherine on my hands.

CROMWELL: Your Grace is of course entirely justified but rather than risk rebellion among your people, or indeed the danger of interference from outside, perhaps we should make one further effort.

HENRY: I'm sick of effort. I offer her my friendship—my love—you'd think with her mother dead—

NORFOLK: Give her a good hiding, sir, that's what I'd do. Girls need a good hiding.

CRANMER: Your Grace, now the Princess Dowager's influence is removed—she's a fine girl.

HENRY: You're too kind, Thomas. Oh, very well. Howard, you shall arrange a meeting with her at Hunsdon. But she must consent to every one of my statutes or I shall proceed against her. Tell her that. Ah, Sir Nicholas, come in.

CAREW (*Entering*): Your Grace. My Lords.

HENRY: How was Greenwich? Is the Queen up from her bed yet? Still moping, I suppose.

CAREW: Queen Anne takes little part in affairs there, sir, she spends most of the day with her dogs, setting them to fight each other.

HENRY: I can imagine.

CRANMER: But I trust her Grace's health is improved.

CAREW: Oh, yes, a little, my Lord.

HENRY: No need to detain you, Cranmer, or you, cousin. (*Waves them off, to Norfolk.*) Better take Bishop Sampson with you when you see my daughter. And she must admit her mother's marriage illegal—and herself a bastard. Nothing less.

NORFOLK: Your Grace. (*Goes out behind Cranmer.*)

HENRY: Well? How did she look?

CAREW: Most charming, sir.

HENRY: Yes. And her answer?

CAREW: Most humble.

HENRY: Don't cozen me. What did Mistress Seymour say?

CAREW: She received your purse of sovereigns in the garden, sir.

HENRY (*Eagerly*): Yes?

Telecine: Exterior. Garden. (Mix to Jane and page.)

CAREW (*Voice over*): She returned it to the page.

HENRY (*Voice over*): And my letter?

CAREW (*Voice over*): She returned.

HENRY (*Voice over*): Unopened?

219

JANE: I pray you beseech the King to understand by my prudence that I am a gentlewoman of good and honourable family, without reproach and have no greater treasure in the world than my honour, which I would not harm for a thousand deaths. If his Grace should wish to make me a present of money, I beg him to do so when God shall send me a husband to marry.

12

Interior. Chamber of Presence, Hampton Court. Day.

(*Henry, Cromwell and Carew.*)

HENRY (*Considering, then greatly pleased*): I like her modesty. It touches me. It shows a seemliness. She has reproved us, and rightly. But what a gentle reproof. Eh, my Lord?

CROMWELL: Most gentle, sir.

HENRY: We will prove our intentions equally worthy. We will not speak to Mistress Seymour in future except in the presence of her relations. I feel better. I shall ride a little today. If we are to return to Greenwich for Easter, I must stir the blood.

CROMWELL: Your Grace. (*Henry stops on his way out, turns.*) I have been considering—my rooms at Greenwich are far larger than my present needs—would they not be more suitable for Edward Seymour and his new wife?

HENRY: But where would you live, my dear Cromwell?

CROMWELL: I can find a room in the friary, your Grace.

HENRY: Master Edward would be forever grateful to you.

CROMWELL: A trifle, sir. And perhaps, since he will be in such proximity to your Grace, the gentleman should be rewarded for past service by election to the privy chamber.

HENRY: My thoughts, exactly, Crum, my very thoughts.

(*And he goes out, smiling and humming to himself.*)

CAREW: Your Lordship never ceases to earn my admiration.

CROMWELL: Sir Nicholas, do you know one of the highest arts of the politician? It is to devise means by which sovereigns can gratify their appetites without appearing to outrage morality.

13

Interior. The private apartment at Greenwich. Day.

(*Jane and Anne Seymour. Anne is playing the lute. She finishes playing.*)

ANNE SEYMOUR: Is that the piece?

JANE: Forgive me, I am not attentive. I have heard that William Dormer is to marry Mistress Sidney.

ANNE SEYMOUR: Within the month.

JANE: Then I think I shall never be married.

ANNE SEYMOUR: Indeed you may—and higher than young Dormer.

JANE: Don't—please—

ANNE SEYMOUR: My dear, there are doubts for the
legality of the Queen's union. They say that she was
previously betrothed to Northumberland and that—

(*Edward Seymour enters quickly through door from
private passage.*)

—Edward—what is it, my dear?

EDWARD: All hell's broke loose! Forgive me, but his
Grace has insulted the Imperial ambassador and now
Cromwell's breathing fire.

(*Anne and Edward exchange look of some understanding.*)

14

Interior. Room of State. Greenwich. Day.

(*Henry and Cromwell in window area of the Room of
State at Greenwich.*)

HENRY (*In full spate*): Can the Pope command angels?
He cannot command me.

CROMWELL: The Bishop of Rome . . .

HENRY: The Bishop of Rome has seen fit to excommunicate me, to anathematize me and pronounce me
unfit to live. Should I now kiss his ring?

CROMWELL: Your Grace knows the sentence is not
yet published.

HENRY: He threatens it like Damocles' sword. Let
him publish. I don't care three straws! We've not

proceeded on such slight grounds as to alter any part of our doings. We've laid our foundations on the Law of God. On nature. On honesty. And we've done this with the consent of the Estate of the Realm in open and high court of Parliament!

CROMWELL: If your Grace will consider calmly, he will see that Signor Chapuys is making the most reasonable proposals.

HENRY: No, no, no! I will not sue to the Emperor. All these years he has shown us nothing but ingratitude, stirring the Bishop of Rome to do us injury.

CROMWELL: There are still advantages to be gained by an agreement with him at this time, sir. And even by an agreement with Rome.

HENRY: Which would destroy our whole policy towards the monasteries.

CROMWELL: There may be greater benefits, your Grace.

HENRY: Have we gone so far in our Supremacy to turn back now? No, by God! I am an Englishman, I cannot say one thing when I mean another.

CROMWELL: I beg your Grace not to reject an imperial alliance merely on a point of etiquette.

HENRY: Are you criticizing me?

CROMWELL: No, your Grace.

HENRY: You do!

CROMWELL: I do not!

HENRY: You reprove our behaviour.

CROMWELL: I merely . . .

HENRY: Take care, Cromwell. No one is indispensable to us.

CROMWELL (*Panting, snorting*): If—If your Grace will allow me, I would drink a glass of wine.

HENRY: Have your drink but do not criticize your Sovereign.

CROMWELL: I only criticize the value of the Queen's advice to your Grace. It shows small policy and less advantage.

HENRY (*Takes hold of him*): I will not be judged by you! You *little* man! (*He shakes him like a dog, pummelling him till Cromwell's hat falls, revealing his shaven poll.*) Do you hear me?

CROMWELL: Your Grace!

HENRY: *I will not be judged by any man!*

15

Interior. Private apartment. Greenwich. Day.

(*Jane in the apartment, waiting with Anne and Edward.*)

16

Interior. Passage. Greenwich. Day.

(*Henry in the passage. He enters the apartment.*)

17

Interior. Private apartment. Greenwich. Day.

(*Henry, greatly disturbed, goes to table, pours wine, waves Anne and Edward out. Drinks. Jane waits patiently, but in some anxiety.*)

HENRY: That Cromwell! That man! That—that wool carder! (*Quietens.*) Jane. (*He turns to her and clumsily seeks refuge in her arms. She as awkwardly half turns away.*) No, be still. I need your honesty. I am a simple man, Jane, easily baffled. Their minds turn me.

JANE: Your Grace is much misunderstood, I think.

HENRY: You understand.

JANE: I think so, sir.

HENRY: I only wish to govern my subjects in my own way. (*After a moment.*) Your brother said you were not well.

JANE: The river mists. I have taken cold, sir.

HENRY: They should keep fires. I will send you a gown, a woollen one.

JANE: No, sir, I thank you.

HENRY: A gown, Jane—a plain thing—you'd take it from a friend.

JANE: Your Grace, I would leave Court.

HENRY (*Looks at her a moment*): And if I will not let you . . .?

JANE: You must, sir.

HENRY: *'Bound to Obey and Serve'*—isn't that your motto?

JANE: I must obey my conscience.

HENRY: We all must. But to leave us . . .

JANE: I would not come between your Grace and his wife.

HENRY: Jane, God is making all things plain to me. I was seduced into this marriage. By sorcery. You know that woman wedded in the power of devils is no lawful wife. That is why I cannot have a son.

JANE: It was a son, sir, that was born dead. And now she blames me for it.

HENRY: No, it was my fall that frightened her.

JANE: I have heard otherwise. So let me go, sir, before I call God's judgement on us.

HENRY: Jane, it was she who urged Fisher's execution and Sir Thomas More's, she who plotted Catherine's death, and now young Mary's.

JANE: *I would not be hers, sir.*

HENRY: No, no, a pension in the country, a life abroad. She always favoured France.

JANE: But if I were gone . . .

HENRY: Her rule would still be ended.

JANE (*After a moment*): When I was young, I did a fearful thing.

HENRY (*Smiles*): You?

JANE: I let one of my sisters visit a house where there was poverty and pestilence. I should have gone. I made her go instead. That night a spot appeared upon her face. Then two. Dark. Horrible. I lived in awe for her. I had no will. I was in darkness. The hours passed while we waited, and she recovered. It was some—some childish ailment. But I knew then the terror of being out of grace, the indecision, the disorder. And I know it now.

HENRY: You have received Your Maker?

JANE: Yes.

HENRY: And made confession?

JANE: Yes.

HENRY: Will you see my confessor?

JANE: Gladly, sir.

HENRY: And will you trust me, Jane?

JANE: Yes, sir.

HENRY: Yes, yes, in obedience you are free. Come to the cross. (*Leads her across room to crucifix on wall.*) Kneel, Jane. (*They kneel.*) Almighty God, grant us thy servants the knowledge of thy Grace—

JANE: Grant us Thy Grace—

HENRY: Restore our will—

JANE: Restore our will—

HENRY: Our good order.

JANE: Our order.

HENRY: Give us to choose aright—

JANE: Give us to choose aright—

HENRY: Give us to *know* the righteousness of our actions—

JANE: To know the righteousness of our actions—

HENRY: And bless us, God, in thy sight.

JANE: Bless us in thy sight.

HENRY: Forever, Amen.

JANE: Amen.

18

Interior. Dining area. Carew's house. Night.

(*The dining table in Carew's house. Laughter. Atmosphere of celebration. Night scene. Candles. The end of supper. Carew at end of table, Lady Exeter on his right, Norfolk on his left. Edward Seymour beyond Lady Exeter. Carew rises.*)

CAREW: My Lords, Ladies, the King's health.

ALL (*Toasting*): His Grace's Health ... Henry Tudor ... The King etc ...

NORFOLK: A fine supper, Sir Nicholas, I wish I could steal your cook.

CAREW: I'm glad it meets with your Grace's approval. I stole him from you, my Lord of Norfolk.

LADY EXETER (*After the laugh*): They've not elected you to the Garter for nothing.

CAREW: Lady Exeter.

NORFOLK: No, a splendid occasion—and timely, very timely.

CAREW (*To servants*): Leave the wine here. You may withdraw. (*To Gardiner.*) My Lord Bishop, will you . . .?

(*Cut to Bishop Gardiner on left side of table. We see that there is another guest, a lady, seated between him and Norfolk but we do not yet see her face.*)

GARDINER: *Agimus tibi gratias, omnipotens Deus, pro universis beneficiis tuis. Amen.* (*Looks to door to see servants have gone.*) Now then to our business. What's this about Cromwell?

EDWARD: He's not been seen for five days.

LADY EXETER: Taken to his bed?

EDWARD: After the unfortunate affair at Greenwich.

GARDINER (*Cheerfully*): So Crum's blotted his copy-book at last.

NORFOLK: Hardly surprising. If you eat cherries with your superiors, you must expect to get the pips in your eyes.

LADY ROCHFORD (*Voice over*): He's clever though. (*Now cut to Lady Rochford, the other guest*). My Lord Cromwell. He'll find his way back somehow.

GARDINER: I suppose we are quite certain of the King's inclination?

LADY EXETER: Oh yes, Mistress Jane's all plainsong, he has no ear for other music now.

LADY ROCHFORD: But you must take care she does not prejudice your cause, Master Seymour.

229

EDWARD: She's well instructed, your Ladyship.

NORFOLK: Surely the only real problem is how to get rid of the night crow.

GARDINER: The what?

NORFOLK (*Emphatic*): The Great Whore.

LADY EXETER: His Grace is making discreet reference to the Queen, Bishop.

NORFOLK: My niece Boleyn. She's a damned rude— whore.

EDWARD: Cromwell's the difficulty. As long as she has him—

CAREW: Yes, if Cromwell trims his sails now as he's likely to, he could be more than dangerous.

NORFOLK: Ah, these new men, Cromwell, Audley, you never know what they're planning. No background, that's why. No breeding.

CAREW: And there's my Lord of Canterbury.

NORFOLK: Oh, Cranmer's quite good family.

GARDINER: Cranmer will do whatever the King and Cromwell require of him. That's why he's where he is.

LADY EXETER: Do I detect a note of rancour, my Lord Bishop?

GARDINER: Pass the wine, Seymour. Does your Ladyship approve this new learning? Cranmer's doing. Or the sermons that she hears? All these books circulated against the holy images and our blessed saints? Cranmer again. Now he's bent on this new translation of the gospel—full of heresy, believe me, your Ladyship.

LADY EXETER: Oh, I do, my Lord, but I still cannot accept Latin as the only language the devil doesn't understand.

NORFOLK: Well, I thank my God I never knew what the Old and New Testament were! There's too many bookworms. That's the whole trouble with the country today.

(*And so it might continue all night but their heads turn to the door.*)

CAREW: Yes?

VOICE: My Lord Cromwell is here, sir.

CAREW: Here?

VOICE: Yes, sir, at the gate.

NORFOLK: Talk of the devil! What's he doing here?

LADY EXETER: That man has agents in every house.

GARDINER (*Rattled*): Is there a way out through the garden?

(*Too late. At this moment Cromwell enters, friendly, on top again, the shark's grin.*)

CROMWELL: Sir Nicholas. Your Ladyship. Your Grace, a pleasure as always. Lady Rochford. My dear Gardiner, a brief trip from Paris, I take it?

GARDINER: Yes, just a day or two.

CROMWELL: His Majesty is delighted with your despatches—in case you have not yet paid him your attendance. Master Seymour.

EDWARD: My Lord.

CROMWELL: All gathered together, eh? I trust you'll forgive my joining your little celebration so unexpectedly, Sir Nicholas, but I felt I must come this moment and offer you my felicitations. (*Taking his hand*.) Yes, the Knights could not have chosen better. Some people expected your husband to be elected, Lady Rochford, but I thought no—no, it'll be Sir Nicholas. (*Taps his head*.) One of my hunches. I'm seldom wrong.

CAREW (*Offering chair*): Will your Lordship be pleased to join us?

CROMWELL (*Taking it*): Thank you.

CAREW: A glass of wine, sir?

CROMWELL: The very thing. It's absolutely freezing on the river.

GARDINER (*Lamely*): Yes, very cold. For the season.

(*The wine is poured. They watch him, masking their deep suspicion.*)

LADY EXETER (*With superb innocence*): We heard your Lordship had not been in the best of health.

CROMWELL (*A sly grin at her*): A trifle indisposed, Lady Exeter. But fortunately my disposition is such that I am now completely recovered. So I came to join your revels. I am at your service. (*Looks at them*.) You doubt me? Come now, you each have good reason for being here. You must allow me mine.

NORFOLK (*Rising*): This is intolerable!

CROMWELL: Pray be seated, your Grace, we are quite alone. I have no armed men or witnesses at the door. (*Norfolk looks to Lady Exeter and then slowly sits. Cromwell has picked up a walnut from the fruit bowl.*

He waits till he has their full attention.) This nut. You desire to eat it. So you must first break the shell. But how? Between your fingers? They're not strong enough. I could of course rub the shell— (*Doing so.*) Slowly—gradually—wear it away—I should eventually succeed. But I am hungry. I'm very hungry. I would in fact be famished long before I ever reached the fruit. (*Puts it on the table.*) And so—(*His fist descends, shattering it.*) And the secret my friends, is not only force but knowing where to apply that force—to the shell's weakness, the protection of its heart.

LADY EXETER: Is there not a danger, my Lord, that too much force may destroy the fruit in your walnut?

CROMWELL: Not if it is applied correctly, madam. You've all been busy rubbing away, trumping up pre-engagements between Queen Anne and Northumberland. It won't signify. There are only two charges that will stick. Treason. And adultery.

EDWARD: But, my Lord, surely—some lesser indictment—carrying a lesser penalty—

CROMWELL (*Like a hammer*): I know his mind. His conscience. You don't. Nothing else signifies.

(*Reactions round the table. A slow and in some cases, notably Edward, a grudging acceptance. But it is the Queen's death warrant.*)

LADY ROCHFORD: May I say we have long needed your Lordship.

(*Cromwell gives her a brief inclination of the head. He is eating the walnut.*)

CROMWELL: You wish to see your sister crowned Queen of England, Master Seymour? Leave it to me. I'm an old hand at it.

18A

(*Limbo, execution and wedding. Drums. Close up of executioner's hands on sword followed by a close up of Anne Boleyn's hands praying and then the executioner's hand swinging sword up behind her shoulders. Her hands part. Wedding bells ring as close up shows Jane's and Crammer's hands and the wedding ring being slipped on to Jane's finger. Cut to black.*)

19

Interior. Chapel. Hampton Court. Day.

(*The baptism. The service continues. The vows. The heartbeat.*)

BISHOP GARDINER : *Tu autem effugare diabole, appropinquabit enim judicium Dei. Eduarde—abrenuntias satanae?*

CRANMER :
NORFOLK : } (*Together, vowing as Godparents*) :   *Abrenuntio.*
MARY :

(*Cut to Mary.*)

GARDINER (*Voice over*) : *Et omnibus operibus ejus?*

MARY (*Voice over*) : *Abrenuntio.*

GARDINER (*Voice over*) : *Et omnibus pompis ejus?*

MARY : *Abrenuntio.*

(*Distort and dissolve to* :)

20

Interior. The Queen's chamber at Hampton Court. Day. August 1536.

(Henry is reading a letter.)

MARY *(Voice over, gruff, almost harsh)*: My most dear father and Sovereign, I have this day perceived your gracious clemency to have overcome my most unnatural proceedings. My poor heart I send unto your Highness to remain in your hand and I will never vary from that submission I made to your Highness in the presence of the Council. I pray God preserve you and the Queen and send you issue. *(Fade voice.)* Your wholly respectful daughter, Mary.

(Open to see Henry with leg up and Jane with him.)

HENRY: Yes, but is she honest? I hate dissemblers. If she's writing to Charles behind my back—

JANE: I'm sure she isn't, sir. Can you not forgive her now?

HENRY: How do I know her mind? She's been forced to this by the Council, by Cromwell, by your letters—and quite possibly at the advice of her own party to save her life. She was always obstinate and disobedient. It's her Spanish blood. How can I believe her?

JANE *(Simply)*: Because she is your daughter, sir. And you need her. *(Henry grunts.)* And then there are the feelings of your people to consider.

HENRY *(He knows it)*: They worry for her.

JANE: Yes.

(Henry shifts his body. It seems larger now. He gasps. Jane rises to him.)

235

HENRY: No, it's nothing. This leg again.

JANE: Shall I rub it for you?

HENRY: No, but stay here. (*She settles, beside him. He touches her hair.*) You know, Jane, you are a fool. You ought to seek the advancement of the children we will have between us, not any others. Why should you care for the Lady Mary?

JANE: I think of her alone. In tears.

HENRY: Nonsense, Mary never cries. They say she's hard as nails, now.

JANE: I think she must cry, sir, not knowing how to keep her—her honour and your Grace's good will. If only—

HENRY (*Interrupts impatiently*): When she places her honour before my—never mind. If only—?

JANE: If you could bring her back to Court—

HENRY: You think she'd thank you for it? Or that you could influence her?

JANE: I think so, sir. I hope so. For ten years now—

HENRY: Go on.

JANE: Ten years she's lived unnaturally, spending her youth in bitterness and anger. I think she needs your Grace's love now.

HENRY (*After a moment, quietly*): How kind you are, Jane. I have never known a kinder soul. Why, if you had your way, my little nun, every villain in the Counter would go free.

JANE: Yes, they'd all be pardoned. Oh, but I should

make a very poor ruler, sir. I'd even believe in Louis' horse.

HENRY: Louis? Of France?

JANE: Why yes, it's an old story my brother Thomas tells. I was sure your Grace had heard it.

HENRY: No, but tell me, Jane. You know I love a good story. And I like to listen to you.

JANE: I can never tell stories, sir.

HENRY: Try. Come. I insist. No, I don't *insist*—but it would please me.

JANE: Well then—oh, dear—it concerns a thief whom Louis had condemned to death—some criminal—

HENRY: Yes, yes.

JANE: And this man, to save his life, said that within a year he could make Louis' favourite horse talk.

HENRY: What!

JANE: 'But that's impossible', says a friend of the thief. 'Keep silent, you fool', says the man, 'for within a year Louis may die, or the horse may die—or I may die—or the horse may talk!'

(*There is a second's pause and then Henry roars with laughter.*)

HENRY: Oh, Jane, that's wonderful! Or the horse may talk!

(*Lady Rochford enters.*)

LADY ROCHFORD: Forgive me, your Grace, but Lord Cromwell is asking to see you on a matter of urgency.

HENRY: Cromwell—send him in, send him in; (*Lady Rochford retires*.) Or the horse may talk!

(*Henry is still laughing as Cromwell enters*.)

CROMWELL: Your Highnesses will forgive my intrusion?

HENRY: What is it, Crum?

CROMWELL: A messenger from York, your Grace. There's been an incident in the city.

HENRY: An incident?

CROMWELL: An armed rising, sir. Thankfully of little magnitude.

HENRY: They've not touched our tax commissioners?

CROMWELL: No, sir. The Lieutenant is in control.

HENRY: How did it happen?

CROMWELL: I believe at the performance of a religious interlude, your Grace.

HENRY: It's those damned Papists again! (*Rising*.) Forgive me, my dear. Is the messenger here?

CROMWELL: Yes, your Grace, but—

HENRY (*Going*): No, no, I can manage. Keep the Queen company. Get her to tell you about Louis' horse.

(*Henry goes. Cromwell looks at Jane, waiting*.)

JANE: It is of no consequence, my Lord.

CROMWELL: What is of consequence to me, madam,

is that I should still be regarded kindly by your Highness.

JANE: As indeed you are, my Lord.

CROMWELL: Yet I cannot avoid feeling that your Highness looks on me of late with some disfavour. I am glad to have this opportunity of seeing her alone.

JANE: But your Lordship knows me for his constant admirer.

CROMWELL: You are naturally discreet, madam. I like that. I am also discreet. (*She looks at him.*) Your Grace perhaps is displeased that her Coronation is postponed?

JANE: No, sir, I would rather go uncrowned than risk the plague in London.

CROMWELL: All our subjects know you for their Queen, madam.

(*Close up of Jane. Troubled.*)

JANE: Do they, sir? (*After a moment.*) This affair at York—

CROMWELL: A pinprick.

JANE: Your Lordship has surely considered it may be on behalf of the distressed monks and friars.

CROMWELL: Ah, now we have it.

JANE: The clergy who have lost their houses—or rather—you will forgive my plain speech?

CROMWELL: Say it, say it.

JANE: The men and women you have caused to be evicted, my Lord.

CROMWELL: Parliament, madam. Not your servant, nor the King, but Parliament.

JANE: And whose servant is Parliament, my Lord?

(*Cromwell smiles. She is faster than he thought.*)

CROMWELL: The clergy have been compensated by Court of Exchequer, madam.

JANE: A new gown and forty shillings.

CROMWELL: Your Grace would defend these strongholds of Popery?

JANE: I was ever taught that Church property is to be held sacred.

CROMWELL: No, madam, for the fifth King Henry confiscated many priories in his time.

JANE: Alien priories, my Lord, whose money he devoted to schools and to the monasteries.

CROMWELL: Ah, you've been at the history books, madam, you're too clever for me! But seriously, isn't it better to support the Head of our Church in his necessities than to support the sloth and wickedness of these monks?

JANE: If you had seen these monks and friars as I have, in hospitals, in prisons, among the poor, wherever there is danger and a total absence of reward, you would not call them wicked or slothful. And even if the King requires this revenue, yet half the land is being given to his friends.

CROMWELL: Of course, madam! We must have their good will. They are the King's right hand, his armour. Oh, madam, I am so besieged by petitioners you would scarce believe it. Why, only this week your brother Edward was granted two manors in Wiltshire and the lands adjoining. (*This stops her. Cromwell grins slyly.*) You see, your Grace, how we are all powerless against the realities of change and State. But any other service—

JANE: There is one.

(*Cromwell can afford to be generous.*)

CROMWELL: Name it, madam.

JANE: The Lady Mary. You have advised her well. Now advise the King. Persuade him, if you will, to bring her back to Court.

CROMWELL: It will not be easy.

JANE: No. But then, as you have said yourself, my Lord, 'a few words from a man of the world are worth volumes of philosophers'.

(*Cromwell grins at being quoted. Henry re-enters.*)

HENRY: It was the Papists! And they'll pay for it. My Lord, I have come to a decision, or rather my wife has helped me to it. If the Lady Mary will write to the Emperor Charles fully acknowledging my statutes, we will fetch her back to Court.

(*Jane goes to him and embraces him. Henry is glowing, his arm round her. Cromwell smiles at her.*)

CROMWELL: Madam, I must correct myself forthwith—a few words from a great lady are worth volumes from worldly men.

(*Dissolve to:*)

241

20A

Interior. The Chamber of Presence at Hampton Court. Day.

(Henry and Jane on throne chairs. The Court present. Cromwell with Cranmer. Norfolk across the room. Present among the courtiers Edward Seymour, Carew with Bryan, Lady Rochford, Bishop Gardiner with Lady Exeter. Chamberlain taps staff. The room centre clears. Conversations cease.)

VOICE: The Lady Mary, your Grace.

(There is a pause while the Court looks towards the door. Then Mary enters with her train. Only twenty, her face is strained, pinched, narrow, and at this moment she is understandably nervous. She makes a low curtsey to the King from the door. She advances, curtseys again in centre of the room. Then comes to Henry and Jane. She makes a further low curtsey and drops to her knees. Mary's voice is hard, gruff.)

MARY: Your blessing, sire.

(Henry raises her, kisses her.)

HENRY: Welcome, my child.

MARY *(Turns to Jane)*: Your Highness.

JANE: Welcome, Mary.

(Henry to the assembled Court.)

HENRY: Some of you wanted me to put this jewel to death.

(And he fastens his eye on Norfolk. Cranmer and Cromwell exchange a look.)

8. *Jane Seymour* (*Anne Stallybrass*) *before her marriage to Henry*

9. *Jane with Archbishop Cranmer (Bernard Hepton)*

10. *Henry VIII carrying his newborn son, Edward, surrounded by Cromwell and the rest of the court*

JANE: That were great pity to have lost your chiefest jewel of England.

(*Mary stands between them, her colour coming and going. Then she falls in a faint.*)

HENRY: The physician.

Mary is laid on a pallet-sofa. Calls of 'Stand back', 'Make room' etc. When room is made Henry stands by her.)

But why should she swoon? (*Doctor comes.*) Ah, Doctor, help her, recover her for us.

(*Pull back as doctor leans over to administer to her to Gardiner and Lady Exeter at edge of the circle.*)

GARDINER: Is she ill, do you think? She looks deathly ill.

LADY EXETER: Wouldn't you be, Bishop, if you'd just renounced your mother and owned yourself a bastard. (*Gardiner blinks.*) She's terrified. She has learnt to be afraid of flattery.

GARDINER: Ah, yes. And then the stink of all these Lutherans!

LADY EXETER: Really, Bishop!

(*Cut to centre of circle where Mary is recovering. Jane holds her gently, helps her to sit up.*)

HENRY: Give us air. She must walk to restore the humours. (*The court stand back. Henry takes Mary by the arm and walks with her, up and down.*) Now there's nothing to fear, my child. We're all delighted to see you here.

MARY: My confessor.

243

HENRY: Yes, yes, by all means.

MARY: He is imprisoned.

HENRY: Then we'll let him out. You shall have all your servants about you again—Mary Fynche, Randal Dodd, the old man who grows your strawberries, what's his name?

MARY: Thomas Crabtree.

HENRY: Yes, a wonderful old man.

(*Cut to Bryan and Carew, watching.*)

BRYAN: Remarkable, quite remarkable.

CAREW: Isn't Cromwell playing a dangerous hand?

BRYAN: My dear fellow, it's the Queen who's playing it—and I'm not sure she even knows the name of the game.

(*Cut to Jane watching. Cut back to Bryan and Carew.*)

CAREW: I'll lay you fifty crowns that she wins.

BRYAN: Done!

(*Cut back to Henry and Mary, walking.*)

HENRY: Yes, you were a good obedient girl to write as you did to Charles. (*He stops. The sudden suspicion.*) You didn't write to him apart from that, did you?

MARY: No, sir.

HENRY: Have you ever written to him?

MARY (*Lying*): Never.

(Henry continuing to walk with her to Jane now.)

HENRY: I believe you. And by God's great mercy you have escaped the hands of that damned poisonous strumpet—Mistress Bulleyn. We shall not lose you from us again, shall we, madam?

JANE *(Taking Mary's hand)*: No, sir.

HENRY: You shall come to Greenwich with us. You always liked it there, didn't you? *(Mary blinks.)* And you like to ride, I remember. You shall go riding with the Queen at Greenwich.

(Dissolve to:)

21

Interior. Mary's room. Hampton Court. Day.

(Bed fragment with table beside it. Jane arranging flowers in small bowl. She does so carefully, lovingly, with a good eye. Dissolve to:)

22

Interior. Chapel. Hampton Court. Day.

(Mary praying before the Virgin.)

MARY: Holy Mother, forgive me. I've gulled you. I'm too weak. I've betrayed you. Forgive me. Forgive me, Holy Mother. Forgive me.

(Dissolve to:)

23

Interior. Mary's room. Hampton Court. Day.

(*Mary has run into the room and is tearing a ring from her finger. Mary throws it down. Then clutches at one of the flowers, taking it and tearing it as she lies on the bed, weeping, a wild masculine weeping. The door is heard to open and Jane comes to her, sits by her, tries to hold her but Mary pulls away. They are almost struggling.*)

JANE: Mary. You've nothing to fear. You're safe here.

MARY: Leave me! Leave me be! Rings! And you dazzle me with flowers!

JANE: He tries to do what is right, Mary.

MARY: You say that? With my mother dead? You loved her. You know the truth. His harlot killed her.

JANE: No, she died naturally.

MARY: Her heart was found black.

JANE: I won't believe it.

MARY: He was responsible.

JANE: Responsible? (*Close up of Jane. Her responsibilities. She returns to Mary.*) You mustn't tax him with that. He's not unfeeling and I won't have him hurt. He's a good man—not always easy—but he loves you, he couldn't bear your reproaches. Do you think he doesn't own them already? (*Mary finally gives way, allowing Jane to hold her, but there is still a coldness, an isolation.*) Rest now. Don't fight him any more.

(*As Jane takes the broken flower from her, dissolve to*:)

Telecine: *Exterior. A bridle path at Greenwich. Day.*

(*Jane and Mary riding palfreys with velvet housings.*

They ride side-saddle, stooping sometimes to avoid a branch.

The scene should have a clean, fresh autumn air, of the early morning.

Jane looks at Mary, smiling at her, for herself, for the ride.

A slow response from Mary which lights up her face and even gives her a certain charm.

As they come down the path, Tom Seymour leaps down from the bank or appears from nowhere after his fashion.

The horses pull up, shying a little.)

JANE: Tom! (*He comes to her, holds her, laughing.*) You're home!

(*Tom, turning to Mary's horse and steadying it, grins at her.*)

TOM: Your Ladyship. (*Turning back to Jane.*) Yes, I came through Wiltshire.

JANE: How were they all?

TOM: Father and Mother still the same, though he's been poorly this month. Dorothy says it's her turn and she'll be married next year, she don't know who!

JANE (*To Mary*): My little sister.

MARY: I believe we must congratulate you, Master Seymour, on being appointed to the Privy chamber.

TOM: Not only that, ma'am, I'm to lead the revels. Make room, Jane!

(*He is up behind her and urging the horse down the bridle path as the scene dissolves to*:)

24

Interior. The Queen's chamber at Hampton Court. Day.

(*Henry and Jane. He is pacing the room.*)

HENRY: Christ in Heaven! First Lincoln, now this. Thirty thousand of them. They're lighting beacons across the hills.

JANE: But they say they have no quarrel with your Grace, only with the Council.

HENRY (*Dangerously cool*): I have never read or heard that Princes' counsellors should be appointed by rude and ignorant and common people. Have you, madam?

JANE: No, sir.

HENRY: Don't we know after twenty-eight years how to govern our kingdom? Oh, they presume! The commons of Yorkshire—Yorkshire, the last place God made! Do they think they are north of the law? Well, my Lord of Norfolk shall show them. He may be a fool but he's a good soldier. He shall deal with Master Robert Aske and his followers.

JANE: Be merciful, sir. They bear Christ's banner, His wounds.

HENRY: Oh yes, they make holy cause of it!

JANE: If you would hear their petitions . . .

HENRY: Their demands, madam. What are you trying to say?

JANE (*Impulsively, on her knees*): I beg you, sir—by the deep love I bear you—I beg you to restore the abbeys. This can only be God's judgment for putting them down.

HENRY (*Icy*): God and my conscience are on perfectly good terms, madam. And if you wish to avoid Mistress Bulleyn's end, you will not meddle in my affairs. You are not yet crowned, madam. Get up.

JANE (*Rising*): Forgive me, sir.

HENRY: You are all ignorant of the truth. But neither you nor any man can make me doubt the justice of our cause. Would Parliament have voted against the abbeys if they had been of benefit to the country? Yet, when the Report of the Commissioners was read to them, there was a huge cry of 'Down with the Church'. The Church for which I am responsible in the eyes of God was denounced as vicious and abominable. (*He is out to break her now like a horse, as he did Mary. So through this scene her reactions, mostly silent, are of great importance.*) Are you afraid to speak? Because I threatened you?

JANE: No, sir.

HENRY: Then you are determined to spite me.

JANE: I have asked your pardon, sir.

HENRY: Will you admit that I am right and that you are wrong?

JANE (*Meekly*): Yes, sir.

HENRY: Meaning no, sir.

JANE: Meaning . . .

HENRY: I know lip-service when I hear it. Do you know what you support, madam? Do you? Prelates who build their great houses with alms money? Who squander endowments, cut down woods for profit, pawn their plate? Their business is the cure of souls and yet service often is not observed because the priest is following his pleasure! We found cases of coining, madam. Coining. In a monastery! Sacred vessels melted into sovereigns, yes. And worse things, I assure you, which I will not mention for modesty's sake. Only your convents are not exempt from this. And several times, when their rules were insisted upon, these same monks declared they were intolerable—their own rules, God thank you—and that they preferred our dispensation! So you curb your enthusiasm with the bridle of reason, madam. Because Christianity and not monkery is to be the religion of this land. Do you know the second commandment, madam?

JANE (*Very quietly*): Thou shalt not take the name . . .

HENRY: That is the third. A natural mistake, seeing the Bishop of Rome expunged the second some time ago. It is, 'Thou shalt not make unto thee any graven image'. God's law. And everywhere the worship of saints and relics and images has led to nothing but dishonesty. To trumpery. Believe me, Cromwell's men found more pieces of the True Cross in England than would make a whole one. Thomas Becket has two skulls, madam, oh yes—one in church and the other in his grave! There are your monks for you—your relics! The Holy Rood of Grace—you have heard of it? Its lips and eyes move at the approach of votaries? Springs and wheels, madam. Springs and wheels! A mechanical contrivance! Do you still maintain the purity of the Abbeys, madam? (*She is praying silently.*) Very well, I will show you a thing. (*And he is holding a Phial towards her.*) My Lord Cromwell procured it for me. He thought it might interest me. Do you recognize it, madam? You should. It comes from Hailes, madam, in Gloucestershire. *Your* Blood of Christ. (*She tries to turn her head.*) No, you look, you look at it. You don't see anything? Not yet perhaps. You have not paid for absolution. But spend your coins and— presto! (*He turns the Phial over.*) There! Now you have it! The glass is clear and you are absolved. Except that it is the blood of a duck which the monks renew once a week! Now—will you still make a God of the Pope's creatures, madam? (*Jane is still silent, the tears streaming down her face. He has attacked her faith. Her roots. And looking at her Henry is suddenly deeply ashamed. He moves away, taking the Phial with him. Puts it down. There is a long silence while his back is to her. Finally.*) Oh. I meant not to show it. Don't cry. I'm a rough man—rough-tempered . . . (*He turns to her and she is in his arms.*) I frightened you, forgive me.

JANE : No, I am bound to obey and serve you, sir.

HENRY : Is it so hard?

JANE (*Frames it, barely audible*): No.

HENRY : Don't make me doubt, Jane. Don't. I'm frightened then. It is as if I am possessed, I don't know what I'm saying—except that I have to strike and I'll use anything at hand. Where can I hide myself?

JANE : Ssh.

(*And now it is she comforting and holding him for he is like a boy.*)

HENRY: Jane— (*And this is his secret terror.*) Am I ill perhaps—in my mind? Am I?

JANE: No, you are only tired and need to rest.

HENRY: Rest, yes. If I could. I feel so old. And first we must put down these rebels. Oh, if only we had met before. For I doubt now we will have any children.

(*As they hold each other, dissolve to:*)

25

Interior. Room of State. Greenwich Palace. Night.

(*New Year's presentation of gifts. Court music.*

Jane is seated with a superb set of sable furs, a present from Henry. Henry, smiling and relaxed now, drinks from a fine goblet which he is admiring and which seems to be Jane's present.

Mary comes to him, curtseys.

The servant behind her proffers cushion and on it a silver inkstand or some gift of this type.

Henry takes it, delighted. Embraces her. In turn he summons a servant who gives Mary a magnificent gold bordering for a dress.

Nearly in tears, she kisses her father. Jane takes her hand, draws her to her.

Dissolve to the main floor of the Room of State. A

dance in progress, a Coranto, slow, stately. Courtiers dancing. See Edward with Anne Seymour, Bryan with Lady Exeter. Then Jane with Henry.

Dissolve to a corner of the room, the window area. Henry and Mary playing backgammon. Jane watches them.

Mary throws dice. Henry looks at situation, looks at Jane, then at Mary, acknowledging defeat and paying his stake. But he is not displeased.

Dissolve to the main floor of the Room of State again. Now the music is lively, a hay or a reel—perhaps 'The Lamb's Wind' or 'The Bishop of Chester's Jig'.

Courtiers, some masked now (among them Jane and Henry), set and turn about and then as the pace of the music increases they form a turning circle in the midst of which is Tom Seymour, fantastic as the Lord of Misrule with scarves, ribbons and laces, gold rings and jewels and with bells on his legs.

The tempo increases as he dances until they close on him and 'Chair' him on their shoulders.

A chant should begin here, started by Tom, in which they are all joining as we

Dissolve suddenly to silence.

Hands. Jane's hands feeling the wall. Cut to her face, blindfold.

She reaches the corner of the room, touches someone's sleeve. Her hands travel up to the face. She removes the blindfold to see whom she has caught. It is Lady Rochford, smiling.

Applause, laughter. The music recommences, fast.

Courtiers come from behind them with a dragon suit.

253

It is put over two courtiers and a line starts, Tom leading the dragon as Lord of Misrule and traditionally beating the drum. The music and the chanting rise.

Jane is carried with Henry along in the crowd beside the dragon.

Tom turns off into a corridor and all follow, beating time, chanting. The noise from the corridor is overwhelming.

Jane breaks away by a side arch into the small private passage that leads to the apartment).

26

Interior. Passage, Greenwich. Night.

(Angles, shadows as she runs from the sound behind her and then she is at the door to the apartment, opening it.)

27

Interior. Private apartment. Greenwich. Night.

(Edward Seymour is sitting alone at the table, holding a letter, a lighted candle before him. His face is grave. The sound of the revels has the insistence of a distant noise. He looks up at her slowly.)

EDWARD: He's dead. Father. He died last week.

28

Interior. Passage. Greenwich. Night.

(She turns, swaying, the door closing on her, and is held by Henry in the narrow passage. He kisses her passionately.)

29

Interior. The Queen's chamber. Hampton Court. Day. Summer.

(Jane, in her sixth month, is seated by the window, looking out. She touches her lips to someone below. Cut to:)

Telecine: Exterior. Day.

(Fragment of garden at Hampton Court.

Henry looking up to her window. He smiles and returns her affection.

See Edward Seymour beside him and a Head Gardener as they move on down the path.)

30

Interior. Queen's chamber. Hampton Court. Day.

(Jane at the window.)

VOICE OVER: My Lord of Canterbury, madam.

JANE (*Turning*): Come in, my Lord.

CRANMER (*Entering*): I could not leave Hampton Court without paying my devotions to your Highness.

JANE: That was kind of you. And you must be busy with Convocation.

CRANMER (*Smiling*): Convocation, madam, is at this minute of less importance than the mother of our future heir. Your Highness keeps good health?

JANE: So I am assured, sir.

CRANMER: And has all she needs?

JANE: Oh, I am very spoiled, my Lord. I venture to express a desire for quail and a cloud of birds descend on us from all parts of the kingdom.

CRANMER: Your Grace must be careful though. A surfeit of game can prove dangerous to a delicate constitution.

JANE: Oh, I am quite strong, sir, really.

EDWARD (*Voice over outside*): This way, this way.

(*Edward enters carrying roses from the garden. He is followed by the Head Gardener who is almost invisible under a load of sallow branches. During the next scene the gardener places these branches round the walls of the room and into corners.*)

JANE: Edward.

EDWARD (*To Cranmer*): Your Grace. (*Gives Jane roses.*) The King wants you to know he chose these himself.

JANE: Aren't they lovely, Archbishop?

CRANMER: Glorious, madam.

(*And with the flowers and the sallow branches the light in the room is all diffused with greenery and summer blossom. Jane arranges the flowers in a bowl.*)

JANE (*To Edward*): The trial is over then?

EDWARD: Yes. (*Answering Jane's look.*) They're all condemned, all the leaders. Lord Darcy is condemned. And Aske.

JANE: Robert Aske? But the King pardoned him. I saw him. At Greenwich. I was there when he gave his promise.

(*There is an awkward silence which Edward breaks.*)

EDWARD: His Grace showed me your new edition of the Bishop's Book, sir. He seemed greatly taken with it.

CRANMER: It should rightly be termed the King's Book, my Lord, for his Highness revised most of it himself.

EDWARD (*Laughs*): I know. He says you criticized his theology *and* his grammar!

CRANMER: His Grace knows me for a great polemicist.

JANE: I was glad the Book admitted Purgatory, sir, and that prayers assist the dead.

CRANMER: Within moderation, your Highness. A single mass is deemed most sufficient.

JANE: Yes, it were a sorry thing if the dead were not to be prayed for.

257

CRANMER: His Grace and I are only anxious to secure an uniformity of religion, madam, according to the Word of God. These are troublous times. (*He bows.*) May God be with your Highness and keep her safely. It is unfortunate the plague has still been so virulent as to delay your Highness's coronation. As soon as your Highness is abroad from her confinement— (*Turns at the door.*) These branches should be sprinkled with vinegar, my Lord, it's sure remedy against the pestilence. Ah, at Lambeth they die at my gate, poor souls, even in the next house. (*He goes.*)

JANE (*Shudders*): I know my Lord Cranmer is the kindest man but why can he never leave without mention of the plague? Oh but I'm glad you're out of it. Come, sit here. So Anne is with child too.

EDWARD: Yes.

JANE: You must be pleased.

EDWARD: Yes.

JANE: Now we must give you sons. The King says a son is worth more to him than all the wealth of the Church. I think he has never been so hopeful, or so happy. Did you see our arms and initials carved at the chapel door?

EDWARD: Yes. (*Turns away.*) You are frightened, Jane. Why?

JANE: Of the plague? I have always . . .

EDWARD: Not that. You have—I don't know, we talk so little now—but you have lost something of your calm. A stillness. When we were young—and what a brood we were tumbling about the house—you hardly spoke, and yet when one of us was in trouble we came to your quiet hands. Am I responsible?

JANE: For what, Edward, dear?

EDWARD: Oh, you know, you know. I've climbed high. From Privy Chamber to the Council. On your shoulders.

JANE: No, on your own merits. And I've been proud of you. I am proud. You're a great man, Edward, greater than Cromwell, because you are scrupulous.

EDWARD (*Almost a groan*): Oh.

JANE: You are. Oh, perhaps I am a little sorry that we no longer agree about the Church, that you accept the destruction of the abbeys. And yes—I am afraid. But you are not to blame, my dear.

EDWARD: Do you fear childbirth?

JANE: No.

EDWARD: The King?

JANE: No.

EDWARD: What then? (*Silence.*) Jane, let me help you.

JANE: I think no one can. I have sought my confessor. I have done pennance. I have asked God's forgiveness—over and over and over again. I've prayed for it, begged for it. I kneel till my legs and knees are raw and my body fails me. I receive absolution a hundred times—and still—I have no—no waking or sleeping moment when I am at peace.

EDWARD: In Christ's name, what is this fear?

JANE (*Slowly, with difficulty*): Of her. The Queen.

EDWARD: The Bulleyn?

259

JANE: She was innocent.

EDWARD: Jane, two grand juries and twenty-seven peers found her guilty. She was guilty.

JANE: Was she? I have heard it was false witness—it was mortal sin. *Don't you understand?* I should be punished. And I'm rewarded. Is this my punishment—to receive none? I don't know, you see. Oh, Edward dear, I'm in such dark. There's no order any more. No grace. No order. Nothing.

(*Dissolve from close up Jane to:*)

31

Interior. The chapel. Hampton Court. Day.

(*Sound of heartbeat. The baptism.*)

BISHOP GARDINER (*Baptising child*): *Eduarde, ego te baptizo in nomine Patris* (*Water and sign of the cross.*) *et Filii* (*Water and cross.*) *et Spiritus Sancti.*

(*Water and cross. During last, distort image and sound and dissolve out to baptism, the Archbishop's blessing.*)

CRANMER: *Eduarde—vade in pace, et Dominus sit tecum.*

ALL: Amen.

GARTER KING-AT-ARMS: God, in his Almighty and Infinite Grace, grant good life and long to the Right High, Right Excellent, and Noble Prince Edward, Duke of Cornwall and Earl of Chester, most dear and entirely beloved son of our most dread and gracious Lord Henry VIII.

(A fanfare of trumpets. The procession starts out of the chapel, the child borne out in solemn state. Dissolve to:)

32

Interior. Staircase. Hampton Court. Day.

(The trumpets deafening. Torches, angels, shadows. Dissolve to:)

33

Interior. The Queen's chamber. Hampton Court. Day.

(Jane lying on the State pallet. She looks ill, feverish, eyes sunken, her head whirling, throbbing dangerously, her hands clasping the mantle. Henry is beside her, solicitous, but smiling and boisterous. The child is brought to her. She blesses him. The trumpets deafening, clashing through her head. Distort sound. Close on candle or torch flame. Distort image. Dissolve all to:)

34

Interior. The Queen's chamber. Hampton Court. Day.

(Candle flame, one of four, beside coffin in chapel. Jane's lying-in-state. Open to chapel hung with black cloth and garnished with rich images. Mourners in attendance, Tom Seymour among them. Ladies in mourning habits with white 'handkerchiefs' over head and shoulders. Close on Mary, chief mourner. Dissolve to:)

35

Interior. The Chamber of Presence. Hampton Court. Day.

(Cromwell with Edward Seymour, Bryan and Carew. Norfolk comes to them.)

NORFOLK *(To Cromwell)*: Thank God you've come, my Lord. We have urged his Grace to accept God's pleasure in taking the Queen and to comfort himself in the Prince but—

CROMWELL: Where is the King?

BRYAN: He rides out alone. Three days now. Says he can't bear to visit the chapel.

CROMWELL: You've fumbled it, all of you. What he needs is a new wife.

NORFOLK *(With a look at Edward)*: God's blood, Cromwell—

BRYAN: Quiet.

(For Henry has entered. He has been riding but he is in black. Cromwell leaves the others and goes to him.)

CROMWELL: Good day, your Grace.

HENRY: Ah, it's you, Crum. We're sad company here, I'm afraid. Even my horse is lame, I had to bring him in.

CROMWELL: Nothing too serious, sir?

HENRY: No. There's a body hung on the bridge by the river. See it's cut down. See them all down through the land. In case of plague. Nothing must touch my son. Have you seen him yet?

CROMWELL: Yes, sir.

HENRY: He'll live won't he? My son. He has to live. Or there's no reason any more. Everything must be carefully planned for his governance. I want his food tasted. They say the Dauphin was poisoned.

CROMWELL: We'll lay down stringent rules, your Grace. In the meantime I would urge your Grace to think of providing for a new wife.

HENRY (*After a terrible silence*): You mock me.

CROMWELL: Indeed not, sir.

HENRY: You mock me, Cromwell. Don't rub too sore on my wound. I shall never be married again.

CROMWELL: But we must consider that the child is weak, sir.

HENRY (*Agonized*): No. No.

CROMWELL: The whole Council urges you to entertain the good of the country, sir. And remember, there would be less danger to the Prince from other sources if he had younger brothers. (*This strikes home.*) At least frame your mind to be impartial, sir.

(*As Cromwell leads him from the room dissolve to:*)

36

Interior. The staircase. Hampton Court. Day.

(*As they descend.*)

CROMWELL: ... Therefore I would urge your Grace to consider the Duke of Cleve's daughter.

HENRY: I said, not now. And a Protestant? We must keep the balance, Crum. A French or Imperial alliance perhaps.

CROMWELL: In that case, sir, the French princess would be well qualified to console your Grace in his deep affliction.

(*They have stopped at the foot of the stairs.*)

HENRY: But not now. (*Thinks about her.*) The Princess Madeleine—

CROMWELL: Yes, your Grace.

HENRY: Or there's Mary de Guise.

CROMWELL: Already spoken for by your nephew, sir.

HENRY: Does that matter? Well, perhaps. And the Emperor's side—?

CROMWELL: Christine of Denmark, sir.

HENRY: Ah yes, who was Duchess of Milan.

CROMWELL: She has dimples.

HENRY: Has she? But I still prefer Mary de Guise. Or Madame de Longueville. I am big in person, I've need of a big wife. For the good of the country. But nothing immediate, you understand.

CROMWELL: Of course, sir.

(*Mary has come out of the Chapel door nearby. Henry sees her and turns to her.*)

HENRY: Are you ill, Mary? You look pale.

MARY: My teeth hurt me, sir.

264

HENRY: How long have you been in Chapel? Day and night, I suppose. Well, we must get the tooth-drawer for you. (*Puts arm round her.*) Or take a new nail and make the gum bleed. Do you remember what you used to say as a child? 'Jesus Christ, for Mary's sake—take away my toothache!'

(*Mary smiles up at him. If she didn't have the toothache, it might be stronger. Cut to Cromwell going to Norfolk and Edward at base of stairs.*)

CROMWELL (*To Norfolk*): Your Grace. (*To Edward.*) My Lord of Hertford. His tender zeal to his subjects has already overcome his Majesty's disposition.

HENRY: Cromwell. (*Cromwell hastens over to him.*) I forgot to inform you of the Queen's last wishes.

CROMWELL: Your Grace?

HENRY: She asked at the end that twelve hundred masses be said for her soul in the city. That is my Lord Cranmer's concern. Her other desire, which we must of course fulfil, will be your responsibility, my Lord, as Vicar-General. The founding of a Benedictine Abbey for her at Bisham. (*Cromwell for once is speechless. He can only raise an eyebrow.*) You see, my Lord—Louis may die, or the horse may die, or I may die (*And then, with difficulty.*)—or the horse may talk.

(*Sacred music from the chapel as the King leaves Cromwell who is smiling ruefully. As Henry passes the chapel door, see Jane's arms with the inter-changed initials H and J over the shield the inscription in English 'Bound to Obey and Serve'.*)

37

Interior. Chapel. Hampton Court. Day.

(Raise music as camera enters chapel and moves slowly toward the coffin beside which Henry is kneeling. Close slowly on to coffin and the cross on its royal covering. Fade out.)

Anne of Cleves

JEAN MORRIS

Anne of Cleves was first presented by BBC Television on 22 January 1970 with the following cast:

ANNE OF CLEVES	*Elvi Hale*
HENRY VIII	*Keith Michell*
THOMAS CRANMER	*Bernard Hepton*
THOMAS CROMWELL	*Wolfe Morris*
SIR THOMAS WRIOTHESLEY	*Patrick Godfrey*
DUKE OF NORFOLK	*Patrick Troughton*
BISHOP GARDINER	*Basil Dignam*
HANS HOLBEIN	*James Mellor*
AMALIE	*Carol Macready*
WILHELM OF CLEVES	*William Maxwell*
SIR CHRISTOPHER MONT	*David Butler*
CHANCELLOR OF CLEVES	*Norman Tyrrell*
LOTTE	*Mollie Sugden*
LADY FRANCES	*Stephanie Lacey*
LADY MARGARET	*Melanie Ackland*
ROBERT BARNES	*Robert James*
PHILIP OF HESSE	*Peter Reeves*
CATHERINE HOWARD	*Angela Pleasence*
HENRY'S GENTLEMAN	*Norman Atkyns*
SERVANT	*Michael Cullen*
PRINCESS ELIZABETH	*Jody Schaller*
PAGE	*Freddy Wilson*

Produced by Ronald Travers
Directed by John Glenister
Sets by Peter Seddon

Characters

ANNE OF CLEVES (*Anna*)
HENRY VIII
THOMAS CRANMER, *Archbishop of Canterbury*
THOMAS CROMWELL
SIR THOMAS WRIOTHESLEY
DUKE OF NORFOLK
BISHOP GARDINER
HANS HOLBEIN, *Court painter*
AMALIE, *Anne's sister*
WILHELM OF CLEVES, *her brother*
SIR CHRISTOPHER MONT
THE CHANCELLOR OF CLEVES
LOTTE, *Anne's servant*
LADY FRANCES ⎫ *her ladies-in-waiting*
LADY MARGARET ⎭
ROBERT BARNES
PHILIP OFHESSE
CATHERINE HOWARD
HENRY'S GENTLEMAN
SERVANT
PRINCESS ELIZABETH
PAGE

Sets

Interior:

Council chamber
Cleves great hall
Anteroom at Cleves
Gallery/King's anteroom
Gallery
Room at Calais
King's room
Anteroom, Rochester
Anne's room, Rochester
King's bedchamber
Queen's room
Central alcove, great hall
Queen's anteroom

Exterior:

Courtyard

1

Interior. Council chamber. Day. Summer 1539.

(The backs of courtiers, including Cromwell, Cranmer, Gardiner, Norfolk, Wriothesley, clustered around an unseen table.)

HENRY *(Unseen)*: And answer me this, Archbishop! *(Camera moves in to show Cranmer in front of the table, still masking Henry.)* If a Christian King were to find himself alone among the infidel Turk, what should he do?

(Hesitating, Cranmer moves to show Henry, confident, grinning, slightly malicious, but very set on his argument. Courtiers exchange uneasy looks.)

CRANMER *(Uneasy too, but more of his conscience than of his King)*: Majesty, after much thought and prayer—

HENRY *(Ruthlessly interrupting)*: He should convert them to our reformed Church.

(Cranmer bows submissively. Henry sits back and enjoys their discomfitures. It is two years since the death of Queen Jane, and he has not improved physically. He is vastly fatter, and his ulcerated leg now troubles him so continually that he has developed various clumsy habits of movement to tender it, but his self-confidence is still so superb that he is not aware of this weakness.)

CROMWELL: Happily, sir, the eventuality is remote.

HENRY *(Suspecting irony)*: Uh?

CROMWELL: Would your faithful Duke of Norfolk—

273

your most reverend Bishop of Winchester—(*He bows mockingly to them.*) ever allow you to go alone among the infidel?

HENRY (*Bursting into mighty laughter*): What, would you all follow me? A pretty pack you'd make!

NORFOLK (*Unsmiling*): To the death, sir.

HENRY (*Not listening*): Ah, I thought of it once: when I was younger and life less full: thought of going on a crusade, as all good Christian Kings should do. It troubles my conscience still.

CRANMER: Sir, there is more than enough to be done for the Church here in Europe.

HENRY: There is, there is. Ah, this burden of ruling; I can hardly find the leisure to amend the dogma of the Church. (*He surveys his cluttered table with satisfaction: something catches his eye.*) And that recalls to me, Cranmer! Your Bishops argue that Christ empowered the Apostles to elect their successors. Is this to say that today only the Church is empowered to elect Bishops?

CRANMER (*Warily*): It would appear logical, sir: the power of the Apostles having descended to the Church.

HENRY: But why did our Redeemer so empower His Apostles, eh?

CRANMER: Clearly because He considered them worthy.

HENRY: Nonsense. Because at that time there were no Christian Kings. Is this not the purest logic?

(*But although he waits for a reply, he is already writing the correction in the margin.*)

274

11. *Anne of Cleves (Elvi Hale) after her marriage to Henry*

12. *Anne of Cleves with Henry, their separation amicably agreed upon*

CRANMER: This is a matter, sir, on which prayer—(*He is aware that Henry's sharp eye has lifted to him. After a pause, with great sincerity.*)—has not enlightened me. It is for the King to guide his people.

(*Henry nods briefly, finishes his correction, in pushing it aside comes by chance on another paper, slashes out half of it and signs the rest, and sits pleasantly back.*)

HENRY: And now, are the horses ready? I need refreshment after this toil.

CROMWELL: One more matter, if your Majesty will permit. On your Majesty's proposed marriage.

HENRY (*Beginning to rise*): Not now, Crum.

CROMWELL (*Moving round the table to him with a letter*): There is new word from France.

(*Henry sits at once, and waves the others away. Camera follows Norfolk, Gardiner, and Wriothesley as they move back out of earshot, speaking low.*)

WRIOTHESLEY: You see, my Lord Bishop! Politics interest him, but not marriage. Two years since Queen Jane died, and he's still making pretence of being dainty about a wife.

GARDINER (*Frowning*): And so, Wriothesley?

WRIOTHESLEY: And so we should change our plans, I say. Forget the women. No Queen of England will upturn anyone's policies again. Ah, he's nearing fifty, and looking more; he's past forgetting everything but a pair of dark eyes. In fact, I have heard—(*He looks cautiously round.*)—well, safest not to talk here. But I'll wager any sum we shall have no more trouble about the women now.

GARDINER: Well, it's true that it's Cromwell who's pushing him now. Cromwell wants a German marriage. There's some sense in that.

NORFOLK (*With hatred*): A Protestant marriage.

GARDINER (*A little impatient*): If France is allying herself with the Empire, England must ally herself with Germany. As for the women—

(*He is plainly in a little doubt whether Wriothesley may not have hit on the truth.*)

NORFOLK: There is only one son.

(*Henry has read Cromwell's document and is slowly nodding over it. He is thoughtful but not at all cast down. Cromwell, though as always watchful not to assume that he knows too much of Henry's mind, is quietly pleased.*)

HENRY: This agreement seems directed at England.

CROMWELL: France is bound to form no new alliance with us without the consent of the Empire. We therefore assume that France rejects our proposals as to your Majesty's marriage. To be just, sir, you were perhaps proposing to marry too many ladies.

HENRY (*Grinning*): Anne of Lorraine, Marie de Guise, Louise de Guise, Renée de Guise—

CROMWELL: Marie de Vendôme, Marguerite de—

HENRY: And who was the little beauty? Ah no, she wasn't French. With the post of Queen of England vacant, don't they expect me to wait for the highest bidder? It would have been a neat stroke—an alliance between England and France, and the Empire's isolated; an alliance between England and the Empire and France is isolated. Well, since they have to clasp one another in brotherly fear of England, it will have to be a German alliance. Ha! Now that I like too.

CROMWELL (*Watching Henry carefully*): If you marry a German bride, which will, of course, involve an alliance with the various German Protestant Princes—

HENRY (*Relishing this*): That'll put the cat among the pigeons. So who is it? I've lost myself in all these Princesses.

CROMWELL: The Duke of Cleves has two sisters.

HENRY: Daughters.

CROMWELL: Since we opened negotiations, sir, the old Duke has died.

HENRY: Has it been so long? Ah, I remember. A fair girl: flaxen. Aye, that would be pleasing—for mark you, Cromwell: the girl must be bedworthy. I am a man as well as King.

CROMWELL: No one doubts it, sir. I fancy that it is not the flaxen lady we were chiefly concerned with. That I think will be the Princess Amalie, the younger sister. Our first approach mentioned the elder sister: the Princess Anna. She is said to be a renowned beauty.

HENRY (*Waving a casual hand*): Our usual procedure, I think.

CROMWELL (*Bowing*): Your Court painter, sir. (*Raising his voice.*) Is Master Holbein here?

PAGE: Holbein! Master Holbein! Call Master Holbein (etc).

(*Courtiers nod in recognition of a known procedure.*)

WRIOTHESLEY: And there it is again—he has to delay matters.

GARDINER: No, I think not. Wriothesley, I think you're wrong. I think the King's an innocent about marriage. (*Wriothesley explodes into laughter.*) Oh, you can laugh. But he looks to find in marriage what others find in marriage, three mistresses, and a brothel at hand. God, the poor fool. How many more years must he suffer this? (*He laughs.*) Good day, Master Holbein.

(*Holbein is pushing his way among the crowd. He is splendidly, even a little too splendidly, dressed, and bows to Gardiner as to an equal. He approaches the King's table as if confident of both his welcome and his worth.*)

HOLBEIN (*Bowing*): Your Majesty has another Princess for me?

HENRY: Was ever King more gracious to artist?

HOLBEIN: Every fresh young Princess in Europe have I had the privilege of seeing on your behalf. Your Majesty wouldn't be thinking of converting a daughter of the infidel? They say their women are marvellous fine.

HENRY: And no one approaches them but eunuchs.

HOLBEIN: My manhood or my loyalty? Majesty, (*Bowing.*) have I not served you faithfully?

HENRY: I'll spare you. No Turk: a couple of flaxen Flemish ladies.

HOLBEIN: Then is your Majesty the Turk?

CROMWELL (*Patient*): I think the first lady in question is brown rather than fair.

HENRY: I know these nordic girls—flaxen everywhere, eh? Ah, Holbein's eye is as good as mine. Which is the elder?

CROMWELL: The Lady Anna.

HENRY: Anne of Cleves. If she's comely, Holbein, take her likeness and bring it back to her ever-adoring betrothed. If she's not, turn your eye to her sister. God's love, man, I am no virgin fumbler; let the girl be straight and let her be sweet-humoured. The rest the King's rank and the King's person will take care of.

(*He holds out his hand. Holbein, bowing, kisses it, and Henry goes. Cromwell comes behind Holbein.*)

CROMWELL: Master Holbein: do your work well.

HOLBEIN: My work, of course. Yours—(*He shrugs.*)

2

Interior. Cleves great hall. Day. Summer.

(*A shot of unbound hair falling untidily down a half-naked back. It is not flaxen: It is an undistinguished brown. A thick plait of flaxen hair comes into shot. The brown-haired girl is sitting on her heels at the hearth while the flaxen girl threads a needle at her shoulder. The brown girl is playing with a puppy and making patterns with a twig in the ashes of the hearth. The flaxen girl looks over her shoulder as she starts to sew: she has written A.R.*)

FLAXEN GIRL: Anna Regina?

BROWN GIRL: Amalie Regina?

(*They both laugh delightedly at their fantasy.*)

FLAXEN GIRL (*Scolding*): Yes, but keep still, Anna.

(*She is the Princess Amalie.*)

(*She begins to sew Anna's gown, which is split under the armhole and has been unlaced in front. It is a plain woollen gown like Amalie's own, and neither sister wears jewellery or any rich clothing. Amalie wears a plain lawn cap, with her hair below in a plait: Anna's hair is so untidy she seems to have thrown off whatever she wore on it.*)

ANNA (*Dreamily, carrying on the fantasy*): And peaches and strawberries to eat every day, and a maid to mend your gowns for you. Two maids.

AMALIE (*Frowning over the difficulty of the sewing*): Two gowns. One to wear and one to mend. Ach! (*She tugs at awkward stitch.*) Why not two wives?

ANNA: One to wear and one to mend. We'll both go to England! (*She embraces the pup at the idea. This is too much for the pup.*) Ach, dirty!

(*She puts down the pup and half-rises to shake out her skirt. Her movement upsets Amalie, who falls back on her haunches with the snapped thread in her hand.*)

AMALIE: Now you've torn it all the way.

2A

Interior. Anteroom. Cleves Hall. Day.

(*Outside the hall, Duke Wilhelm, half angry and half uneasy, is remonstrating with Holbein and Christopher Mont.*)

WILHELM: But on such an errand the Princesses my sisters should have been warned.

MONT (*Bored, but doing his duty*): My dear Duke, ladies of the beauty—(*He inspects his finger-nails.*)—of the reputed beauty of the Princesses of Cleves are never unfit to receive admirers. Discerning admirers.

WILHELM: My sisters are not your idle Court ladies, with nothing to do but sit in their jewels and sing idle songs. They are good German daughters of the house, who leave their adornments—

HOLBEIN (*Irritable*): God's truth, man, I paint women, not jewels.

MONT: And if I have to explain to the King my master that because of the absence of Court dress the Princesses once again refuse to see his ambassador—

HOLBEIN: And his portrait painter.

(*Angry, Wilhelm throws open the door.*)

2B

Interior. Cleves Hall. Day.

(*Long shot of the two girls. Amalie is giggling on the floor and Anna has risen and is examining the wet stain down her gown.*)

WILHELM (*Grim*): Sisters, the embassy from the King of England.

(*Amalie scrambles up, horror-stricken, and automatically smooths her gown and feels that her cap and hair are tidy. Anna looks up and automatically also pulls her torn gown together.*)

WILHELM : I present to you, sisters, the envoys of his Majesty of England, on this proposed marriage between our countries. Sir Christopher Mont, Master Hans Holbein. My younger sister the Princess Amalie.

(*Amalie curtsies and Mont kisses her hand. Holbein, who keeps behind Mont for the better look at everything, contents himself with a bow and a good look. He nods to himself, as if he finds Amalie sufficiently pretty but not interesting.*)

And my elder sister, the Princess Anna. Anna!

(*Anna comes into shot beside Amalie and curtsies. During the next lines the camera stays on Holbein's face from between and behind Anna and Amalie, so that it is clear which of them he is looking at at any moment. As Anna curtsies he takes a short look at her. He studies Amalie and feels for the tablets and silver-point he carries at his belt.*)

MONT : Ladies, we are most happy to be privileged to see you. The negotiations between your noble brother, the Duke, and my royal master, the King, having reached a fortunate state, it is the earnest wish of my master to behold the likeness of the lady he aspires to marry. With your permission and good will—

ANNA : And which lady is that, sir?

(*Holbein's eyes switch to Anna. He leans forward in interest: slowly, during the next lines, he begins to stare in a mixture of fascination and pleasure.*)

MONT (*Treading with care*): Madam, it must not be thought that the King chooses his bride solely as a King. As a King he must take thought for his realm, but as a man he must take advice from where none other can give it, from his own heart. (*Pull back to show that Anna, under pretence of putting her arm*

*round her sister's waist, has taken Amalie's fingers
and is pinching them to mark the humour of what
Mont is saying.*) And as his Majesty, to his own deep
sorrow, is prevented by the cares of State from
coming to Cleves himself, he sends Master Holbein
here. If you will permit him, my ladies both—

(*Holbein unceremoniously pushes Mont aside and
goes quickly to Anna. Ignoring her surprise, he
studies her full-face, takes her chin to turn her to look
in profile and three-quarters, stands back to look her
completely up and down, seizes her by the shoulders
to stand her full-face to him, steadies her chin, and
takes his silver-point.*)

ANNA (*Clapping her hands to her insecure gown*): Not
now!

MONT: Master Holbein!

HOLBEIN (*Irritated by the interruption, but resigned to
the necessities of being a Court painter*): Madam,
forgive me. I am not an ambassador, I am not, alas, a
lover; I am merely an artist. (*He makes it clear that
this is irony, since he would far rather be an artist
than anything else.*) When I see beauty I have neither
words nor alas deeds; I have only my hands. His
Majesty of England commissions me to take the
likeness of his beautiful Princess. When may we begin
work?

ANNA: (*Surprised*): Beautiful?

WILHELM (*Thunderstruck*): You think my sister—my
sister Anna—might please the King?

HOLBEIN (*Arrogant*): Please? My portraits tell truth
about more than a face, sir, and what I paint now
will please men four hundred years in the future.
Please . . . one King? Generations will lament that
they did not live to be Anna von Clev's lover.

(*Close up of Anna, stunned: It is the first time she had taken the idea of being Henry's Queen with any seriousness. Amalie puts her arm round her and kisses her cheek with pleasure.*)

ANNA (*To Holbein*): You are very kind, sir. . . . Here in our simple life in Cleves—I had not seriously thought. . . . But it seems that I must. Perhaps you will be even kinder and instruct my ignorance. I know nothing of England.

WILHELM: You know everything a high-born German maiden needs to know.

MONT (*Taking him discreetly by the arm and drawing a step back*): English queens, sir, are not precisely high-born German maidens.

WILHELM: Then your King has something to learn. My sister has been most carefully taught. She knows nothing of music, and dancing, and dress, and such doings. They only encourage lovers and lead to expense.

MONT (*Discreetly*): Which reminds me that there is still to be discussed the Princess's dowry. If the ladies will forgive us—

(*But Holbein and the ladies are absorbed: Amalie is trying to coil Anna's hair behind, and Holbein has his tablets and silver point, taking notes from all angles, while Anna is worried about her torn bodice.*)

MONT: Now sir, the dowry—

WILHELM: The dowry: yes. But I was saying, Sir Christopher. Our father, now, was a man of great foresight. I make no secret of it, we are a noble family but it was my father who established us thus in the eye, as you might call it, of Europe.

MONT: More than the eye. The pivot. The Cockpit.

WILHELM: Cleves, he said, might one day dictate the fortunes of Europe. Yes; he was a man who liked to dictate.

MONT: It is a manly liking.

WILHELM: A woman, he said, could be as powerful as a man, so long as she were knowledgeable. So he educated her. She is a most exquisite needlewoman, but she sometimes takes too great an interest in men's affairs.

MONT: Men's affairs?

WILHELM: Politics.

(*Cut to Anna, Amalie, and Holbein. Anna has found a stool to sit on, though she is still silent. Amalie is behind her, having got her hair up, and is taking out her own pins to secure it.*)

AMALIE (*Her mouth full of hair pins*): And in particular you must tell us about the King. Oh, we are provincial here, but we come to hear about such things.

ANNA: They say that King Henry is the handsomest and most courtly King ever born.

HOLBEIN (*Looking up from his work*): The handsomest and most courtly King ever born.... Now how, madam, am I to tell you about the King?

3

Interior. Gallery. Day.

(*Close up of Henry bellowing in a rage.*)

HENRY: Norfolk! Norfolk!

(*Pull back to show that he is outside a door and shouting both ways along a corridor. Down the corridor, Norfolk is talking urgently to Catherine Howard. He waits for a last threatening word of command before hurrying to Henry.*)

HENRY: Ha! I do not call a third time.

NORFOLK: Sir, your pardon. I needed a word with my niece—newly come to Court, Lady Catherine Howard.

HENRY: I have no time for nieces. Nor for so many Howards. (*Watching Norfolk maliciously.*) I'm a betrothed man, Norfolk, or very nearly.

NORFOLK: The Protestant woman—princess?

HENRY (*Grinning*): The contract's not signed yet.

NORFOLK: (*Disdainfully refusing to be teased*): But your intention is firm.

HENRY: Unyielding. Mont writes from Cleves that Holbein's more than happy with the Princess Amalie. Or is it Anna? (*He thrusts a paper at Norfolk.*) You petition for employment.

NORFOLK: We Howards, sir, live to serve our King.

HENRY: And your family. I know my needs; and my tools. When I need your services, I'll take them.

NORFOLK: Yet you use men like Robert Barnes: use them continually.

HENRY: Who?

NORFOLK: A Lutheran—and a heretic, a rank heretic. A friend of Cromwell's.

HENRY (*Mildly*): Barnes. Nonsense; he's no heretic: he's a learned man and a good diplomat. I use him to the German courts. You'd be no use to me there, Norfolk. You'd be like a thunderstorm to a bowl of fresh milk. (*He gives Norfolk his petition.*) Ah, marriage is the only estate for a man. Jane, sweet Jane! And sons, Norfolk, more sons! This girl's young; we'll have a string of lusty princelings around the throne!

NORFOLK: Is the Prince's health no better, sir?

HENRY: Edward's health—nonsense. A childish cough; all children have them. But a king needs sons: sons. When I marry my adored—God's body, but I have to know the girl's name! Where's the man can tell me? Crum!

NORFOLK: My Lord Cromwell is likely with his Lutheran friends.

HENRY (*Smiling broadly*): I rule this kingdom, Norfolk; I say when one Protestant or one Catholic is too many.

NORFOLK: Sir.

(*Cromwell appears in the doorway, Norfolk bows in leave-taking to Henry and goes, ignoring Cromwell.*)

CROMWELL (*Mock repentant*): I offend his Grace of Norfolk.

287

HENRY: You exist. And you don't urge me to marry a Howard.

CROMWELL: Aye, he's just brought another to court, a Lady Catherine.

HENRY: And he hints that you favour heretics.

CROMWELL (*Patient*): On your Majesty's orders I negotiate with the Lutherans. But you, sir, know that I am a faithful son of the English Church.

HENRY: Oh, I know who is heretic and who is not. (*In amusement.*) And who do you imagine he accuses with you as a heretic? Robert Barnes!

CROMWELL: Barnes? (*For a moment he is startled and apprehensive: then realizes that Henry is really amused.*) The Duke's invention begins to fail him.

HENRY: No, it's his intelligence. Take warning from Norfolk, Cromwell! Never give way to malice; it turns the best of men into fools.

CROMWELL: Malice, sir?

HENRY (*Sparkling with malice*): To be such a fool as to think I could be persuaded to give up a tool as useful as Barnes. Or as yourself. (*Cromwell smiles composedly.*) And while it's in my mind—when are we to have the portrait? I'll sign nothing until I'm satisfied of her beauty. My little Amalie.

CROMWELL: Anne, sir.

HENRY: Uh?

CROMWELL: Your little Anne.

HENRY: Oh.

4

Interior. Cleves Hall. Day.

(*Dissolve from Henry's face to Anna's. Wearing the dress of the Louvre portrait, but without jewellery, she is looking anxiously down at Amalie, who is kneeling in front of her struggling with the belt of the dress.*)

AMALIE (*Sitting back on her heels in despair*): It's the clasp, it's broken right through.

ANNA (*Speaking over Amalie's shoulder*): We do not much use our Court dress here, Master Holbein. Paint the clasp tomorrow, when we shall have mended it. And the lace too. (*She lifts her hands to show that her lace cuffs are torn.*) But at least you find the dress proper for a portrait? Then as for jewellery—

(*She lifts to her lap an iron chest fastened by a chain and lock, and drops the chain. Amalie at once clasps one hand to her mouth to indicate dismay and the other hand on Anna's, shaking her head violently.*)

AMALIE (*Mouthing in silence*): Sold.

ANNA (*To Holbein*): You must paint me without.

(*Holbein is at his easel and already making notes. He is now on excellent terms with both princesses, and flirts constantly with them both, but is plainly fascinated by Anna, and perhaps half in love with her.*)

HOLBEIN: No. Impossible.

ANNA: Nonsense.

HOLBEIN: If I paint you without Court jewels, then I must paint you as I first saw you, without—(*He makes an illustrative gesture.*)—practically anything. (*Persuasive.*) It would be the fuller portrait.

AMALIE (*Shrieking with laughter*): And for a husband!

ANNA: Very well. Amalie, this—

AMALIE: Oh!

ANNA: And this—(*She seizes the chain from the chest and the discarded belt with its buckle, and puts them round her neck, the belt as a choker with the buckle in front as a pendant, and the chain in two loops hanging lower, as in the portrait. To Holbein:*) These are my richest jewels. Paint them!

HOLBEIN (*Promptly making notes*): A double chain of the purest gold; and a linked necklace of golden circles; a pendant crucifix of the finest rubies—

ANNA: Ah, if I'm to be given jewels let me have diamonds.

HOLBEIN (*Serious*): Madam, you should wear rubies with your colouring. (*He drops his hands in despair.*) Oh the devil take them! The King will give you all the jewels in England. I am painting you.

AMALIE: Then paint in a crown!

(*She kisses Anna and runs away laughing. With her departure they grow more serious. Holbein comes to pose Anna.*)

HOLBEIN: Facing me exactly, yes; you will look at me all the time, if you please. Hands—so—You must hold a rose, of course, an English rose: so—ah—

ANNA : So.

(*He shows her how he wants her to hold the rose, between thumb and forefinger, and she obediently imitates him, but as he leaves her nervously clasps her hands, as in the portrait.*)

HOLBEIN : Madam.

ANNA : Oh—your pardon. Like this. This—

(*She tries to regain the pose but cannot.*)

HOLBEIN (*After a pause*): I was wrong. Hold your hands as seems natural to you.

(*She at once clasps them as before. He returns to his work.*)

ANNA : You can talk as you work?

HOLBEIN : If you will stay still, yes.

ANNA : Then tell me about England.

HOLBEIN : England; yes. Well, your Highness must understand first that all the King's troubles are concerned with France—

ANNA (*Laughing heartily*): I don't need to know that! I am the seal on the alliance of England and Germany against France and the Empire. No, no, Holbein—tell me what I need to *learn*! The clothes. The manners. The games. The dances.

(*Holbein rises from the easel.*)

4A

Interior. Anteroom. Cleves Hall. Day.

(Wilhelm and his Chancellor are pacing as they talk, out of sight but not out of earshot of the sitting.)

WILHELM: I'm not easy: I confess it. He has even agreed to waive the dowry.

CHANCELLOR: We couldn't have paid it.

WILHELM: But my sister will be penniless. Ah, he needs the alliance—now. But God's truth, this league between France and the Empire will last no longer than the decorations they put up to celebrate it. The King must know this.

CHANCELLOR: Is he the man to wait cap in hand for friends?

WILHELM: There's a good deal in that. And then he's been unmarried for two years.

CHANCELLOR: Do kings need to marry to find bed-fellows? Though it is true that the King of England has shown a curious passion for marrying his paramours.

WILHELM: He imagines his presence in the bed sacrament enough. Whom the King decides to take God, Pope, and Church must acknowledge. But mark me, Chancellor!—

CHANCELLOR: I have, my Lord. The contract will be unbreakable. Our lady may go to a doubtful husband, no friends, and no money; but once the contract is signed she will be safe. I swear to that: married to the King of England to the end of his days. (*Laughter and singing from the hall attracts Wilhelm's attention. To himself:*) Or, of course, to the end of *her* days.

WILHELM: What's here?

(*He opens the door on a view of Anna and Holbein*).

4B

Interior. Cleves Hall. Day.

(*Long shot down the hall of Anna dancing with Holbein. He is singing; they are both laughing delightedly and unaware of being watched. Miming breathlessness, Holbein collapses to the floor under the windows, pulling Anna down with him.*)

WILHELM (*Striding down to them*): Master painter, you were engaged to paint.

HOLBEIN (*Refusing to rise for him*): My Lord Duke, the Princess needed my help on a matter of importance. Madam.

(*He rises for Anna, and offers her his hand with dignity.*)

ANNA (*Rising without self-consciousness*): The dances, Brother, the fashionable dances—the King is fond of the dance. How am I to learn in time? And oh Brother, the lacks in my education! No dancing, no music, no knowledge of fashions—what am I to do?

WILHELM: Sister, I have been applying myself to the matter of your marriage contract. When that is signed, no lack of music or dancing can harm you.

(*He stalks away, Anna watches him go, and her hands clasp themselves nervously. Holbein unclasps them and kisses them.*)

ANNA: I am afraid, Holbein. What am I going to?

5

Interior. Gallery/Great Hall. Day.

(Dissolve to gallery at Court. Courtiers etc. busily passing. Cromwell is standing waiting alone.)

WRIOTHESLEY *(In passing)*: The King is delighted with the portrait, I hear. Your usual good fortune, Master Crummle!

(Cromwell acknowledges with a slight bow. Norfolk and Gardiner approach.)

GARDINER: The marriage contract is to be signed, then. Our congratulations, Master Crummle, on your success.

CROMWELL: Thank you.

NORFOLK *(In barely-suppressed rage and hatred)*: The girl is a heretic.

CROMWELL: My Lord, she is nothing of the sort. She is a faithful daughter of the Church; like us, she does not acknowledge the authority of the Pope.

NORFOLK: It is part of your plot, Crummle; you take us all into league with heretics. You will regret it.

(He stalks off. Gardiner follows him more civilly, amused. Cranmer comes quietly to Cromwell's side.)

CRANMER: So the King approves the little German princess. I hope he finds the happiness with her he found with Queen Jane. And the Princess herself?

CROMWELL: Delighted with her fortune, I suppose.

CRANMER: You should think more kindly of your— tools.

CROMWELL: Your tool, too, Archbishop of Canterbury. The King is committed to the Protestants in Europe now.

CRANMER: Cromwell, you press very hard for this alliance. You don't hurry the King too fast?

CROMWELL: No one hurries the King. I am his servant. Nothing else remains to me.

CRANMER: Norfolk troubles me.

CROMWELL: Sighing always for the England of his fathers. He has some foolish plot with a pretty Howard girl as bait. Do they think the King will be caught again by a pretty face and a guarded maidenhead?

CRANMER: No, I suspect more's afoot than a pretty Howard girl. There's persistent talk about Robert Barnes being a heretic. Barnes is known to be a friend of yours.

CROMWELL: Barnes is safe enough. He's the King's man.

CRANMER: The King's man?

(*He ponders in distress.*)

6

Interior. Room at Calais. Day. Mid-December 1539.

(*The sound of high winds and rough seas.*

Anna is looking dismally through a snow-blurred window. On a table at her side are a lute, cards, embroidery.

She opens the window and leans out. Wind and sea up.

Lotte, Anna's personal maid, comes into the room, carrying a bowl with a linen cloth.)

LOTTE (*Horrified*): Madame, madame! Your complexion! (*She runs to the window and closes it decisively.*) Wind—snow—cold: the worst of things for the brown complexion.

(*She takes the bowl and tenderly moistens the cloth and approaches Anna with it.*)

ANNA (*Pulling away*): Lotte, have done! This face of mine has taken the German air for twenty years, and ten minutes of Channel snow will make no difference.

LOTTE: The King's complexion, as we all know, is most delicately fair. His bride's must not offend him. Be graciously pleased to sit down.

ANNA: I am not graciously pleased to do anything: here in this dull Calais, delayed by the dull weather, overlooking this dull, dull, *dull* English Channel. I have learnt a card-game; well, you put down the cards, you count the points, you win or you lose; so? It passes the time. It's better than this. (*Picking up the lute with an expression of hatred.*) Is that in tune? (*She plucks a note.*)

LOTTE (*Wincing*): No, madame.

ANNA: Why not? I am willing to learn, why will no one *tell* me, *what is in tune?*

(*She plumps discontentedly down in a chair, and Lotte at once seizes the opportunity to come behind her, lift her chin, and start sponging her face.*)

LOTTE: For whitening, for softening, this lotion of

mine has not its peer in Europe. Many queens have begged me for the recipe. If you had used it before, madame, against so many years of neglect, of riding in all weathers—

ANNA: The King likes women to ride in all weathers.

LOTTE: He does not. He likes women of a delicate complexion.

ANNA: Queen Catherine—

LOTTE: Madame, will you never learn! The Princess Catherine of Aragon!

ANNA: We are not in England yet. Queen Catherine he dearly loved, and she was a good rider.

LOTTE: She invariably wore a veil against the weather. And no doubt the reason why she was eventually divorced was that not even that preserved her complexion. Now—(*She finishes Anna's face, examines it tenderly, puts aside the lotion and linen.*)—let us come to your hands. You are using the cream night and morning? Empresses in person—

ANNA (*Tearing herself free*): Enough, enough of it all! I am what I am, and nothing will change that! If this gale would only drop, if we could be quickly on our way to England!

LOTTE (*Sentimental*): My little bride! Longing for her bridegroom! And how do you suppose the bridegroom is feeling?

(*Anna turns hopefully to her: her face brightens.*)

7

Interior. King's bedchamber. Day. Fire going. London. New year 1540.

(Distant music and revelry. Close up of Henry drinking and smacking his lips in satisfaction. He is in a good mood. Pull back to show that he is in a chair in his bedchamber, surrounded by his gentlemen, who are removing his boots after hunting.)

HENRY: A good hunt, yes. The King was always the finest rider in the realm. I can remember times when I—Man, take care! (*He winces as a boot comes off, and then is overtaken by greater pain and holds to the arms of the chair with closed eyes.*) Footstool. Quickly.

(With practised skill the gentlemen slide a padded stool under his leg to support it, and watch him anxiously. As he remains with his eyes shut, trembling with pain, First Gentleman goes out. Cromwell comes in, First Gentleman anxiously behind him. Henry breathes more easily. He opens his eyes to see Cromwell standing in front of the fire.)

CROMWELL: I hear it was a good hunt, sir.

HENRY (*A little dizzily*): Good—good—that music?

CROMWELL: The New Year revels.

HENRY: Revels eh?

CROMWELL: You've ridden far, sir. You should rest a little.

(He goes down on his knees and with a movement of complete devotion adjusts the stool to Henry's leg.)

HENRY: Better. (*With his eyes closed again he sits relaxed. Pause. Suddenly alert.*) New Year?

CROMWELL: The music, sir.

HENRY: Fool! Why should I remember New Year, that's what I ask.

CROMWELL: The Princess Anne of Cleves is in England.

HENRY: Oh yes.

CROMWELL: She will lie tonight at Rochester. Tomorrow—

HENRY: *Tomorrow!* You say tomorrow to a bridegroom awaiting his bride? (*He struggles to his feet and roars to his gentlemen.*) Clothes! Clothes fit for the bridegroom! More wine! Food!

(*The gentlemen bustle to obey.*)

CROMWELL: Sir? Rochester is thirty miles away. You've been riding all day. Sir, I beg you—

HENRY: Beg? You think your King a weakling?

CROMWELL: The Princess will be taken unawares, not dressed to receive you—

HENRY: —Ready for bed—what could be better? That's a picture we couldn't send Holbein to take. (*To the gentlemen.*) Riding dress in half an hour and horses in an hour. The gifts we chose for the Princess—quick, let me see them as I eat.

(*He sits to the table of food and wine the gentlemen have prepared. The gifts are brought to his side on a tray.*)

299

CROMWELL (*After a pause*): Will you permit us to ride with you?

HENRY (*Carelessly; as he begins to eat hugely*): Those of you who can keep up with me. And so long as you are secret! No announcement, no state! We will say—we will say that I am a messenger sent by the King. She receives me, when we are alone I reveal myself—not the King but the lover, who can wait no longer. (*Mumbling with a mouthful.*) Aye Cromwell, you shouldn't have let me forget: today I am an ardent lover.

8

Interior. Anteroom to room at Rochester. Night. Winter.

(*Rochester, the same evening.*

Outside Anna's bedchamber. The gifts are being arranged on a table, ready to be carried in and presented to her.

Also preparing, by a mixture of gentlemen and very confused lower servants of the house, wine for two.)

FIRST GENTLEMAN (*To Servant*): Now . . . you understand?

SERVANT (*Blankly*): No.

FIRST GENTLEMAN (*With elaborate patience*): It is *not* the King. You will *not* use court ritual. But you will *not* raise your eyes, you will *not* speak, and you will *not* turn your back on him.

SERVANT: But you said I wasn't to come out backwards.

(*With great patience the First Gentleman illustrates what he must do, daintily miming the carrying-in of the wine, the putting it down, and the withdrawing with a crab-like sidling step. The Servant watches mystified.*)

FIRST GENTLEMAN (*Sharply*): The Princess's maid. Careful!

(*Instantly the Gentleman and the servants either vanish or become elaborately casual: the gifts are whipped out of sight and the wine hidden behind someone's back. Lotte, unaware, approaches carrying her usual cloth and cup of lotion: she curtsies civilly to the gentlemen still visible as she taps lightly on the door and goes in.*)

9

Interior. Room at Rochester. Night.

(*Anna's bedchamber. Anna is in the last stage of her preparations for going to bed, with her hair down and wearing a loose gown. She is absorbedly rubbing cream into her hands and inspecting the results hopefully.*)

ANNA: What was that noise in the courtyard below?

LOTTE: A messenger from the King, to enquire after you. Let me see to your hair.

ANNA: I can't receive any messenger like this!

LOTTE (*Who is pulling Anna's hair and gown even looser*): Pooh, you're not in your shift. And he can carry back more news of you like this than your husband's heard yet. Or why should he be sent so late?

(*A knock.*)

ANNA: *Ja?*

(*Enter First Gentleman.*)

FIRST GENTLEMAN: Madame, his Majesty the King has been graciously pleased to send a messenger to enquire after your health. May I admit him?

ANNA (*Weary but courteous*): Willingly.

(*The Gentleman goes out. Anna keeps her eyes on the door. As it opens she rises and curtsies.*)

HENRY (*Voice over shot of Anna curtseying: Gently*): So this is to be the Queen of England.

(*Anna lifts her head and looks at Henry. Shot from her point of view. Henry is mud-splashed and sweat-stained, puffed with fatigue, wheezing with over-weight, and standing clumsily to ease his leg.*)

ANNA: His Majesty has sent you, sir; that was most kind. I see the journey has tired you.

HENRY (*Delighted to have deceived her*): Twice as far would have been nothing so long as it was to your side, madam. (*He feels a twinge of pain, and in advancing into the room has to support himself by the furniture. This does not in the least diminish his bridegroom's self-confidence.*) Does England please you as much as you will please England? The journey, these lodgings, your attendants . . . are they all you could wish? One finger lifted and all England is yours.

ANNA: Everything is most comfortable, thank you.

HENRY: And to hear your views on England, we will take a cup of wine with you.

(He claps. The Servant, eyes fixed on the wine he is carrying and lips moving to remember his instructions, brings in the wine, puts it down, makes two blind bows in the wrong directions, and stops to think about how to get out of the room correctly. Henry takes him by the collar and pitches him through the door.)

Your woman may leave us.

LOTTE *(Shocked)*: Leave her Highness alone, sir?

HENRY *(Amused)*: It's not manners in Cleves, mistress? Well, just here *(He taps himself on the chest.)*, manners are different.

(He starts to pour himself a drink. Lotte looks dubiously at Anna. Anna shrugs resignedly, indicating that no doubt English manners are unrefined.)

LOTTE *(With meaning)*: I shall be within call, madame. *(She withdraws.)*

(Henry has meanwhile poured one cup of wine and taken a hearty drink. Seeing that Anna is watching this with chilly outrage, he refills, lifts the cup to her, takes a shorter drink, and passes it to her. She civilly takes it, but makes no move to drink. Henry, filling the other cup, does not see this.)

HENRY: For to become Queen of England, madam, what happier destiny could any woman wish? When I was young, what was England? A little country absorbed in its own affairs: disregarded in the councils of the world. Who feared England then? When we signed the Treaty of Lille in the year fifteen fourteen—

ANNA: Thirteen.

HENRY: Madam?

ANNA: The Treaty of Lille was signed in the year fifteen thirteen.

HENRY: Uh?

ANNA: October.

HENRY: Uh?

ANNA: The seventeenth.

HENRY: Uh. It was a pretty thought to prepare yourself for marriage by familiarizing yourself with your husband's triumphs. (*Anna's eyebrows lift, but she succeeds in saying nothing.*) But there are better ways of pleasing a husband.

ANNA (*Chilly*): I am not dressed to receive visitors so late at night.

HENRY (*Closing on her*): That's a mighty pretty silk, but nothing so fine as what it covers.

ANNA (*Angry*): Sir, this is too much. If the King were here himself—

HENRY (*Opening his arms to her*): But he is, sweetheart!

ANNA (*At once eager, looking beyond him*): Oh, where?

HENRY: Behold him!

(*Close up of Anna speechless with revulsion.*)

10

Interior. Anteroom. Rochester. Night.

(Outside Anna's room.

As before, but an air of boredom everywhere.

Cromwell and Cranmer stand apart, speaking low.)

CROMWELL: That marriage contract! I tell you, it's becoming a new profession—tinker of marriage contracts for Queens of England. No one is going to break this one, believe me.

CRANMER (*Uneasy*): This is no way to think on the eve of a Christian marriage.

CROMWELL: On the *eve* it is: if only for the sake of the bride. As for the morrow—

(Henry's voice heard in Anna's room. They freeze. Inside the room, Anna laughs hysterically.)

CRANMER: The Princess—?

CROMWELL (*With a sigh of relief*): My procuring has been successful, then.

CRANMER (*Disturbed*): But why are you so uneasy?

(Cromwell laughs, and passing his hand over his forehead holds it out to show that he has been sweating.)

CROMWELL: No, there was no need, was there. He's set on the German alliance, and he's signed the contract, and—Did you catch a sight of her?

CRANMER: Yes. I thought she had a sweet face.

CROMWELL: It may be that she's what he needs. What we all need. Can I rest easy for a night or two, I wonder?

CRANMER (*Affectionately*): You haven't the trick of it. Do you ever rest?

CROMWELL (*Simply*): No. I'll work myself into my grave, if they let me live so long.

(*Anna's door opens and Henry comes out. Everyone springs to attention. Henry is dangerously expressionless. The gentleman takes up the gifts, ready to carry them in to Anna.*)

HENRY (*Waving him away*): Tomorrow. Let the servants take them in tomorrow.

CROMWELL (*Too astonished for discretion*): Sir!

HENRY: I am ashamed that men have so praised the Princess. I like her not.

CROMWELL: *Sir?*

HENRY (*Loudly and defiantly*): I like her not! I will see you in the morning.

(*He goes, with a very wavering and painful stride. Cromwell and Cranmer exchange amazed and dismayed glances.*)

CRANMER: But that sweet lady—

CROMWELL: And that sweet contract—

(*Cranmer turns towards Anna's door, his attention caught by a sound within. After a pause he goes quietly in. Anna is on the floor, shuddering and sobbing. Fade to black.*)

11

Interior. King's bedchamber. Day. Fire going. Winter. London.

(The wedding morning. Henry is in his chair, sheeted and in process of being barbered. A Gentleman is combing his beard, and Cromwell stands by him.)

HENRY (*Shouting*): By God, I should have trusted no one but myself! This matter touches me too nearly.

(The Gentleman stops combing and sprinkles perfume.)

CROMWELL: Sir, the portrait pleased you well enough. And it is admitted a most lively image. For that which did not enter into the portrait—

HENRY: Like the evil smells about her.

CROMWELL: Her form is most exquisite, her—

HENRY (*Goaded by the reminder*): Enough! (*He sweeps aside Cromwell's words, and with them the Gentleman with the perfume. Submissively, the Gentleman takes the brush from the tray and resumes brushing Henry's beard.*) I complain not of—of—I complain only of the marvellous good words I have heard of her. Her face—her form—her bearing so queenly, her voice so—(*He dashes the tray to the ground. The Gentleman holds a mirror for his inspection.*) I have not been well handled.

CROMWELL: Sir, the Princess is a stranger in this realm, and most likely confused at her great destiny. She will learn, she will learn; she will bear you sons; and can we doubt that the Majesty of England will be the best of teachers?

(*Henry takes the mirror and contemplates himself.*)

HENRY: And is this the happy bridegroom, who—
(*Forgetting Cromwell.*) Catherine—Anne—Jane—
three happy brides. . . . And it was not so long ago!

CROMWELL (*In horrified comprehension*): Sir!

(*In the mirror Henry sees Cromwell's face behind
him. At the understanding it shows he turns coldly
angry.*)

HENRY: So I must put my neck in this yoke you have
prepared for me? (*Cromwell drops on his knees and
seizes Henry's hand. Henry deliberately takes it away
before he can kiss it.*) My Lord, if it were not to
satisfy my realm, I would not do that I must this day
for none earthly thing. (*He rises and takes off his
sheet, revealing his wedding clothes.*) The bridegroom,
gentlemen, is ready.

(*He turns his back on the kneeling Cromwell.*)

12

Interior. Queen's bedchamber. Day. Winter.

(*At the same moment, Anna in her own room is also
dressed and very wretched. She sits on a chair, with
Cranmer, robed for the marriage service, at her side.*)

CRANMER: And in Christian matrimony, must the
wife not be submissive to her husband?

ANNA (*Cold and determined*): A signed contract is not
yet Christian marriage.

CRANMER: It is a promise you have to put your hand
to in the name of God.

ANNA (*Turning on him*): Archbishop: how is it with your wife?

CRANMER (*Shocked*): You *know* I am married?

ANNA: It was whispered about in Germany. I know you hide it in England.

CRANMER: Yes, we hide it. I had hoped that—there were times when the King seemed to favour a married clergy. Why do you ask this?

ANNA: Archbishop: remember your wedding night, and then imagine mine.

CRANMER: Madam, my dear wife lives in obscurity and danger; we can meet seldom; we bear this unhappiness because we think it our duty. (*Anna bursts into tears.*) Oh my Lady Anne—Anna: we work for peace and toward the Protestant Church. We think this worth much unhappiness. Can you not bear your share?

(*Anna stops crying and considers.*)

ANNA: Peace and the Protestant Church. I will fix my eyes on one thing alone. I have promised to marry this King. (*Rises.*) Archbishop, the bride is ready. Only do give me your hand.

12A

Interior. Gallery. Day. Winter.

(*The sound of wedding bells.*

The bridal procession forms.

Below the great window, Henry and Anna step into

309

silhouetted profile, facing one another, both cold and withdrawn.

Zoom between them, as the wedding bells fade, to the wintry trees outside the windows.)

13

Interior. Queen's bedchamber. Night. Winter. Fire going.

(The same evening.

The marriage chamber. Music and laughter from outside.

Anna is in bed, with her ladies-in-waiting and Lotte around her.

The curtains of the bed are looped up on both sides, and on the side opposite to the door are chairs, a table, wine for two, a lute, and cards.

Anna's shift has a neck on a drawstring, which is now arranged at its lowest.

A stir outside indicates that Henry is arriving.

The ladies arrange themselves in two lines to the door.

As attention is diverted from Anna, Lotte leans over her and they execute a brief alteration in her dress.

When Lotte withdraws, Anna's shift is high under her chin. She waits in a grim composure, but her hands are nervously clasped.

Henry, glum and silent, enters, in his night-shirt and furred robe.

The ladies curtsey.

He is followed by his gentlemen and courtiers, who are rather drunk and very noisy.)

GENTLEMAN: No music in the marriage chamber? What is love without music? Let the musicians come nearer!

(Word is passed back and the music grows louder and drowns any words, as Henry greets Anna and the ceremony of bedding the groom is carried out. Four men remove Henry's fur robe and 'lift' him to the bed with fingers to shoulders and elbows. Here Henry abruptly sits on the edge of the bed and waves them away.)

HENRY: Enough! *(Silence falls.)* Wedding done. Bedding done. Ladies and gentlemen, you have our leave.

(The music resumes for a ceremonial retiring of the Court, backwards in order of rank, gentlemen bowing and ladies curtseying. Cromwell is last but for Cranmer; as he passes Henry gives him a hard stare. Last of all, Cranmer, at the door, raises his hand in blessing.)

CRANMER *(Making the sign of the Cross)*: Benedicat vos omnipotens Deus. Pater et Filius et Spiritus Sanctus.

HENRY: Amen.

(Cranmer withdraws and the doors are closed. At the door, Henry broods for a moment, then turns to the bed. It is empty. Anna is now seated at the table, placidly pouring wine.)

ANNA: A tiring ceremony, sir.

HENRY: It is our duty, madam. The most tiring part is yet to come.

311

ANNA: You will take some refreshment?

HENRY: No. Come here, wife.

ANNA: Then you will allow me. (*As he begins to frown.*) I am not used to these long hours. I must revive myself a little. (*She drinks, then takes up the cards, as if idly.*) I have heard you are very skilful at card games.

HENRY: I have all the skills of a man, wife.

ANNA: I learnt a card game before I came to England. For your pleasure, sir.

HENRY: My pleasure, wife—

ANNA (*Hurrying on*): But I am not very skilful. If you would graciously please to instruct me—

HENRY: I will indeed. Here. (*He is seated solidly on the bed still.*)

ANNA: Kind. (*She seizes her cup and takes another sip. Desperately taking up the lute.*) But in music I fear not even the greatest of masters can teach me much. (*She touches the strings, which are appallingly out of tune.*)

HENRY (*In genuine pain*): Madam!

ANNA (*Innocently*): That is not in tune? It sounds well enough to me.

(*She plays some notes as loudly as she can. This so excruciates Henry that it brings him off the bed to snatch the lute from her and painstakingly tune it.*)

ANNA: And surely you will play to me? The King is reputed such a wonderful master!

(*Henry, flattered, makes to play: then sees that he is being fooled. He puts down the lute.*)

HENRY: No, wife, I will not play to you. We are not here for music. (*Anna stiffens herself. Even Henry cannot miss that she is frightened, though making a brave shot at not showing it. He softens a little as he looks at her.*) Come—Anne. We are married now. When we met at Rochester we—we didn't agree. Let it be forgotten.

ANNA (*Coldly*): Sir, our meeting at Rochester is the subject of gossip throughout the Court.

HENRY (*Seizing her in fury*): Gossip! What do they say?

ANNA: That *I* do not please *you.*

(*In relief Henry lets her go.*)

HENRY (*Slightly ashamed of himself*): I ask your pardon, Anne. I thought you had meant—

ANNA (*Very distinctly*): No, no. I meant *I* do not please *you,* my Lord. How can you bed with a woman who does not please you? Can even the Church command that?

HENRY (*Interested*): That's true. Such an impediment might hinder—(*His eye strays to Anna.*)—I say—no, no, let that be forgotten.

(*He tries to embrace her, but at her frantic backward step gets no nearer than a hand on each shoulder.*)

ANNA (*Struggling to regain her composure*): Can any honest woman thrust herself upon a man who is repelled by her ugliness?

HENRY: Yes, if it is her duty. You are my wife.

ANNA: Repelled by her ugliness. Particularly in view of the bad news from Germany?

HENRY: Eh? What bad news?

ANNA: The League of the Protestant Princes is about to break up. Hesse is going over to the Empire.

HENRY: Hesse? Impossible! It's one of the leading members of the League.

ANNA: You don't believe me? Very well. But are you satisfied with the reports from Germany? Is there no wavering in the League?

HENRY (*Uneasy*): League! As ramshackly a league as—(*Turning on her.*) Then what is amiss in Hesse? Do you know that?

ANNA: No. Would they advertise it? But Hesse is of the Empire, however Protestant its ruler may be. Now if the German League breaks up—

HENRY (*Dismayed*): And England tied to it—

ANNA (*Smiling in growing confidence*): Not yet. Ours is a political marriage, sir.

HENRY: It is celebrated.

ANNA: But not consummated.

HENRY (*Slyly smiling*): Not consummated? Ah, that would fox them! To keep them guessing about my intentions—France and the Empire can't agree for much longer. Am I married to the German alliance or am I not? (*He looks again at Anna, and suffers a last pang of regret.*) But we are married, Anne.

ANNA (*Decided*): No.

314

(*Mix to later the same night. Lights out, only moon-light in the room. Henry is sprawled across the bed. In a chair by the window, wrapped in Henry's fur robe and shivering with cold, Anna is patiently wait-ing for the night to pass. She stares at the moon in calculation.*)

HENRY (*Murmuring in his sleep*): Jane. Sweet sweet Jane.

(*Fade to black.*)

14

Interior. Queen's anteroom. Day (Spring).

(*Anna is seated in an armchair in the afternoon sunlight by the window. She is richly dressed and her manner is now one of unstrained dignity and com-posure; her once-nervous hands lie relaxed in her lap. She is watching, with deep affection, a small bundle on the floor at her feet.*

Track down to the bundle, revealing it to be the Princess Elizabeth, aged 7. She is working on an embroidery frame.

It seems that she is not a very good needlewoman. She nearly turns to Anna for help, but finally is too proud. With a sigh she turns up the frame and unthreads the needle.

Four o'clock strikes.)

ANNA (*Putting her hand on the frame*): My pretty, you must run away now; besides, you shouldn't sew in this evening light. Let me look. (*She takes the frame in her lap and Elizabeth stands dubiously beside her.*) Yes, my Lady Elizabeth, that will be a

very fine shirt for your brother the Prince, and your
father the King will praise you for it. Just one tiny
knot here; shall I—not letting anyone see—put right
just that tiny knot? Hush, then!

(*She puts a large sweetmeat into the child's mouth.
Elizabeth gives her a grave curtsey and then a smacking child's kiss, and runs skipping to the door. At the
door she remembers herself: stands straight, smooths
her skirt, and goes out with great sedateness. Anna
wipes her sticky cheek and with a smile shakes her
head over the frame. With loving care she takes a
bodkin and starts unpicking the stitching. The sunlight outside attracts her now: with the frame in her
hand she goes out into the courtyard.*)

14A

Exterior. Courtyard. Day.

(*Anna sits on the stone bench and lifts her face to the
late sunlight.*

Distant, music and laughter.

*She listens, grows wistful, and for a moment sits sad
and desolate.*)

15

Interior. Gallery Great Hall. Day.

(*Gardiner and Wriothesley, in a similarly sunny window, are irritably squabbling, but with every effort to
conceal it from the court around them. Norfolk,
gloomily aloof, listens but takes no part.*)

WRIOTHESLEY: You must be mad! You work against the German alliance, which was made by Cromwell; you work against the Queen, because the marriage was made by Cromwell; God help us, you even work against that harmless man Robert Barnes, because he is a friend of Cromwell's. Yet when was Cromwell ever stronger? He has the King's favour in everything he does!

GARDINER: You have it wrong. We work against Cromwell through Barnes.

WRIOTHESLEY: But he's done nothing!

GARDINER (*Shrugging*): What does innocence matter? Barnes has a foolish tongue. I can see to Barnes.

WRIOTHESLEY: And then?

GARDINER: He'll burn.

WRIOTHESLEY: Burn him twice over for all I care. How will that bring down Cromwell? And the Queen? For mark this—to bring down Cromwell you must first demolish this German marriage.

NORFOLK: It is no marriage.

WRIOTHESLEY: It may be none.

NORFOLK: It is no marriage.

WRIOTHESLEY: Well you have your spies in her household, I suppose. That flaxen-haired niece of yours? But the contract is signed, the Queen is living at Court *as* Queen.

GARDINER: No. The King seldom goes near her, the Court ignores her. She is neither married, divorced, nor beheaded.

WRIOTHESLEY: Christ, can we go through that again?

GARDINER : If we have to.

NORFOLK : We have to.

GARDINER : The alliance between France and the Empire is weakening. At any time now the King must make up his mind, is he with the German Protestants or is he not: is he married to this German girl or is he not. And so—and *so*, Wriothesley—this is our time to strike. Bring down the German girl, and we bring down the German alliance, and Thomas Crummle at the same time. So, we attack Barnes as soon as may be.

NORFOLK (*Abrupt*): We should not be seen plotting.

WRIOTHESLEY : It seems the plots are yours. Very well, I'll leave you. (*He goes, annoyed.*)

GARDINER (*Amused*): The Howards always had a brief way with them. Wriothesley's right, you know. The King looks on Cromwell with all his favour.

NORFOLK : He looked with all his favour on Wolsey too.

GARDINER : Times are very different now. The Pope— the so-called Queen—

NORFOLK : Times, Popes, Queens—they have nothing to do with it. The King will have no strength in his kingdom greater than his own. Cromwell is the most faithful of servants; but the lion of the forest strikes down every rival.

GARDINER : That is very true.

NORFOLK : So that our plots need do nothing but keep the victim well within reach of the lion's paw.

GARDINER : Norfolk: do you ever give thought to

what follows when we are successful? When Norfolk is the King's greatest servant?

NORFOLK: Do you remember Flodden, Winchester? It was the Howards who won that great battle. Ah, times were merry in England before this New Learning came in. I see little hope of merriment in the future. Perhaps the Howards will go where the other great families have gone, into the urns and sepulchres of mortality. . . . No, one chance of merriment I do see! To pull down that peasant's son Crummle with my own hands!

16

Exterior. Courtyard. Day.

(*Anna's hands on Elizabeth's embroidery. Pull back to show that she has been crying a little. She shakes her head, wipes off the tears, and with determined cheerfulness rises, goes indoors, and sits down to her task.*)

16A

Interior. Queen's anteroom. Day.

(*She works at it with genuine concern. Laughter is heard outside. Lady Frances and Lady Margaret, two of Anna's ladies-in-waiting, burst in as if racing. Lotte follows them.*)

LOTTE (*Remonstrating*): Ladies! Ladies! What is all this noise?

(*The ladies check as they realize that Anna is there.*)

FRANCES: We didn't know you were here, madam. It was so quiet; and coming from the Court—

ANNA: Yes; the Queen's apartments are not gay, like the King's court. Well, and so the new caps have arrived fom the milliner.

MARGARET: Yes, and the new silks from abroad too—such colours!

FRANCES: Would it please you to see them?

ANNA: From abroad? (*She shoots a swift look at Lotte.*) Yes, have them fetched, Lotte.

MARGARET: Can I help?

ANNA: No, no, they are too heavy for you. Show me the caps.

(*Lotte goes out. Margaret and Frances fetch the caps and kneel in front of Anna as they examine them.*)

FRANCES: This is the one with the seed pearls. Too plain, *I* think.

MARGARET: But very rich. Though if there had been knots here and here, in gold perhaps—

ANNA (*Decisive*): No knots; that one is altogether to my favour. The others—(*Lotte returns, herself carrying a roll of velvet and followed by attendants with bolts of silk. She nods swiftly to Anna.*) Oh, beautiful, beautiful. Yes, we must think carefully about these.

(*She examines the silks with deep pleasure and attention: the girls follow her with squeals of pleasure.*)

MARGARET: Oh this! Now thickly worked in gold—

FRANCES: Criss-cross—a pearl in each space—

MARGARET: Madam, trimmed much more thickly than ever you wear!

ANNA (*Firmly*): Such fashionable trimmings don't suit me. They are for little fair girls like you. So are these.

(*She gives them each a cap.*)

FRANCES (*Dazzled*): For us?

MARGARET: Madam, you are always so kind.

ANNA (*With the third cap ready*): But where is the fairest of the little girls? The flaxen one? This one was for her.

FRANCES: Catherine Howard? She will be here this evening. Shall we take it?

ANNA: No, no, I'll give it her myself, and I shan't need you for an hour now; run away and try on your new caps. (*They curtsey and run happily out. To Lotte*:) Safe for an hour.

LOTTE: It's the flaxen one is the Howard spy.

ANNA (*Careless*): Ah, they're all spies for someone. Now Lotte—the roll of green velvet.

(*From the centre of the roll of velvet Lotte extracts a letter. Anna breaks the seal and reads.*)

LOTTE: The truth from Hesse, I hope? If we know that—

(*Anna drops the letter in exasperation.*)

ANNA: No news at all. My brother is sending a messenger.

LOTTE (*In dismay*): A messenger, to you? Haven't you told him the danger?

ANNA: I have written in words of blood until my

fingers ached! Your sister is in danger, I have written, send me news, all the news you have, but do nothing, *nothing* until I tell you.

LOTTE: No man could ever take *that* advice. This messenger, how is he to come?

ANNA: He tells not even that. He recommends me to keep his stay secret. And I have told him my ladies report every move I make. Ah, God! (*She puts her hands round her neck.*) Lotte, some plan to hide this messenger.

LOTTE: Plan? When six spies watch if you speak to a gardener?

ANNA: Have I even found a gardener who'll speak to me? Oh Lotte, and I thought I was coming to a gay country! Oh for some merry company!

LOTTE (*Warning*): Madam, the letter! There is someone at the window.

(*She moves to cover Anna, who swiftly hides the letter, and then goes to the courtyard door and opens it. Outside stands Robert Barnes, looking uncertainly about him. He is dressed in the dark gown of the scholar.*)

Sir, you are intruding. These are the Queen's private apartments.

(*Barnes bows to her. In spite of his dress, he has the manner of one accustomed to courts.*)

BARNES: Mistress, I am at fault. I was waiting in the pleasant evening air, and strayed in here ignorantly. I hope I have not disturbed her Majesty. (*Lotte curtsies civilly, reassured, and is about to come in.*) But would it be possible to make my apologies in person? (*Lotte stops.*) Her brother the Duke has honoured me with his friendship and—

(*Anna approaches.*)

ANNA: My brother? Lotte, the door.

(*Lotte nods and goes quickly in to guard the main doors. Anna beckons Barnes to step inside.*)

BARNES: Majesty, it was never my fortune to be in Cleves at a moment when I might be presented to you, but to see a daughter of that Protestant Church we have fought for for so long—

ANNA: Sir, my movements are watched. Give me your message, please, as quickly as possible.

BARNES: Message?

ANNA: From—my brother?

BARNES: It is several months since I saw your brother. Since I was last in Cleves on embassy. My name is Barnes, Robert Barnes.

ANNA (*Masking her mistake*): You—you disappoint me, Master Barnes. I have been long gone from my home. I hoped you had seen my brother later than myself. I think I have read some of your works.

BARNES: We are of the same Protestant Church. But I am sorry I disappoint you. I will be truthful. I was walking outside awaiting Master Cromwell, and when I thought I could reach your windows unobserved I made so bold as to try. I had no message; I have only a message of loyalty to our Protestant Queen.

ANNA (*Drily*): Is it so impossible to obtain audience of me?

BARNES: Madam, no one knows. So it is safer not to try. You must not blame men for regarding their own safety.

323

ANNA: I do not. I sympathize. But the King has employed you, I know, Master Barnes, on many embassies to Europe. What late news have you?

BARNES: Little new. The German alliance is uneasy, and I have forebodings. These Protestant princes, they are weak alone, they must unite to hold up against the Empire. More: they must have England behind them. It would be to the advantage of the King, it would clinch his great reforms of the Church, but he hesitates, he hesitates. I greatly fear that the hope of some worldly success may tempt him—

ANNA: Master Barnes. I have heard much good of you, but one thing evil. You talk unwisely.

BARNES (*Astounded*): Madam? But I preach only the dogma propounded by the King himself. For his great wisdom in reforming our church, his Majesty has my most profound devotion. I think I have proved that; I have worked faithfully for him these many years.

Anna: You put your trust in princes. I honour you as an upholder of the Protestant Church.

BARNES: Its life is precarious, madam; we must all give of our best. Night by night I think of it; day by day I work for it.

ANNA: *I* sit at home and think on my Maker.

BARNES (*In genuine humility*): You rebuke us all. Man's chief end in life is to glorify God. Yet, while we sit and think of Him, the Pope has slipped in with some curst alliance that separates city from city, or treacherously subtracts taxes from the faithful—

ANNA: Some matter of Mammon rather than of God. Is this battle of churches all that there is in life, Master Barnes?

324

BARNES (*Astonished*): What else is there?

ANNA: Why—saving a child from unhappiness. Lotte—my work; it must be done before tomorrow.

(*She intends a civil dismissal: but Barnes stands in doubt.*)

BARNES: A child: one single child. . . . It would be against scripture to deny that this is acceptable to Christ. But to us who have spent our lives working for the true Church, what is a child's misery?

(*Anna turns, stops as his meaning dawns on her.*)

ANNA: Master Barnes, you seem to me a good man, but you have said one of the most wicked things possible. Pray say something to restore my liking for you.

BARNES (*Miserable*): Madam, what can I do? My life has been given to the true Church.

ANNA: Then you are the stuff of martyrs. Let you be happy while you burn.

CROMWELL (*Out of shot*): Burn? Robert—

(*Anna and Barnes turn to the courtyard door. Cromwell is standing there horrified.*)

ANNA (*Sharply*): And it seems that the Queen's apartments are becoming a thoroughfare.

CROMWELL: Madam, I—I came to guard your privacy rather than break it; I saw that Robert here had come this way and would have taken him off. You were talking of burning?

ANNA: I spoke in irritation. We will leave you to your tryst with Master Barnes; whom I am happy to have met.

325

(*She bows to both, indicating that they may go.*)

CROMWELL: I had also hoped to obtain an audience.

ANNA: Of the *Queen*?

CROMWELL: We have interests in common.

ANNA: We visit the same merchants, but bargain for different goods.

CROMWELL: And lower our voices in the open air.

ANNA: If my Lord Cromwell risks coming to the Queen, then the Queen must risk my Lord Cromwell. Lotte, the wine.

(*She seats herself, with Elizabeth's embroidery in her hands. Lotte brings wine. At Anna's nod of permission Barnes sits: Cromwell remains uneasily standing.*)

CROMWELL: Madam—

ANNA (*Sewing placidly*): You have travelled much in Europe, Master Barnes.

BARNES: For the last ten years, madam. I was first in Wittenberg to see Master Martin Luther in—let me see—the year thirty-one. Then later to secure—

CROMWELL: Robert, Robert!

ANNA (*Coolly*): To secure for the King approval of his divorce from Queen Catherine: I beg pardon, from the Princess of Aragon. The King's inclination to the Protestants is far from new.

BARNES: But Luther would not approve. His argument was an interesting one; there were those who maintained that the marriage could not be dissolved because it had been consummated, even though—

CROMWELL (*Losing his temper*): Robert, will you never learn to be discreet!

ANNA (*Composedly*): Be quiet, Master Cromwell. The subject of kings' divorces is of interest to me. Am I wrong in thinking it pertinent to your errand here?

CROMWELL: Madam, I wish half of my clerks had half of your good sense. I take it that there is nothing in the situation that I need explain to you?

ANNA (*Sewing tranquilly*): You have had a grand design: an alliance of all the Protestant powers of Europe against all the Catholic powers. And I am a small part of this design.

CROMWELL: You are not a small part. I need your help.

ANNA (*Mocking*): The help of Anne of England, whom not even the King ever visits?

CROMWELL: Madam, I know why. I shaped your fate, Majesty, but you shape mine. If I fall, you fall; if you fall, I fall; and with us both falls the English Church.

BARNES (*Shocked*): You? Never say it! Queens are one thing, but *you*—

CROMWELL: Robert, your tongue!

BARNES: Tongue! Perhaps I spoke in haste, madam, but—

ANNA (*Waving away the apology*): Cromwell, they say you have never been higher in your King's favour.

CROMWELL: So I smell my danger. Do neither of you yet know this King? Do you hear none of the things that are said of him in the land? This land that thirty years ago adored him? Ah, I read the reports as they come to me. When the King has a fall they wish it

had broken his neck for him. If he knew his subjects'
true feelings, they say, he would quake with fear
when he rode amongst them. Jesu, they even say that
Thomas Cromwell had been an honest man if he had
had an honest master, and what worse condemnation
can there be than that? And they are right. You are
married to a monster, madam. God and his holy
church defend us, a monster who knows nothing, sees
nothing, cares for nothing but his own will.

ANNA: And you remain his servant.

CROMWELL: What other kennel would hold me? And
now my ruin is in your hands. I have been speaking
treason.

ANNA: I take it that you have honoured me with your
confidence. You've also mightily puzzled me. Why
have you come to me?

CROMWELL: Madam, I do not enquire into the secrets
of the marriage bed; but I know my master. Will you
hear my conclusion on the state we are all in, and the
one solution that I see? (*Anna nods non-committally.
He has to wipe the sweat from his face before he can
go on.*) Madam, you are the only solution.

ANNA (*Coldly*): The King does not visit me.

CROMWELL: No, but he needs you. A wife who
offered him quiet at his day's end, peace at his life's
end—I think she could be my King's salvation. And
in his peace would be England's hope of peace.

ANNA (*After a long pause*): You speak persuasively;
almost as persuasively as his Grace of Canterbury on
my wedding morning. You set me three problems;
whether I agree with your view; whether I have
the—the will to act as you think I should; and
whether I have also the ability. You must give me
time.

CROMWELL: Time! The spring draws on, troubles mount up in Europe; the German League squabbles, France disagrees with the Empire, what is going on in Hesse God alone knows. And you talk of time!

ANNA (*Turning on him*): If you forgot your papers sometimes you would discover that more things go on in the world than politics. Yes, you and I, Master Barnes, have had words on this.

CROMWELL (*Puzzled*): Words?

ANNA: Young children shamed, honorable ladies brought to death or despair—God bless us, Cromwell—God bless all the kings and rulers of the earth—have you never counted how sweetly life goes on with never a thought of your existence? Did the milk ever curdle in the mouth of the Protestant babe? Did the wheat ever grow higher because it was sown by a good Protestant?

BARNES (*Severe*): God, madam, is merciful to the sinner, in the hope of his amendment.

ANNA: And man, sir, takes on too much in speaking for his Maker.

BARNES: But the Protestant Church is founded upon the very word of God!

ANNA: And I would rather comfort a shamed child than save a dozen churches!

(*In the angry pause that follows this, a sound from the door makes all three turn to look. The door bursts open and Frances almost falls into the room, followed by Lotte, who pulls her roughly to her feet and boxes her ears. Anna looks at Cromwell who discreetly takes Barnes's arm and retires with him to the screen by the window.*)

FRANCES (*Shrieking*): Peasant, clod, loutish serving-woman!

329

LOTTE: Bitch, doll, simpering spying little trull! (*Taking a firm hold of Frances. To Anna:*) Madam, your pardon. This—this lady would have interrupted you on a matter of no moment.

FRANCES: Witch, kitchen woman, German dolt— (*She kicks Lotte's ankles so violently that Lotte lets her go.*) Madam, it is not the place of your serving-woman to say whom you will see or not see.

ANNA (*Mildly*): If Lotte chances to know that I am occupied, Lady Frances, your good sense will lead you to listen to her.

LOTTE: Your Majesty—

FRANCES (*Looking over her shoulder and raising her voice formally*): Majesty, an envoy from your august brother of Cleves. His Excellency the Chancellor of the Duchy of Cleves-Jülich with Gelders.

(*Philip of Hesse comes gaily in: Lotte and Frances withdraw behind him. He is wearing the long gown proper to his assumed character (that worn by the Chancellor in scene 4A), but with much jewellery and a gallant and martial air.*)

PHILIP (*With extravagant bows*): Madame, I bring you so flowery a garland of greetings that it will add lustre even to that very moon of beauty that was born the adorable Anna von Clev. Ah, sad, sad Cleves to have lost her, happy England to have her for ever beaming upon them!

ANNA: Cleves, sir, seems to have gained a new Chancellor since I left.

(*Philip kneels at her feet and kisses the hem of her skirt.*)

PHILIP: Here, madam, is the humble devotion of every soul in the land you once graced. Here—(*He rises and kisses her hands.*)—the homage of the life-long servant of your beauty now at your feet. And here—(*He rises and kisses her left cheek.*)—the fraternal embraces of your ever-loving brother. (*He kisses her right cheek as she frees herself.*) And there are yet two sisters, a brother-in-law and several dogs.

ANNA (*Delighted*): Dogs?

PHILIP: At least do not disappoint the dogs!

(*He drops again to his knees laughing, Anna lets him kiss her hands.*)

HENRY (*Voice over*): So! (*Thundering.*) Guards! (*He comes into shot as he strides towards the door. His guards crowd into the room.*) So, madam! This is how you pass your time in your husband's absence!

PHILIP: I see a lucky man, Madam, your noble and fortunate husband. Majesty of England—delighted!

(*He bows to Henry as to an equal.*)

ANNA (*To Henry*): My Lord, I present to you an envoy from my brother: the Chancellor of our Duchy.

HENRY: Whom you, madam, receive alone. By God, madam, is this not treason in a Queen?

ANNA (*Composed: her fear shown only by her clasped hands*): Am I alone where my husband can enter unannounced?

CROMWELL (*Appearing*): And her Majesty is not alone, sir. I had withdrawn to the window while she heard her family's greetings.

331

(*After an angry stare, Henry ungraciously waves the guards away. They leave, the doors closing behind them.*)

HENRY: And what kind of conference is this, eh, behind my back? Plots, eh? What business have you, madam, to talk to my minister?

ANNA: My talk was with Master Barnes, sir. I have read his works with interest.

(*Barnes advances and bows to the King.*)

HENRY (*A little mollified*): Ah, Robert Barnes: good day to you. Well, if you must read divines, madam, you can do no better than Robert Barnes. He is thoroughly sound; he knows my mind.

(*Barnes bows again.*)

ANNA: And forgive me, I have not yet presented these gentlemen. My Lord Cromwell, Master Barnes, his Excellency the Chancellor of Cleves.

(*Cromwell bows to Philip. Philip bows jointly to Cromwell and Barnes, less deeply as he has forgotten he is not supposed to out-rank Cromwell. Barnes looks around in surprise.*)

BARNES (*Innocent*): I am, of course, well acquainted with his Highness here.

(*He bows deeply to Philip.*)

HENRY:
CROMWELL: } His Highness!

(*Philip for the first time looks directly at Barnes.*)

PHILIP (*Unabashed*): Well, what a devilish chance!

(*In undisturbed good humour he removes his beard.*)

HENRY (*Thundering again*): A disguise? In my wife's apartments?

BARNES (*To Henry*): Sir? You are not acquainted with his Highness the Landgraf of Hesse?

PHILIP (*Acknowledging the introduction*): Your Majesty.

HENRY:
CROMWELL: } Hesse!
ANNA:

BARNES: I wonder if he has come to enlighten us about the situation in Hesse?

HENRY: Perhaps he has. But first of all he will enlighten us why he is here in my kingdom, disguised, unannounced, and in secret conference, with my wife—who has just tried to hide his identity from me. Queens, madam, may commit other treasons than adultery.

PHILIP: Secret conference, with a *woman*? D'you think me mad? Madam, I beg your pardon, but let us retain our good sense. Certainly I came to England in secrecy, but to the King. And how better to approach him discreetly but by way of my German compatriot, his beloved wife?

(*Anna closes her eyes in relief but speaks with tolerable steadiness.*)

ANNA: I am delighted at the success of your scheme, sir. Let me wish your conference equal success.

(*She turns to Henry ready to curtsey to him.*)

HENRY: Wait. Are your women discreet?

ANNA: They were chosen by your Majesty; it is for you to judge them.

HENRY: Then we will so far try your patience, madam, as to use your apartments for a little time. Instruct your servants not to disturb us.

ANNA (*With a spark of malice*): Then, sir, I must either summon my ladies to my bedchamber, or join the Court outside.

HENRY: Eh?

ANNA: Or it will be thought that you and I—(*She smiles placidly.*)

PHILIP: But why should the Queen not hear my troubles? Feminine wit for feminine matters; she may even be of help.

HENRY: *Feminine* matters? Your country's twisting in the Protestant League has troubled Europe for months, and you talk of feminine matters?

ANNA: It has happened before.

PHILIP: And will again, I have no doubt. No, pray let her Majesty stay, let my Lord Cromwell stay, it will concern him soon, no doubt; and Master Barnes knows the German courts as well as any Englishman. Brother Henry, I need all the help I can find.

HENRY: Herr Landgraf, we have been hoping for months that you would take up your position as one of the leaders of the German League.

PHILIP: And defy the Empire. I would be very willing to do it, if I could rid myself of one obstacle: one woman. And so I come to your Majesty for advice.

HENRY: To me? Why?

PHILIP: She's my wife. Brother, advise me. How am I to divorce her?

(*Barnes, Cromwell, and Anna all turn to watch Henry.*)

17

Interior. Gallery. Council chamber. Day.

(*Close-up of a chess-board with the game nearing its end. A hand (Gardiner's) picks up the Queen, hesitates. Gardiner is playing with Norfolk, among a crowd of courtiers. As he hesitates, Norfolk watches sardonically. Gardiner plays his Queen. Without hesitation, Norfolk moves and takes a piece. The courtiers applaud and comment. Wriothesley, very nervous, comes into shot, trying to attract the players' attention.*)

WRIOTHESLEY: My Lords.

GARDINER (*Rising*): I fancy the Duke believed that the game was his in any case.

(*Courtiers retire to background. Gardiner joins Wriothesley.*)

WRIOTHESLEY (*Speaking urgently and low*): The Queen is moving. The King is with her in her rooms. There are instructions that they are not to be disturbed.

(*Norfolk joins them.*)

NORFOLK: (*Unmoved*): They are not alone.

WRIOTHESLEY: They are together. The King dismissed the guards. Her ladies are refused entry.

GARDINER: You suggest?

WRIOTHESLEY (*Angry at their denseness*): She's young. She's comely. He's been a bachelor two years. And, Lord help you for fools, do you never take account of a woman's fears? She can entice him to her bed, or she is cast off. And what happens to cast-off queens in England? Divorce or death.

18

Interior. Anna's anteroom. Day.

PHILIP: And it is divorce or death for me.

HENRY: Landgraf, I cannot advise you. I have never been divorced.

PHILIP (*gaily embracing Anna*): Madame, you are free! The King has never had a divorce, you cannot be his wife.

CROMWELL (*Intervening*): Highness, when the King married the Princess of Cleves, he was a widower. Queen Jane was dead, and his two previous marriages were null.

BARNES (*As tactless as ever*): In any case both ladies concerned were dead.

PHILIP (*Tolerant*): Well, annulment, divorce, execution, the effect is the same. You rid yourself of them; and you did it legally. How? I need to rid myself of my own wife. If I can't I must submit to the Empire.

CROMWELL (*Deeply distressed*): Submit? Renounce the Protestant League, give up the cause of the Church—

BARNES (*Equally distressed*): The Church, the true

Church in Europe—it will go down. The King will never consider an alliance—

(*Past patience with his indiscretion, Cromwell turns to Henry.*)

CROMWELL (*To Henry, as minister to king*): I am sure the Landgraf has your attention, sir.

(*Henry nods, as king to minister.*)

PHILIP: I thank you. Briefly, I have got myself into a damnable tangle, and all because of this wife of mine. Master Barnes, you know her.

BARNES: She seemed—an amiable woman.

PHILIP: She is; so execution is out of the question. I've no complaint against her except that I can't abide her. I can't bring myself to her bed; and God save us, but a man must have a bed he can climb into at his day's end.

ANNA: Sir, we feel for you.

HENRY: Madam! Landgraf, the solution of your difficulties seems to us simple. Get yourself a mistress.

PHILIP (*Shocked*): But I can't! That is, of course I have. A charming little love. But I can't go on sleeping with her as my *mistress*.

HENRY (*Baffled*): Why not?

PHILIP (*Surprised*): It's a mortal sin. I can't take the sacrament. Madam—do you suppose that every time this fortunate man, your husband, came to your bed, a consciousness of mortal sin impeded you both. Would you not both long for more—comfort?

ANNA: We were speaking of the German alliance.

PHILIP (*Slightly defiant*): I haven't finished my story. I took advice elsewhere. I consulted Master Martin Luther.

HENRY (*Interested*): And what was his advice?

PHILIP: To commit bigamy.

HENRY: Pooh. I always said Luther was no scholar.

CROMWELL: I think the same solution once occurred to you, sir. In connection with the Princess of Aragon, was it not?

HENRY: It also occurred to the Pope. There were Biblical precedents.

PHILIP: There were indeed. Luther named them all. So I did.

HENRY: Did what?

PHILIP: Commit bigamy. And if one wife was hell, two turned out to be hell, death, and damnation. It leaked out; and what we had all forgotten is that I am by law a subject of the Empire—and in the Empire bigamy is punishable by death.

ANNA: Death?

PHILIP: I am on a short rope. I abandon the Protestant alliance, or I am executed for bigamy.

BARNES (*Distressed*): And I had always thought Luther a man of God.

ANNA (*To Barnes and Cromwell*): Were we not talking of what politics does to men of God?

PHILIP: And life or Luther—what sensible man would hesitate to choose life?

338

BARNES: Men have chosen Luther, Herr Landgraf, and died in the fire for it.

PHILIP: Master Barnes, there is only one man you have a right to urge into martyrdom, and that is yourself.

CROMWELL (*Distressed*): Robert, there is no talk of your burning.

BARNES (*Haunted but courageous*): I hope not. I am a good subject of my Lord the King. (*Henry grunts.*) But those flames disturb my dreams sometimes. I beg pardon. I interrupted the Landgraf.

PHILIP: So to get my divorce, I must once more become a faithful subject of the Empire, unless your Majesty can advise me of a way out of my tangle. Can you?

(*Henry sits meditating: his eyes run round them all and finally a look of crafty satisfaction comes over him.*)

HENRY: Landgraf, I can't.

(*A pause of consternation.*)

PHILIP (*Philosophical*): Ah well: then it's the Empire for me.

BARNES (*Unable to believe him*): And not the Protestant Churches?

CROMWELL (*Shocked to the heart*): And not the German alliance?

HENRY: That you and I must discuss further—my Lord Earl.

CROMWELL (*Dazed*): Sir?

HENRY : So faithful a servant, Cromwell; you are now the Earl of Essex, by my pleasure.

CROMWELL (*After a pause*): I know how your Majesty rewards his faithful servants. My gratitude will be as long as my life.

(*Henry laughs uproariously.*)

PHILIP (*Turning to Anna*): To the continuing glory of so pre-eminent a Queen.

ANNA: Drink, please, Landgraf, simply to the good fortune of Anna. And my thanks, Master Barnes, for your spiritual advice.

BARNES (*Surprised*): We did not agree, madam.

ANNA: No; but it cleared my mind wonderfully. (*To Cromwell.*) My Lord Earl, you have my leave.

CROMWELL : You dismiss me?

ANNA: It has all been said.

(*Cromwell drinks his cup silently to her and kisses her hand. He turns to Henry.*)

CROMWELL: Your Majesty.

(*Henry gives him a long look and then points to the door. Cromwell bows and goes.*)

19

Interior. Gallery. Day.

(*Cromwell comes swiftly through and Gardiner, and Wriothesley surround him. He stops.*)

GARDINER: My Lord Earl of Essex.

WRIOTHESLEY: Our felicitations to you, my Lord Earl. The King indeed holds you high in his favour.

CROMWELL: I thank you. Of your kindness—

GARDINER: Kindness, my Lord Earl?

CROMWELL: Is his Grace of Canterbury within?

GARDINER: I believe so.

CROMWELL: I have an urgent need of him. Forgive me.

(*As he passes Norfolk's hand comes out and grasps savagely at his collar.*)

NORFOLK (*Recovering himself after a pause*): you had—a speck of dust there, my Lord Earl.

CROMWELL (*Savage*): Dust, which some would call decorations.

(*He thrusts past Norfolk, and comes to a quiet corner. Cranmer is sitting reading.*)

19A

Interior. King's anteroom.

CRANMER (*Rising in pleasure*): My Lord Earl—

CROMWELL: Not from you, Archbishop. Stand silent a little.

(*His hand goes blindly out, clutches Cranmer's, and holds it.*)

CROMWELL (*After a pause*): For a learned man you're mighty slow in the wits, you've done some shameful things in your life and likely you'll do more before you die. So how is it that I find such a comfort in you?

CRANMER (*Abashed*): Comfort? I have never any to give.

CROMWELL: No? I fancy that when that King in there, that arrogant bag of diseased guts and crazed pride, at last comes to die, he will only go in peace if he has your hand in his.

CRANMER: But what comfort can you need?

CROMWELL: I've seen the warrants ready, and the pen dipped to sign them. Well, few can be favoured with such clear notice of death. Will you pay a debt for me, Archbishop? Will you pay a debt for me?

CRANMER: You have credit with me.

CROMWELL: Stay, Tom, until the King has left the Queen tonight. Whatever happens, there will be a lady in dire need of comfort.

CRANMER: Comfort again! And my hands so empty. But what will happen?

CROMWELL: The more I see of that lady of Cleves, the more I wonder.

(*Mix to:*)

20

Interior. Queen's anteroom. Night.

(*Anna is placidly pouring a steaming cup of punch. Henry drinks, faintly suspicious, but very comfortable in his chair.*)

ANNA : Punch seems good on an April night.

HENRY : You try to keep me with you.

ANNA : But you haven't dined, sir.

(*She moves to the table to refill his cup. At the table Lotte is finishing the setting of a sizeable meal. Henry rises to look.*)

HENRY (*Nostrils quivering as he smells the punch, eyes going over the table*): Is that chicken seethed with almonds?

ANNA : Yes.

(*He takes the punch and sits. Anna nods to Lotte to withdraw and serves Henry herself with the chicken. Lotte withdraws. Henry sits and eats. His eye falls on Anna. She is sitting cosily opposite him, eating. His eyes go round the room: they are alone.*)

HENRY : We are alone. Is this some trick?

ANNA (*Placid*): Husband : we were alone on our wedding night.

HENRY : What do you mean?

ANNA : If our marriage is to be valid, it was consummated. If it was consummated, it was on that night : when we were alone.

HENRY: So, madam, you think you have me?

ANNA (*Smiling*): Only if I want you, husband. If, now, I were some foolish young girl, thinking only of the title of Queen; or if I were so forlorn as to be frightened by what happens to unwanted Queens in England—why then I might affirm that our marriage had been consummated; might mention that my brother spent so many hours—

HENRY: That contract!

(*He drinks heavily at the memory, and throughout the next lines continues to help himself from the punch bowl and drink freely.*)

ANNA: But then I'm not so foolish, husband. Not all the brothers and churches and kingdoms in Christendom can contradict us. So long as we agree that our marriage was never consummated, then it should be easy enough to have it annulled.

HENRY (*Astounded*): Annulled? You think I—would divorce you?

ANNA (*Ticking off on her fingers the stages of her argument*): You can't help Philip of Hesse. Hesse will fall to the Empire, and without Hesse the German League will fall apart. Ah, you never really liked that League, Henry. The part was too small for you. You want to be one of the great three of Europe, not simply a leader of many small states. So!—the reason for our marriage no longer exists. The marriage may be as if it had never been.

HENRY: You dictate to me?

ANNA: I assure your Majesty that I understand his pleasure.

HENRY (*Bewildered*): You mean you—you would accept—

ANNA: Yes.

HENRY: Would you really? You would really—without resistance, without legal battles, years and years of senseless arguing—

ANNA: Yes.

HENRY: You would do as I wish?

ANNA: Yes. I have been saying so for some time.

(*Henry is by now slightly drunk.*)

HENRY (*Moved*): Madam! Anne—Anna: give me your hands: both of them. (*He kisses them. He finds this pleasant: kisses them again: then is overtaken by caution.*) Mind! I do that without prejudice. In homage merely to a woman who can discuss marriage without—without—

ANNA: With sense.

HENRY: I salute you. But I won't accede to your demands.

ANNA: I have made none. I have acceded to yours. Oh, you won't be ungenerous, you are too great a King for that. (*She refills his cup.*) You'll give me an establishment of my own, so that no one can say there was ill will between us. You'll let me stay in England; you'll let me see your children. I love your children; they are all so like you. In their different ways, of course. The chief point now is to free you of this marriage. Then when you make another approach to the Empire, which by then will be free of the French alliance—

HENRY: Anna. Anna. You are right. You are perfectly right. I am no petty German princeling, thinking myself mighty because I defy the Empire. I am

345

emperor and pope myself in all but name; what other man in England has ruled both kingdom and Church? Yes, I need to talk and walk with emperors, or I am not all that I can be. But Anna: I need also a wife. (*He sits by Anna. She rises and moves from him, slightly dismayed.*) We laughed at Philip of Hesse. Quite right; he is petty. What do you think happens, eh, when he gets into bed and the consciousness of sin begins to—(*He rolls about with laughter: then grows serious.*) But he's right. A married man should be faithful to his wife. Utterly, utterly faithful. (*Drunkenly singing.*) 'As the ivy groweth green and changeth not of hue, so am I, have ever been, unto my lady true.' I wrote that. I forget who for.

ANNA (*Wary*): But Philip of Hesse.

HENRY (*Slapping the table, so that his empty cup bounces off*): By the Passion of Christ, he is right! All men are sinners, and kings—kings—(*In an access of self-pity.*) How the women thrust sin upon kings! (*Anna stoops to pick up the cup, and sits well away from him.*) And all—all—all for their own glory. . . . No, there was one; and it ended too soon; but if it had not ended. . . . What was I saying? Yes, about peace.

ANNA (*Momentarily lost*): Peace?

HENRY: For I am not as other kings—not as other men are, in anything I pursue—I pursue. . . . I can find women; but peace. . . . Yet it came. It did come, once, twice, even three times, and always with women. Anna! (*He leans toward her; she hastily leans back.*) If I had a wife: a wife I could be faithful to: a beauty, yes, but chiefly kind to me; quiet at my day's end, peace at my life's end—(*Tearful.*) Ah God, what will my life's end be? (*Anna is watching him attentively.*) Peace, where can I find peace? Peace so that I can attack France—(*Anna's expression har-*

dens. Maudlin.) And Anna, Anna, for the love of
Christ save me from these women! Because they will
have me married. They'll pick some pretty wench
from some great family, and they'll parade her in
front of me, and I'm an old man, and she'll make
such a fool of me, oh such an old fool of me. Anna,
Anna, save me from that! And if I find the man who
called you ugly I'll have him hanged as a traitor. My
beauty, my Queen, my wife!

(*He seizes her hands, rolls over and falls at once into
a drunken sleep. Anna looks around. Henry is snor-
ing. Gently Anna releases her hands from his, rises
and goes out through the courtyard doors.*)

21

Exterior. Courtyard. Night.

(*Anna comes to the stone bench. She sits, then drops
her head sobbing.*

*Cranmer comes into shot behind her. He sits at her
side and strokes her hair.*)

CRANMER: Anna. There there, my child. Come now.
Come. You don't need comfort, you know.

ANNA (*Sobbing*): Oh yes, yes.

CRANMER: Oh no, no. Just to cool your head a little.
Come, that's enough weeping now.

ANNA (*Looking up at him*): Tom? Yes, that's enough.
(*She dries her eyes.*) Listen. Tell Cromwell that his
cause is lost. Tell him to save himself.

CRANMER: Anna. Cromwell knows this. He has seen
his death already.

ANNA: And Robert Barnes—

CRANMER: Barnes too? Yes, perhaps it must be. I pray that it will not be the fire for him; for anyone; we all dread those flames.

ANNA (*Urgent*): They have a little time. Tell them! Let me have no martyrs!

CRANMER: Every good needs its martyrs. Even the hatred of martyrdom. Leave us all to the ends we need to find. And now you must go in. I am happy for your salvation. *In nomine Patris, Filii*—

(*He blesses her as she kisses first his ring, and then his hand, and watches her quietly as she runs in through the window.*)

22

Interior. Anna's anteroom. Night.

(*Anna returns through the courtyard door and shuts it behind her. Henry is sleeping peacefully. Anna tidies her dress and cap, shakes Henry, and sits at his feet on a stool.*)

HENRY (*Waking reluctantly*): Uh?

ANNA: Oh? Oh dear, sir, I must beg your pardon.

HENRY: Uh?

ANNA: I must have dozed a little.

HENRY: Uh?

ANNA: And in the middle of so important a talk.

HENRY: Uh?

ANNA: And with so much business so well settled.

HENRY: Uh?

ANNA: The annulment of our marriage.

(*Henry stares: remembers: remembers more. A great wave of relief comes over him.*)

HENRY: So it was settled?

ANNA: Yes. Our marriage was never consummated. But we remain friends.

HENRY: Friends? (*He stares at her. She returns his look steadily.*) Well—we must agree. (*Mumbling.*) Friends.

ANNA: Yes. I could call myself your sister. Your Majesty's most loving and obedient sister. (*She sinks formally in a curtsey.*) May I ask your Majesty's leave to call my ladies and retire?

HENRY: Madam my sister, your brother—your loving brother wishes you a very good night. (*He rises, affectionately kisses Anna, and slowly and painfully makes his way to the door. Turning at the door.*) Sister. (*He goes out.*)

(*Close up of Anna. She is smiling.*)

Catherine Howard

BEVERLEY CROSS

Catherine Howard was first presented by BBC Television on 29 January 1970 with the following cast:

HENRY VIII	*Keith Michell*
CATHERINE HOWARD	*Angela Pleasence*
DUKE OF NORFOLK	*Patrick Troughton*
DOWAGER DUCHESS OF NORFOLK	
	Catherine Lacey
LADY ROCHFORD	*Sheila Burrell*
THOMAS CULPEPER	*Ralph Bates*
WILL SOMERS	*Howard Goorney*
FRANCIS DEREHAM	*Simon Prebble*
STANTON	*Bill Riley*
ANNE CAREY	*Julia Cornelius*
1ST SURGEON	*John Richmond*
1ST LADY-IN-WAITING	*Sue Bishop*
AMBASSADOR OF THE ORDER OF ST.	
JOHN OF JERUSALEM	*Alberto Colzi*
TWO CHILDREN	*Ruth and Paula Mills*
	Frederick Clemson
	Alistair Meldrum
KNIGHTS & SOLDIERS	*Michael Pattern*
	Bill Jenner
2ND SURGEON	*William Curran*
2ND LADY-IN-WAITING	*Unity Grimwood*

Produced by Ronald Travers and Mark Shivas
Directed by Naomi Capon
Designed by Peter Seddon

353

Character

ANNE CAREY, *Catherine's cousin*
CATHERINE HOWARD
LADY ROCHFORD
DUKE OF NORFOLK
DOWAGER DUCHESS OF NORFOLK
HENRY VIII
FRANCIS DEREHAM, *Catherine's secretary*
THOMAS CULPEPER
WILL SOMERS, *the King's Fool*
STANTON, *an officer*
TWO YOUNG CHILDREN
TWO SURGEONS
TWO LADIES-IN-WAITING
AN AMBASSADOR OF THE ORDER OF ST.
JOHN OF JERUSALEM
AN OFFICER

Sets

Interiors:

An upper room in Lambeth
Corridor and staircase in Lambeth
Lambeth Hall
King's bedroom
Queen's bedroom
Queen's anteroom
Council room
King's anteroom
A cell
Queen's prison

1

Interior. An upper room in Lambeth. Night.

(*Moonlight shines through a narrow window into a low, bare room.*

In a broad bed lie three girls: two of them children. They sleep in each other's arms. The third—Anne—a girl of fifteen sleeps with her face towards the window.

In the far corner of the room is a second narrow bed.

Here—Catherine Howard lies awake. She is a beautiful girl of eighteen. Beautiful but sallow; vain and proud like all the Howards.

She draws back the bed-covering and eases herself out of bed.

Catherine Howard pads across the bare floor to the window. She stares out at the moonlight.

Anne wakes, and calls softly to Catherine.)

ANNE: Catherine! What is it?

CATHERINE: Nothing. Go to sleep.

ANNE: What can you see?

CATHERINE: Nothing. The moonlight woke me. Then I thought I heard someone calling from below ... calling my name. But it was only a waterman out there on the river.

ANNE: Who would call your name in the middle of the night?

CATHERINE: No one here in London. But last summer, in Horsham, there was a young man stood under my window night after night.

ANNE: A young man?

CATHERINE: A beautiful young man who swore he would die if I would not love him. (*Anne giggles. Catherine turns angrily.*) Don't you dare to mock me!

(*Anne shrinks into the pillows.*)

ANNE: No, Catherine! Don't strike me! Not again!

(*The two younger children stir and moan in their sleep.*)

CATHERINE: Be silent then! I tell you there was a young man loved me. And more! One night he climbed the wall—up to my room—and stayed with me through the night. All night. And we lay together. he kissed my neck and put his hand here—between my breasts—

ANNE: Then . . .

CATHERINE: Begged me to let him look on them. And he watched me as I stood and lifted my shift up over my head, and he knelt down before me. He wept—

ANNE: Why?

CATHERINE: He said he had seen nothing so beautiful as my body. And I let him kiss and fondle me. And all the time, he wept like a child—a little boy. There were other nights. We did such things together—but you would not understand.

ANNE: Who was he?

CATHERINE: I promised never to tell. And I shall never see him again.

ANNE: But what if the Duchess had discovered you?

CATHERINE (*Smiling*): She found us one morning near the Chapel—holding each other by the hand. She boxed my lover's ears and sent me to the Chaplain for 'correction'. And that very night we two had lain, naked in each other's arms—heart to heart—in a room over her very head. While she snored and mumbled, we two clung to each other—(*Catherine shivers at the memory*.)—would to God I were back at Horsham!

ANNE: I should be afraid.

CATHERINE: Why, so was I. But fear is part of love. Without fear, there is no true passion.

ANNE: How can you know that? You've loved but once.

CATHERINE: I know it in my bones. That first night when his hands were on my wrists and I could feel his fingers gripping me so tightly that I thought my arms would break, and I could see the veins in his throat stand out hard and sharp, I thought the pain must kill me. I was afraid. Afraid for myself. Afraid that the Duchess must hear us. Yet it was magnificent too.

ANNE: You will go to Hell for thoughts like that.

CATHERINE: Not I. I confessed to the Chaplain. Old Sir Edward gave me absolution. He took my chin in his shaking hand and prayed for me. He dribbled and could not look me in the eye—I sometimes think he was praying for himself—(*Then she laughs and hugs herself*.)—all men are brothers—in the dark.

(*The door to the room creaks open, and Lady Rochford shuffles in carrying a lantern. She is an ugly short woman of little intelligence but with the cunning of a natural bawd or pander*.)

LADY ROCHFORD: Not asleep! Catherine—you will surely breathe some sickness there by the window. The river is foul and brings plague and mischief. And here's your uncle, the Duke below with his mother, come straight from Whitehall—from the King. They wish to talk with you.

CATHERINE: With me?

LADY ROCHFORD: And no time to dress yourself. Here, cover yourself with this—(*She holds out a heavy furred cloak.*)—and be swift. Your uncle Norfolk is an impatient man—(*Wondering, Catherine puts the cloak about her shoulders and moves towards the door.*)—You, Anne Carey, you've no business awake at this hour. Go to sleep, child. Cover your head and say your prayers. Ask God for a rich husband and fine, tall sons. Ask God to make you clear-skinned and bright-eyed—as pretty as your cousin, Catherine! Come with me.

2

Interior. Corridor and staircase.

(*Catherine, barefooted and with the long furred cloak trailing behind her, follows Lady Rochford. The lantern casts long weird shadows down the bare corridor and long stairs.*)

3

Interior. A room at Lambeth.

(*A tall echoing hall. A fire sparks in an open grate.*

By the fire, in a high-backed chair, sits the old Dowager Duchess. Her parchment face is as still and expressionless as an effigy on a tomb.

Facing her is the impressive vision of her son Norfolk. A large and powerful aristocrat with the bearing and briskness of a soldier. He is ambitious and ruthless, but not without enormous charm.

Down the staircase and into the body of the hall, comes Catherine—following Lady Rochford.

LADY ROCHFORD: Catherine Howard, my Lord Duke.

NORFOLK: Catherine—

DOWAGER DUCHESS OF NORFOLK: Your brother Edmund's daughter—you surely remember her?

NORFOLK: She has grown—I would not have recognized her. Come here, child—here by the fire where I can look at you.

DOWAGER: Lady Rochford. You may go to bed.

LADY ROCHFORD: Believe me, it is no hardship to stay—

NORFOLK: My mother ordered you to go. Be off with you then.

LADY ROCHFORD: My Lord—

NORFOLK (*Suddenly exploding*): God's teeth, woman! Are you deaf as well as old! You are ordered to leave us—then, in God's name, go! (*Frightened Lady Rochford retreats up the staircase. She stumbles in her haste. Norfolk laughs.*) Foolish, mischievous—

CATHERINE: She has a kind heart.

NORFOLK: That's no great quality in times like these. What's needed is a strong heart, a hard heart—a Howard heart. (*He smiles and holds out his hand to Catherine. Shyly she moves towards him.*) Are you a Howard, child? A *true* Howard?

DOWAGER: She's stubborn enough.

NORFOLK: And before God, I swear she's pretty enough. (*He stares at her. She looks back at him— calm and unafraid. Norfolk circles her slowly. He reaches out and jerks the cloak from her shoulders. It falls to the ground leaving the girl standing in her thin shift. Norfolk approves.*) Fine-boned—and her skin is perfect—pale, but with a sheen to it. (*Catherine lowers her head. Norfolk lifts her chin.*) Look at me, child—there—now walk over to the stair. (*Catherine obeys. She walks slowly to the foot of the staircase. There she pauses, then turns and walks back towards Norfolk. Again he nods his approval.*) She's perfect, madam. More than I expected, or hoped—there. Now you may wrap yourself in your cloak. (*He puts the cloak about her shoulders. Catherine lifts the hair from her eyes.*) I asked if you were a *true* Howard, Catherine.

CATHERINE: Yes, my Lord?

NORFOLK: And you know me—the *first* of the Howards.

CATHERINE: Yes?

NORFOLK: We are a remarkable family—and I say this, not from a desire to boast or to confound anyone with empty bombast, but because it is truth— a remarkable family. Close-knit, powerful and loyal. Above all—*loyal*. When the father of our present 'much-loved' King cut down Richard Plantagenet at Bosworth Field, *my* father—your grandfather— fought on the wrong side. He was led before the victor and told that he had championed a tyrant. My father said 'Richard was my crowned King, and if the Parliamentary authority of England set the Crown upon a wooden stock, I will fight for that stock. And as I fought for Richard, I will fight for you, when you are established by that same authority' . . . and he lived to prove his new loyalty. As *I* did in my turn, which the scars of old wounds, here on my arms and shoulders, must witness—the marks of Flodden, Morlaix and Brest. I have served the King for many years—with thoroughness, and, what is more important, with success—and he in his turn has been generous in his gratitude. Now, Catherine, I would like to do him yet another service. A service which, if successfully concluded, will certainly make his Majesty more grateful than ever before—which must make *our* family the most powerful in the land, and which will finally rid the King of certain evil men like Cromwell, who at present fill his ears with slanders, lies and wrong-counsel. To prosper this wish of mine to assist the King, I need your help, Catherine.

CATHERINE: My help, my Lord? But there is nothing I can do.

NORFOLK: Be guided by me.

CATHERINE: I will do whatever you wish.

NORFOLK: *Your* reward, Catherine, will not be insignificant.

CATHERINE: I want no reward.

NORFOLK: What have you heard of the Queen?

CATHERINE: They say the King dislikes her—that he is not pleased.

NORFOLK: The King wants no more to do with her. Another divorce is in the air. Friend Cromwell looks pale. He sweats and trembles. The Queen was to be the key to his plan for a grand German alliance: an anti-Papal Crusade. Now that plan is in the fire and Cromwell fears that he will follow it. The Crusade is abandoned. For the moment, and who knows how long the moment will last, I—and my few friends— have the ear of the King. We could wish for a more reliable, a more permanent opportunity. The King's ears are open to many whisperers. We would have his ears, his eyes, his heart—if possible, his soul. We would have him find another Queen, choose another wife, Catherine. To speak plain—we would have him choose *you*.

(*Catherine stares at Norfolk.*)

CATHERINE: Me—? But he has never paid me any attention.

NORFOLK: He has not seen you since the spring. He has not looked on you as I look on you *now*. Were he to see you now, I swear that he could not fail but be enchanted by you—moreover you are a Howard. The Earl Marshal of England—(*He bows mockingly.*)—is your uncle. Everything in life depends on the moment. One must know 'how', 'who', and 'when' . . . our moment is *now*. A month ago—too soon. A month's time—too late. For you, Catherine, the stars are perfect! *Now!* You bring no devious foreign entanglement as part of your dowry. You seem strong and healthy—fit to bear a fine male heir. For it is rumoured the Prince will not live to succeed. But your son would have my blood in him. He would be a Howard . . . you say nothing. Does the thought of becoming a Queen not please you? Or is there some young man lurking in your mind? (*He turns to the Dowager.*) Is there? The girl is not known—?

CATHERINE (*Strong*): No one. There is no one.

DOWAGER: There were a couple of young admirers last summer in Horsham.

CATHERINE (*Strong*): No one. There is no one.

DOWAGER: A scholar—Francis Dereham—and a teacher of music, one Mannox. They pestered Catherine. I had to box Dereham's ears and dismiss Mannox.

CATHERINE: They were nothing.

NORFOLK: You swear to that?

CATHERINE: By all I hold dear and holy.

NORFOLK: You relish the thought of being a Queen then?

CATHERINE: It frightens me—my cousin Anne Boleyn was Queen.

NORFOLK: She was foolish and reckless. She ignored the advice of those who could have helped, even saved her. She deserved to die. Think no more on her—think instead of the splendours and the powers. You will have rich clothes and fine jewels, women to wait on you, noblemen to kneel to you, a king to love you.

CATHERINE: But *will* he love me?

NORFOLK: I know the King—he must love you. (*He takes the girl by the shoulders.*) You will be ruled by me?

CATHERINE: Yes.

NORFOLK: Now—*and* after?

CATHERINE: Yes.

NORFOLK: Then now return to your bed. I shall send for you tomorrow. Bless you, Catherine.

(*Catherine bows to Norfolk and to the Dowager, then turns and walks away up the long staircase. Norfolk watches her as she goes, then turns to the Dowager.*)

Do you think she understood anything of what I was saying?

DOWAGER: She understood that you were going to make her a queen.

NORFOLK: So I will. But does she *know* what it means?

DOWAGER: How can she? She's so very young.

NORFOLK: Poor innocent—

(*The Dowager Duchess says nothing. Norfolk turns to warm himself at the fire.*)

4

Interior. Corridor and staircase.

(*Catherine, walking as in a trance, returns slowly to the upper room.*)

5

Interior. Lambeth. Bedroom. Night.

(*Anne Carey sits up as Catherine enters the room and crosses to the narrow bed.*)

ANNE: Was it really the Duke? What did he want of you?

CATHERINE: It is late—go to sleep.

ANNE: I cannot sleep. I keep thinking of the boy at Horsham; how he wept, how you let him into your bed—

(*Catherine crosses swiftly to lean down over Anne.*

Her eyes are wild and furious. She takes the younger girl by the hair and pulls her head back over the edge of the bed. She hisses in her frightened cousin's ear.)

CATHERINE: Never dare speak of that again! Never, do you hear! If you do so much as whisper anything to anybody, I swear I shall poison you! Swear to keep silence—swear!

(Dumbly, and in pain, Anne nods. Catherine lets go of the younger girl's hair. She stands up. Her face relaxes into its usual enigmatic half-smile.)

6

Interior. King's bedroom. Day.

(King Henry VIII dozes in a chair. One leg is swaddled in bandages. His cross face is swollen. He is an old man: diseased and ugly. Will Somers crouches nervously in a corner. Norfolk stands beside the chair—staring down at the King with evident disgust. The King snores. Norfolk coughs diplomatically.)

NORFOLK: Your Majesty—?

(The King grunts and wakes. He winces as he reaches down to stroke his ulcered leg.)

HENRY: This ulcer bites into my leg like the teeth of a dog.

NORFOLK: Still no improvement?

HENRY: The ointments do nothing. They dry the sore for a day or two, but the poison is working away all the time. The poison is there as foul and malicious as ever—I can stomach the pain, but the need of sitting

367

all day in a chair with my leg swaddled in bandages is
my real enemy. I am bored, Norfolk. Sick and worn
with doing nothing. No sport. No hunting. Nothing but
gloomy surgeons with long faces and no remedies—I
feel old, Norfolk.

NORFOLK: But your Majesty will surely enjoy many
years yet—

HENRY: Save me that. You sound like Cromwell.

NORFOLK: You are simply fretting because your
wound keeps you inactive. You need some new
interest—

HENRY: But what?

NORFOLK: A new occupation—a new face. You have
surrounded yourself with surgeons far too long. And
we others—your counsellors and courtiers—you have
seen too much of us. Believe me, I hate being sealed
up here in Whitehall almost as much as you, your
Majesty. I sometimes pray for a good war. A commission to go hang a few rebels or knock loyalty into
some arrogant and ambitious Scot. But failing a
campaign, the best remedy—nay, the only remedy—is
a woman.

HENRY: No—no—not again. Cromwell's last blunder
has cured me of women. God's blood! The very
thought of it sets my leg throbbing! (*Will Somers
sniggers. Then, quickly, checks himself.*) My only
comfort is that the divorce will be swift and uncom-
plicated!

NORFOLK: Hear me out, your Majesty. Cromwell
forced the German woman on you for his own
devious policy. You had no need of an anti-Papal
alliance. All the world respects and fears us. For the
first time in many years your people are enjoying the
rich blessings of peace and, under your guidance, they

work and sleep secure with no dreams of domestic rebellions or foreign wars to disturb them. You have no need to make another political marriage. At long last, you are perfectly free to marry for other motives. *Personal* motives—for you truly need a woman to love and care for you. Someone to nurse and comfort you. Your grim surgeons will never heal you. A gentle and considerate girl would do more good than a hundred surgeons.

HENRY: But where am I to find such a paragon?

NORFOLK: Look about you. You have your whole kingdom to choose from. Invite some new faces to court. Young people. Rid yourself of the old and the miserable. Banish the ugly. Banish Somers there . . . Banish me! (*The King begins to chuckle. Norfolk presses on.*) Why, only last night I saw such a girl here in London. A sweet young child of—oh, I suppose, barely seventeen—fresh from a summer in the country. Just to look at her made me feel ten years younger. Your kingdom is ripe with girls like her.

HENRY: Who was she?

NORFOLK: My brother Edmund's daughter Catherine. She was at Court last year—in these last few months a miracle has happened. She has blossomed. Changed from a pretty girl into a beautiful young woman. A transfiguration, your Majesty. Mark you, I am only a soldier. The beauty of women has meant little to me. I may be over-praising her—

HENRY: Let me be the judge of that. Let her come to Court again—

NORFOLK: Your Majesty. (*He goes.*)

(*Somers comes to Henry.*)

SOMERS: Your surgeons would be wiser to ignore your leg.

HENRY: Why?

SOMERS: Then they could cut open your head and look into your brains—a *fifth* wife? Surely it's your wits that are rotten and not your leg.

HENRY: I said nothing of marriage.

SOMERS: But the Duke most certainly meant marriage. The girl is one of his tribe—a Howard. And then, what is worse, she is young—she'll have no time for me.

HENRY: No?

SOMERS (*Bitter*): No—the young do not need fools to make them laugh—

(*The King smiles. Cut to*:)

7

Interior. Lambeth Hall. Day.

(*Watched by the Dowager Duchess and Lady Rochford from below, and by Anne Carey and the two wide-eyed little girls from above, Catherine comes down the long stairs. She is dressed now in a fine costly robe. As she advances towards the Duchess, Norfolk enters. Catherine curtsies to him.*)

NORFOLK: Too solemn—when you meet the King. remember to smile as you rise from your genuflection. Do not be afraid of him. Smile, you have every reason to be brave. You already *look* like a Queen— though I would he had seen you as I first did. The gown is magnificent but it makes you older—more 'knowing', less vulnerable. But no matter—come now—to Whitehall.

(He takes her hand and leads her towards the door. Catherine looks back once—up at Anne Carey and the two little girls on the stairs. She smirks triumphantly; rather as a modern school-girl would stick out her tongue.)

8

Interior. King's bedroom. Day.

(The King, in evident pain, grips the arms of his chair. His leg is stretched out on a stool and a thin gloomy surgeon peers at the hideous ulcer.

A second elderly surgeon stands ready with a bowl, ointment and bandages beside a tray of crude, terrifying surgical instruments.

Will Somers stares with horror at the knives and forceps.

The surgeon sniffs the ulcer.)

SURGEON: I am certain it is less noxious now, your Majesty.

SOMERS: Then your nose is as useless as your skill.

HENRY: There! Even Somers has more knowledge. I say there is no change! The poison is as malevolent as ever it was.

SURGEON: I fear that to drain it again would only anger the wound.

HENRY: And I tell you that to leave it as it is makes no sense. God's blood! You'll not be satisfied till my whole leg is poisoned! Then you'll rub your hands eagerly enough, eh? Out with your saws and knives

371

and off with the leg! I know you butchers! *Cut,* I say. Cut now and drain the poison—or do I have to be my own surgeon?

(*The two surgeons look at each other. The second surgeon selects a scalpel and hands it to his colleague. The thin surgeon bends to probe the ulcer.*)

Swiftly, man. Be quick about it—

(*The surgeon cuts. Henry bites his lips in agony. The second surgeon bends to assist his companion. Enter Norfolk, followed by Catherine. She is nervous and half-hides behind her uncle.*)

—God's wounds!

SURGEON: The cut is made, your Majesty. The poison is draining free. The pain will ease now.

HENRY: Who is there by the door? Is it Norfolk?

NORFOLK: Your Majesty . . . And my niece, Catherine.

HENRY: Here—come stand by me. I remember you. But your uncle tells the truth. You have grown up. It is generous of you to come and visit an old sick man, Catherine.

CATHERINE: Old? But you are surely younger than my uncle here. And *he* is not old, your Majesty.

HENRY: Ah! but the Earl Marshal has led a healthy spartan life—long campaigns, months at sea. He has not had to carry my burden of care. Politics wear a man to a shadow.

CATHERINE: You seem broad and strong enough to me, your Majesty. Perhaps it is only your wound that depresses you at the moment?

372

HENRY: If you had seen me as a young man. There was no one in all England to match me for strength and for skill-at-arms, and for other—'talents'. Now look at me—tied to a chair like a useless old woman!—(*He lashes out in a sudden spasm of pain at the kneeling surgeon—sending him flying.*)—Devil take your clumsy fingers! I'll have your hands lopped off at your elbows if you can't learn tenderness!

SOMERS: A surgeon would surely prove an excellent executioner! To sever a head with a knife would take longer than a headsman's axe.

HENRY: You hold your tongue! Or I'll have these butchers cut it out of your head!

CATHERINE: Let me finish this work. I think these gentlemen are frightened of you—

HENRY: And you are *not*?

CATHERINE: No—why should I be? (*She kneels beside the King's leg and begins to complete the bandaging. Henry, enchanted, stares down at her.*) You must tell me where the core of your wound is—or is the whole leg inflamed?

HENRY: There—where the linen is stained.

CATHERINE: It should be washed and soothed with oils of herbs. If I could send to the garden at Horsham—I'm not binding the linen too tightly?

HENRY: No. There is no need to trouble the Duchess of Norfolk's gardener. You shall have whatever you need from my own gardens at Hampton.

SURGEON: With respect, I doubt very much if—

HENRY: These fools prescribe richer ointments. This morning they suggested a paste of ground pearls!

CATHERINE: No. Marjoram and Lady's Mantle—they will help in the healing. And then Marigold—that is to ease the scab. If you press the leaves you find a soft sweet-smelling oil. Lady Rochford says that to *look* at the oil is enough—it drives away *all* evil humours. She cured a stable-boy once who had cut his thigh on a scythe—*his* wound was healed in a week—(*Using her teeth, she tears the linen and secures the bandage.*)—There. (*She looks up at the King and smiles.*) The gardens are most wonderful at Hampton! I saw them last spring.

HENRY: Would you like to visit them again?

CATHERINE: I could perhaps talk to the gardeners and find those herbs that might help your Majesty.

HENRY: So you shall. And what is more, *I* shall come with you! We will go tomorrow, Catherine.

CATHERINE: But your Grace's leg—!

HENRY: To the devil with the leg! I swear to heaven that it seems stronger already. I will walk through my gardens with you, Catherine, or turn monk and eat stewed fish and sing psalms for the rest of my days!

(*He struggles up in his chair. The surgeons and Somers rush forward.*)

SURGEON: Your Majesty! We consider it most unwise—

(*The King, in answer, roars and strikes out with his stick at the table of instruments—scalpels and saws go flying.*)

HENRY: I *will* walk! (*He stands swaying for a moment. The sweat leaps on his face. Then, deliberately, he throws down his stick.*) Catherine—give me your hand.

(She holds out her hand. Henry takes her hand and they move towards the door. Norfolk watches.)

9

Interior. Lambeth. Bedroom. Night.

(Anne Carey and the two younger children are tucked up in their bed.

Lady Rochford is chuckling away by the window.

There is a distant thunder of kettledrums and trumpets.)

LADY ROCHFORD: . . . So many lights, the river is like fire! They say the King has commanded music and dancing every night this past week. Old Lord Thomas Mortimer dropped dead of apoplexy last night. Fell under the banquet table and was only discovered this morning! Oh! I shall be happy to leave this gloomy house.

ANNE: Why must you go?

LADY ROCHFORD: Your cousin Catherine has asked for me. And her request is a command these days. Tomorrow, she will be the Queen of England—but I promise I will talk to her. Just a few more months and I'm certain she will send for you to come to Court and wait on her.

ANNE: Will I have fine gowns and jewels too—like Catherine?

LADY ROCHFORD: Indeed, you will. The King is young again. And giddy! I saw the jewels he has given Catherine—one brooch has thirty diamonds and more

375

than fifty rubies in it, all edged with pearl. And for tomorrow, for the wedding, she is to receive a truly magnificent gift.

ANNE: More jewels?

LADY ROCHFORD: Much, much better.

ANNE: What then?

LADY ROCHFORD: The head of Cromwell! (*Anne trembles. Lady Rochford laughs.*) At the very hour of the marriage ceremony, Cromwell is to be taken from the Tower to Tyburn.

ANNE: Why to Tyburn?

LADY ROCHFORD: Cromwell is of common origin. He is to die among his own kind.

ANNE: Poor man—I wonder if he can hear the music there in the Tower?

LADY ROCHFORD: He will never hear music again.

(*She slams the window shut.*)

10

Interior. The King's bedroom. Day.

(*The King—magnificently dressed—is preening himself. He seems fit, buoyant and upright.*

Somers holds a mirror for him.

Norfolk stands with him, holding a document. As he reads from it, Henry is apparently disinterested. He continues to straighten his doublet, admire his calves and arrange his heavy gold garter collar.)

NORFOLK (*Reading*): To me you have been most bountiful, more like a father than a master. I ask mercy where I have offended, but I have done my best, no one can justly accuse me of having done wrong wilfully. I acknowledge myself a miserable sinner towards God and your Majesty, but never wilfully . . . Written at the Tower, this twenty-seventh day of July, with the heavy heart and trembling hand of your Highness's most heavy and most miserable prisoner and poor slave, Thomas Cromwell . . . Most Gracious Prince, I cry for mercy, mercy, mercy—'

(*The King sniffs.*)

HENRY: You think I look like a bridegroom, eh?

SOMERS: Magnificent, your Majesty.

HENRY: That villain of a barber cut my cheek this morning. There's a speck of blood here on the silk—

NORFOLK: I see nothing.

HENRY: Perhaps I could teach my Catherine to shave me. Her hands are so gentle and her touch so tender—she could surely put all the barbers and surgeons in England out of office. A perfect girl—my Rose without a thorn.

NORFOLK: There's not a man who loves you who does not envy you, your Majesty.

HENRY: Many a young man will get drunk tonight, eh?

NORFOLK: They will be happy for you.

HENRY: And not a little jealous! (*Laughs wickedly.*)—God knows. Norfolk I tell you I am as nervous as a green boy. My hands are trembling at

377

the thought of my Catherine's sweet young body. There'll be no long feasting tonight, I promise you. I want that girl more than anything in my whole life. She must have those lordships and manors I gave to Jane.

NORFOLK: Your generosity to my niece is most bountiful, your Majesty.

HENRY: For your own services—I have decided to name you Lord Treasurer. Also Lord-Lieutenant of the North—(*Norfolk bows.*)—to replace Cromwell, your cousin Sussex shall be Great Chamberlain. And for Lord Privy Seal?

NORFOLK: I would suggest the Earl of Southampton— a firm ally . . . to both of us.

HENRY: An excellent choice. What time is it now?

NORFOLK: Patience, your Majesty. Another hour—

HENRY: And we shall both be satisfied no doubt! (*He laughs. Norfolk looks at him as if uncertain of the King's meaning. The King crosses to the Duke and takes Cromwell's last message from him.*) No need to brood further on this? (*Norfolk shakes his head. Henry glances at the letter, then tears it in two and throws the pieces away.*) His lands and property shall be given to Catherine.

(*Norfolk bows impassively.*)

NORFOLK: Most generous.

HENRY: Hoping for them yourself, were you?

NORFOLK: Your Majesty?

HENRY: Be satisfied with his head—you have worked for it long enough. I'm not certain about these silver slashings. I think I prefer the white and crimson satin. Somers! Fetch my servants—I still have time to change. Would to God it was night—

11

Interior. The Queen's bedroom. Night.

(The high, bare room is dominated by the curtain-hung bed.

Catherine waits. She wears a stiff cloak, trimmed with fur and embroidered with seed pearls, over a simple virginal shift.

Catherine's hair is loose about her neck and shoulders.

The ecstatic Lady Rochford is with the young Queen She helps arrange the famous brooch of diamond and ruby—worn now as a pendant on a fine gold chain— about Catherine's slim white neck.)

LADY ROCHFORD: Lift your head, child—the clasp is difficult to secure.

CATHERINE: Your hands are shaking.

LADY ROCHFORD: I'm thinking that the next person to touch this chain and finger your pretty throat will be the King himself! But how cold you are! Your skin is like ice!

CATHERINE: I took no wine today. And I could not bring myself to eat.

LADY ROCHFORD: Well, the King will warm you soon enough. I've heard say he's a very Turk with women—you'll find little rest tonight, my angel. I envy you. My husband now, God rest his soul, was a poor thin creature with no blood in him. He spent our wedding night on his knees—praying to the Lord for a son. (*Catherine giggles.*)—I told him the way to ensure a son was not to pray to the Lord but to save his breath for his wife. But he went on crossing himself and protesting. And the Lord rewarded him with ague pains in his chest and legs ... *Your* husband will not waste time praying I promise you. I watched him during the ceremony—he could hardly bear to keep himself from caressing you there and then, before the clergy, the Court, and even the Archbishop!

CATHERINE: You think he really loves me?

LADY ROCHFORD: His Majesty is besotted! You could ask him anything at this moment and he'd not refuse you. And I pray he'll be of the same mind tomorrow morning!

CATHERINE: Amen to that—

LADY ROCHFORD: Let him do as he wants, child.

(*The door to the bedroom opens. And two young ladies-in-waiting hurry in—both tremendously excited. They curtsey breathlessly to Catherine.*)

FIRST LADY: The King has left his room! He has dismissed the guard.

CATHERINE: Close the door when his Majesty knocks, wait till I tell you before you open to admit him—hurry now! (*The two ladies-in-waiting obey. They shut the door. As they do so, we hear the sound of marching men and the swish of long trailing robes over stone floors. The four women wait. There is a thunder at the door. The two young ladies move to the door. Catherine stamps her foot. Harsh whisper.*) Wait, I tell you!

HENRY (*Off*): Catherine!

(*The ladies obey. A pause, then a second more urgent knocking. Catherine smiles mischievously.*)

CATHERINE: Very well—now you may open the door.

(*The ladies open the door and immediately curtsey— as does Lady Rochford. The King enters. He wears a heavy furred robe over his nightgown. He is followed by Norfolk and Will Somers, and a handsome young gentleman—Thomas Culpeper. Somers lurks by the doorway. The King advances slowly towards Catherine. As he moves, so she curtsies low. Henry eyes her with obvious relish. She slowly lifts her head to look up at him. They look at each other. The King gestures for her to rise. As she does so, the heavy brooch falls from around her neck to the floor. She stoops to pick it up. At the same time, Culpeper darts forward. On the floor, their hands meet over the brooch. They look at each other. Catherine slowly rises. Kneeling, Culpeper holds up the brooch to her. She takes it from him.*) I thank you.

HENRY: We'll not need you more, Thomas.

CULPEPER: Majesty.

(*Culpeper moves back to stand beside Norfolk and Somers at the door.*)

HENRY: Nor any of you. You may leave us.

(*All bow. Lady Rochford goes out, followed by the two ladies-in-waiting, Thomas Culpeper, and Will Somers. The Duke of Norfolk is the last to go.*)

NORFOLK: Good night . . . your Majesties.

HENRY: God save the King?

NORFOLK: I am sure your Majesty has no real need of any further aid—human, *or* divine—

(*Henry laughs. Norfolk bows, and goes. The door closes. Henry turns to Catherine. He puts his hands out to her shoulders, then gently touches her hair.*

HENRY: . . . I thought you beautiful when your uncle brought you to me, and when you and I walked that first morning through the gardens at Hampton Court. And again today, when we stood together before the Archbishop, you were magnificent. Diamonds and gold helped dazzle me. But now, when I see you like this with your hair loose about your throat, the sight of you hurts my heart. You are the most perfect possession I have ever owned. And perfect in yourself alone. You need no jewels to complement you, you are—perfection. (*He takes the cloak from her shoulders and lets it fall to the floor, then takes the brooch from her hand and drops it onto the cloak. Catherine stands slim and straight in her shift—looking at him.*) Let me see you. Let me look on you. You shall have all the diamonds, rubies, pearls and gold you wish. But for the moment, let me look on you as you are—without even your shift to hide you.

(*We see only the face of the King as Catherine takes off her shift. We hear the rustle of cambric. The King's pig-eyes blink. It is apparent that he is sincerely moved by the vision of his young wife. He stumbles towards her, and reaches out to hold her in a clumsy bear-like embrace. He mumbles her name and buries his huge face in her hair.*)

12

Interior. Queen's anteroom. Night.

(*The Duke of Norfolk and Thomas Culpeper sit together by a dying fire. They are drinking. The young man is plainly drunk. Norfolk is calm and smooth as usual.)*

NORFOLK: Go to bed, Master Culpeper.

CULPEPER: Too late and too drunk.

NORFOLK: I'm certain there'll be no need for any Gentlemen of the Household to present himself for duty before noon.

CULPEPER: She cannot be more than eighteen.

NORFOLK: You are talking of the Queen?

CULPEPER: Yes. Were she thirty-five, she would still be too young for the King!

NORFOLK (*Amused*): I excuse you, Culpeper, because you are plainly drunk. But watch your tongue— statements like that have the reek of treason about them.

CULPEPER: Not treason, your Grace. Forgive me—we are all jealous.

NORFOLK: *We?*

CULPEPER: We who attend the King. We who see the Queen—and are envious.

NORFOLK: I never understand you young gentlemen of the Court. Never did—but then, when I was your age I served my father against the Scots. I had no time to lurk in palace corridors and sigh for young women. Too occupied in keeping alive. What you need, Master Culpeper, is a long hard campaign in a cold climate.

CULPEPER: Would to God there *was* a war! Believe me, your Grace, I'd raise a company tomorrow—for

France, or Ireland, or even against the Turk! But in these miserable days of peace what else can a young man do but mope after women—and drink too much? Oh, for a crusade!

(*Norfolk laughs. He rises from his chair and strolls across to the window. He peers out at the darkness.*)

NORFOLK: There's a glimmer of dawn beyond the Tower—and a smell of rain.

CULPEPER: There's one among us who'll not notice the sunrise—or heed the rain.

NORFOLK: The King?

CULPEPER: I was thinking of Cromwell. They've spiked his head over London Bridge. The officers were ordered to set his face to the East—towards the sun and away from Whitehall—so he should not spy on the King's wedding night. Not that he would see for very long; the crows will soon be at work on his eyes—

(*He chuckles drunkenly. Norfolk continues to stare out of the window.*)

13

Interior. The Queen's bedroom.

(*It is now near dawn. The King is standing by the bed looking down on the sleeping Catherine. She stirs, and wakes.*)

HENRY: Catherine—

CATHERINE: For a moment, I was afraid. I could not see your face.

fort you. (*Catherine runs to her and buries her face against Lady Rochford's bodice. The ugly old woman leads her to the edge of the bed and sits down—cradling the young girl in her arms like a small hurt child. Catherine is sobbing now.*) There . . . tell me what it is. My poor, darling, little girl . . . there now. Your heart will break, my angel. What is it now? . . . tell me . . . tell me.

CATHERINE: I cannot, must not tell you.

LADY ROCHFORD: But, yes, you must—who else can you tell? I've cared for you for three years now. Cared for you, and loved you. You are the dearest soul in the world to me—no one could love you as I **do.**

(*Catherine hugs her. Lady Rochford strokes the girl's hair.*)

CATHERINE: He called me his Shunammite—

LADY ROCHFORD: God have mercy!

CATHERINE: He tried to tell me about King David and Abishag.

LADY ROCHFORD: What are you saying, child?

CATHERINE: I did as you told me. I let him do as he wanted. I lay down, and lifted my arms to him—invited him to lie beside me. And he threw off his clothes and held me for a moment, then stroked and caressed me with his hands.

LADY ROCHFORD: He was gentle?

CATHERINE: Yes. But he seemed to be continually at a distance; as if he were afraid to hold me in his arms for very long, as if my skin were made of fire. And it was only then that I dared look at him; and I was appalled—I had not understood how *old* he was. Oh, I had bathed and bandaged his ulcered leg, I had seen him tired and evil-tempered at the end of a long day—but to see him there without the satins and the gold—his very skin is old—yellowing, scarred, loose and coarse. He is *ugly*. His breath is pocky and stale. He has no grace any more. I had seen him dressed like a king, standing proudly and magnificently before his Court, and I could believe that here was a man who was *truly* a king; who could ride and hunt and fight all day. I had imagined that there was still the body of a Hercules beneath the gold and velvet. But it is not true. There is only the hulk of an old fat man.

LADY ROCHFORD: You must be patient, child!

CATHERINE: How can I? I have given myself to a sick, impotent, old man! I am condemned to a mock-marriage. I might as well take vows as a Nun or become the bride of a ghost!

(*She weeps. Lady Rochford hugs and rocks her in her arms. The door opens, and the two ladies-in-waiting return. The two ladies-in-waiting curtsey, and Thomas Culpeper enters between them. He essays a graceful bow and salute.*)

CULPEPER: Your Majesty!

LADY ROCHFORD: What is it?

CULPEPER: I am commanded by his Majesty to ask if you would graciously be present at the audience of the Ambassadors from the Knights of St John at Malta—at noon.

(*Catherine slowly rises and composes herself.*)

CATHERINE: Tell his Majesty that I shall be honoured to salute the representatives of so holy and gallant an order—at noon. Thank you, Master Culpeper.

CULPEPER (*Bowing low*): Majesty—

(*He strides out. The ladies-in-waiting close the doors behind him.*)

CATHERINE: He has a fine swagger about him—as if he hadn't a care in the world.

LADY ROCHFORD: A handsome boy. He'll break many a heart before he's much older.

CATHERINE: He reminds me of . . . oh, well, no matter. What shall I wear for the audience? Black, do you think—out of respect for the Knights' saintliness?

LADY ROCHFORD (*Doubtfully*): Black? So soon after the wedding?

CATHERINE: I am pale today. Black will do very well.

LADY ROCHFORD: There's no danger that the King might think you've chosen to go into mourning?

CATHERINE: I have told the King that he must be merely tired after his long illness—all will be well again soon.

LADY ROCHFORD: Do *you* really believe that?

CATHERINE: I do not know—but *he* must be made to believe it.

LADY ROCHFORD: My poor angel—! But thank God you are so sensible and understanding. These men are shallow, foolish creatures! All as vain as peacocks, unfeeling as cattle. Now my late husband was just such a buffoon. One winter, I forget the year, but it was very cold. The river was frozen over for more than a month. We were travelling to his estates in the north—

(*Catherine is not listening. She finds the diamond and ruby brooch, and looks at it as it swings, pendulum-like, on its broken gold chain.*)

16

Interior. Council Room. Day.

(*Henry sits on his chair. Henry is flanked by Norfolk and Culpeper and a group of gentlemen to receive the ambassador and his retinue. The knights are resplendent in their long black cloaks embroidered with the white Maltese cross. The knights listen impassively to the King.*)

HENRY: We would wish you to convey to your Grand Prior our earnest promise of good will and our hopes that he and his gallant brothers in God will long continue to deny the Ottoman power—(*Catherine enters—magnificent in black velvet embroidered with pearls—followed by Lady Rochford and the two ladies-in-waiting. Henry holds out his hand to the Queen. All bow low.*) Here—come stand by me. I shall need your beauty to charm these good representatives of the Grand Prior—or they will bleed me dry.

AMBASSADOR: We ask only for restoration of that which is rightly ours ... for compensation—money, and men—

(*Norfolk looks quizzically at Catherine from behind the King's shoulder. Catherine shrugs, then catches the inquisitive Culpeper's eye.*)

The situation of our Garrison at Malta is critical. Our galleys bring certain reports that the Turkish power is assembling in every port in the East. Its destination must surely be Malta—and its purpose can only be the destruction of the Knights of St. John—

(*Catherine stares calmly at Culpeper. He looks away. Catherine smiles. She puts her hand possessively on to the King's shoulder. He strokes her fingers.*)

—Our need is for money. Money for arms, for labour and materials for fortifications, for artillery, for galleys. And we need men. Men to use those arms, guard the fortifications and fight the galleys—

(*The Ambassador stops. Pause. All look from the Ambassador to the King and Catherine. For the King is no longer listening. He is looking up at Catherine. He is holding her hand—and is obviously oblivious to everything but the vision of his young wife. He kisses her hand. The Ambassador looks round at his colleagues and cynically cocks his eye.*)

17

Interior. Queen's bedroom. Day.

(*Part of the Queen's apartments. The anteroom adjoins the bedroom. A young man—Francis Dereham walks up and down impatiently. The door to the bedroom opens and Lady Rochford enters, followed by Catherine. Dereham kneels.*)

DEREHAM: Majesty!

CATHERINE: Francis Dereham—(*To Lady Rochford.*) Leave us alone. (*Lady Rochford obeys. Dereham takes Catherine's hand and kisses it. Catherine pulls her hand away.*) Look at me—(*Dereham, still on one knee, obeys.*) You've grown fat. Last summer—was it really only last summer?—*then* you had the look of a saint. The skin was stretched over the bones of your face like the carving of the dying Saint Sebastian.

(*Dereham stands. He is shifty and embarrassed.*)

DEREHAM: Last year I *was* Saint Sebastian. Shot through with arrows, and near to dying for the love of a girl—

CATHERINE: But now the agony is vanished?

DEREHAM: I had to banish it. Put all thought of her out of my mind.

CATHERINE: That was wise, Master Dereham—politic. Be sure she continues to stay out of your mind. That girl is no more.

DEREHAM: As lost as St. Sabastian.

CATHERINE: We understand each other.

DEREHAM: Yet I shall find silence difficult.

CATHERINE: Why?

DEREHAM: Because I cannot rid my mind of you. Because there's not a single night passes that I don't dream of you; hardly a moment of the day that I don't think of you—you in my arms—

CATHERINE: You corrupted me.

DEREHAM: You were willing, even eager, to be corrupted. But that's not a word I'd have chosen ... It was a magic summer for me. Too innocent to be sinful.

CATHERINE: But treasonable.

DEREHAM: Only because you are now the Queen.

CATHERINE: You must swear to be discreet. No one must ever know.

DEREHAM: My absolute discretion and continued silence could be made certain.

CATHERINE: Surely . . . I could have you poisoned—or order your throat cut.

(*Dereham laughs nervously.*)

DEREHAM: Then people would ask 'why'—

CATHERINE: What then do you want?

DEREHAM: I would be honoured to serve you.

CATHERINE: How? My household is complete.

DEREHAM: It is reported that you have not yet appointed a personal secretary.

CATHERINE: You?

DEREHAM: I am skilled in Latin and French. I am trustworthy—I would make a good secretary.

CATHERINE: A secretary . . . Alas, Francis, I fear you would . . . Attend the Court tomorrow. I will give you my decision then.

DEREHAM: I am grateful, Majesty—truly grateful—

(*He bows and goes—rather shamefaced. Catherine watches him go. Lady Rochford enters.*)

CATHERINE: Lord! Lord! To think that once upon a time I would have faced hell-fire for a touch of his little finger! For *that*! Saint Sebastian; and now a plump clerk skilled in Latin!

LADY ROCHFORD: You'll not appoint him secretary?

CATHERINE: You were listening?

LADY ROCHFORD: I only heard the word 'secretary'. Anyway, I can hold my tongue to keep my head.

CATHERINE: And so must he—I shall make him my secretary. To speak the truth, I feel sorry for him—

(*She turns and walks back into her bedroom. Lady Rochford shakes her head gloomily and then follows.*)

18

Interior. The King's bedroom. Evening.

(*The bedroom is empty. The door is flung open and Henry enters, leaning on Culpeper—his arm round his gentleman's shoulders. Both are in mud-stained hunting-clothes. Will Somers follows them.*)

HENRY: Gently, Thomas—help me to the bed. (*Henry reaches the bed and sits himself heavily on the edge. He rubs his side and groans.*) Aiee! One would think the villainous brute had kicked me rather than fallen on me!

SOMERS: Shall I send for your surgeons?

(*Lady Rochford enters.*)

HENRY: Where is the Queen?

LADY ROCHFORD: Majesty! You're hurt!

CULPEPER: His Majesty fell. His Majesty's *horse* slipped in the mud and fell.

HENRY: Fell on me!

(*Catherine enters—brisk and cool as ever. She crosses to the bed.*)

CATHERINE: Not your leg?

HENRY: Catherine—No. But my shoulder.

CATHERINE: Let me see—(*She pulls at the shirt.*)—your hunting-sword, Master Culpeper—

(*Culpeper hastily gives his shortsword to the Queen. She cuts the seam of the shirt and exposes an ugly, vivid bruise on the King's side. She touches it gently. The King winces.*)

No ribs broken.

HENRY: You're certain of that?

CATHERINE: Certain. But you'll not be riding for a week or more. You must rest now. Master Culpeper—

CULPEPER: Your Majesty?

CATHERINE: Help me, if you please.

(*Culpeper quickly obeys. Catherine assists the King back on to the pillows. Somers also tries to help. Catherine to Henry.*)

Send this man away—

HENRY: Somers?

CATHERINE: Send him away—I do not want him near me.

HENRY: But he's my buffoon. He's supposed to make me laugh.

CATHERINE: He never makes me laugh—he disturbs me. In truth, I would have him whipped and banished.

HENRY (*To Somers*): Leave us.

(*The anxious Somers scuttles away.*)

CATHERINE: I *hate* him—I never want to see his sly face again.

HENRY: As you wish, I'm in pain—I will not argue with you.

CATHERINE: Lady Rochford. I shall need a basin of hot water, sufficient linen for a poultice, and some Hypericum—to draw the bruise.

(*Lady Rochford turns to go. The King shouts after her.*)

HENRY: And bring me some wine! Hypericum?

CATHERINE: St. John's Wort. A wild flower with a slender stem and bright yellow flowers. We make a tincture from it which is the surest remedy for an outward bruise—

HENRY: There, Thomas—you wanted me to send for my surgeons. They would have shaken their heads and prescribed leeches!

CULPEPER: St. John's Wort sounds far pleasanter, your Majesty.

HENRY: And what of the *nurse*, eh?

CULPEPER: I would *I* had fallen, Majesty, had I been sure of such a nurse to attend me.

CATHERINE (*Unsmiling*): You may go now, Master Culpeper.

CULPEPER: Majesty—

(*He bows and withdraws.*)

HENRY: You were harsh with Somers, Catherine— and cruel to the young man.

CATHERINE: Because he is foolish. I do not care for empty compliments. (*Henry laughs. But this aggravates his side, the laughter becomes a groan.*) You must lie still.

HENRY: Where is that woman of yours? And the wine?

(*Lady Rochford enters with a basin, the two young ladies-in-waiting follow one with linen and tincture, the other with the wine. All three bustle round the stranded hulk of the King. Catherine stands aside. She takes up Culpeper's hunting-sword and balances it in her hand, then puts it down on a chair with a deliberation that suggests she has a future use for it. The King takes the wine. Lady Rochford swabs the linen and presses it against the King's side.*) Take care, woman! Do you want to burn a hole in me!

CATHERINE: Give it to me—(*She takes the linen from Lady Rochford, and kneels beside the bed.*) Lie back now.

HENRY: You will stay with me?

CATHERINE: For a little—until you are asleep. (*Henry scowls.*) You must have complete rest. You'll be sooner recovered if you are undisturbed . . . (*The King looks petulant.*) . . . Lie back now.

(*She gently puts the poultice against the bruise. The King grunts and closes his eyes. Catherine turns and looks up at Lady Rochford. Both women smile, then Catherine picks up sword.*)

19

Interior. King's anteroom. Evening.

(*Culpeper is alone. He appears moody and bored. He yawns. Dereham enters. The secretary is carrying the hunting-sword. His attitude to Culpeper is smug and patronizing.*)

DEREHAM: Master Culpeper.

CULPEPER: Well?

DEREHAM: I am ordered by the Queen to return this to you.

(*Culpeper takes the sword.*)

CULPEPER: Nothing else?

DEREHAM: What else should there be?

CULPEPER: No message of thanks?

DEREHAM: Not that I can remember. I was simply instructed to return the sword.

CULPEPER: Well, there was no real need. I suspect we shall have little enough hunting for the present—if ever again.

DEREHAM: The King is recovering.

CULPEPER: I was riding with him when he fell. He blamed his horse but the true blame lay with the rider. He is not able to sit a saddle all day any more. Yesterday, he bruised his shoulder. Next time, he could well break his back.

DEREHAM (*With a snigger*): If the Queen does not break it first.

CULPEPER (*With menace*): Tread softly, master secretary—the Queen is divinity to me.

DEREHAM: Then you are a poor foolish mortal. Divinity!

CULPEPER: I will not caution you again.

DEREHAM: Come man, open your eyes. The Queen is a woman just as you are a man. She feels, suffers, laughs, eats, drinks, functions, dislikes, desires—just as any other woman.

CULPEPER: You speak as if you shared some secret with her.

DEREHAM: I do.

CULPEPER: *You*? A secretary?

DEREHAM: I knew her before she came to Court. Last year in Horsham I was in her company daily.

CULPEPER: Your brain must have rotted with too much scholarship—

DEREHAM: Sneer if you wish, but I speak the truth.

CULPEPER: And I say you lie!

DEREHAM: God's pity, man! Why should *you* be so piously arrogant? I have watched you stare at her. You want her but you are afraid. You dream of her. You lust after her. But you know well that she is beyond you, as remote as the Holy Grail. She was *not* beyond me, however.

CULPEPER: I'll not believe it!

DEREHAM: Tush, man. Why shouldn't I speak truth? The nights were long. I was bold and nimble enough to climb a wall. The girl was hot, eager and curious. I politely obliged—(*Culpeper grasps the hunting-sword and advances on Dereham with evident menace.*)—What?—what are you thinking?

CULPEPER: I'm thinking I shall cut off your lips before you speak any more blasphemy!

DEREHAM: Be sensible, Master Culpeper. (*Culpeper shrugs and throws down his hunting sword. Mocking.*) Shall I inform the Queen of your humble gratitude for her graciously returning your hunting-sword to you?

CULPEPER: Say what you will.

DEREHAM: Then I shall tell her Majesty that I found you disturbingly pale, that, in my opinion, Master Culpeper is sick in love, but that I can suggest no possible remedy—(*He turns to go. Then his voice loses its mocking note. He is suddenly serious and bitter.*) For there *is* no remedy. You will have to burn, Master Culpeper. *Burn*—just as I do—

(*He goes. Culpeper picks up the hunting sword.*)

20

Interior. Council Room. Night.

(*A small, cluttered room half library, half study. Norfolk is seated at his table. He is pensive and troubled. He looks up and across to where Culpeper is standing.*)

NORFOLK: Do you think the Secretary was speaking the truth?

CULPEPER: I thought he was boasting of an imaginary

13. *Henry in infirm old age with his jester, Will Somers (Howard Goorney) and the Duke of Norfolk (Patrick Troughton)*

14. *Catherine Howard (Angela Pleasence) with Norfolk after being told of his plans for her to become Queen*

15. Catherine Howard as Queen

relationship to try and impress me; or perhaps to rouse me to jealousy. But when he left me, his last words were spoken with such bitterness, such real agony, that I came near to believing him.

NORFOLK: Whether imagination or reality, it was equally foolish . . . No—dangerous.

CULPEPER: That is why I came to you, my Lord; and not to the King. Above all, I want nothing to harm the Queen. As you are her kinsman, as well as the King's first councillor—

NORFOLK: You acted wisely. I think your second opinion of the Secretary was probably the more accurate. I have my mother's word, as that of the Queen herself, that there was no history of any previous entanglement. I would take their word rather than that of Dereham's.

CULPEPER: But what if he repeats the slander?

NORFOLK: There will be no repetition. I shall speak to the Queen tomorrow—

21

Interior. The Queen's bedroom. Night.

(*The Queen is sitting. She is tense and angry.*)

CATHERINE: I deny every detail of my Secretary's foul story. I shall have him repeat it before the King and see his head on London Bridge before he's a day older . . . !

(*Norfolk stands before the Queen—quiet and calm.*)

NORFOLK: Why trouble the King? Take my advice

403

and send your Secretary away for a time. Let him
visit your many estates and take inventories—or
whatever secretaries are supposed to do . . . Keep him
occupied and away from the Court for a half-year or
so.

CATHERINE: I would prefer him silenced for ever!

NORFOLK: Then people would ask 'why'.

CATHERINE: I've heard that argument before.

NORFOLK: Who from?

CATHERINE: But what if Dereham repeats his lies to
others?

NORFOLK: I do not think he will. I understand this
whole foolish, but dangerous, business was only oc-
casioned because of some youthful quarrel or rivalry.
And I will make certain that the Secretary is
cautioned before he leaves the Court.

CATHERINE: Is it not possible for some accident to
overtake him on his journey?

NORFOLK: But you tell me his story was imagined?
Then why are you so afraid? *Is* the story a lie?
Answer me!

CATHERINE: You have no right to question me in this
manner.

NORFOLK: I have every right. Had it not been for my
ambition for you, you would still be an unknown girl
in my mother's household. I made you Queen,
Catherine, and I could *un-make* you just as easily.
Remember your cousin Anne. Her neck was just as
pretty, just as slender as yours. *She* ignored the
advice of her family and she died on the block. Now
then, tell me the truth. My mother listed two names—

Mannox and Dereham. She dismissed the incidents as innocent—*were* they innocent?

CATHERINE: In spirit—yes. I never dreamed of marrying the King!

NORFOLK: You swore to me you were chaste. The King believed you to be untouched. Now I must understand that Dereham was *not* lying? That you were lovers?

CATHERINE: Yes.

NORFOLK: And what of Mannox?

CATHERINE: We were never lovers.

NORFOLK: What then?

CATHERINE: He—once or twice . . . kissed and caressed me.

(*Pause.*)

NORFOLK: How many people knew of your dealings with these young men?

CATHERINE: Nobody *knew*—some may have guessed.

NORFOLK: I should imagine every servant-girl and stable-boy in the house! I can silence one man, I cannot silence a household of servants.

CATHERINE: Then what am I to do? Confess everything to the King before he learns anything from someone else? Beg him on my knees to forgive me?

NORFOLK: Come now, you've been close to him long enough to understand that above all he is vain. He must never know. Or if he is to know, then you must be in such an impregnable position that no former scandal can harm you.

CATHERINE: How?

NORFOLK: Give him a son.

CATHERINE: Impossible.

NORFOLK: Why 'impossible'?

CATHERINE: He is incapable.

NORFOLK: I cannot believe it.

CATHERINE: Nor will he. He sleeps with me; lies with me as a husband does with a wife. But I'm certain that he can never be more to me than was King David to Abishag. He can never give me a child. I can never have the protection of a son.

NORFOLK: No—not *his* son.

CATHERINE: What do you mean?

NORFOLK: When you lied to me, and through me, to the King, then you committed yourself, Catherine. You committed yourself rather as a soldier commits himself to battle. There are only two possible conclusions—victory or death. My advice—the advice of a seasoned and successful soldier—is to place yourself in a defensive position . . . with a son on your knee.

CATHERINE: But the danger—

NORFOLK: As you now stand, one danger looks much like another.

CATHERINE: But *how* . . .? And *who*?

NORFOLK: *That*, I would have thought, will be the least of your problems. Two young men and the King of England, all within a year, would seem to me to indicate a remarkable talent. Make use of it—for my part, I cannot help you. I, alas, am a simple soldier with no skill in bedroom intrigue. You must fight this battle yourself. Be sure that you win. Nowadays, war is a dedicated affair. No ransom. No general pardon. To the victor, the glory. To the loser—the axe. (*He goes out.*)

(*Lady Rochford enters. Catherine stands pale and still as Lady Rochford undresses her.*)

LADY ROCHFORD: What now, my angel? So silent—

CATHERINE: When you are old, do you think often on death?

LADY ROCHFORD: More than when I was young. Then I never bothered with thoughts of the life to come.

CATHERINE: But now you think of it?

LADY ROCHFORD: At night. And when the Lord in his wisdom reminds me of mortality—another grey hair, a pain in my bones when the east wind blows.

CATHERINE: Do you think it is so terrible to die?

LADY ROCHFORD: To die young would be sad. How pitiful to go into the next world knowing nothing of this world. Such ignorance. Such waste.

CATHERINE: *Is this* world worth knowing?

LADY ROCHFORD: I believe so, my angel. And especially so for someone like you. A queen. Adored. Beautiful—

CATHERINE: If I were to die adored and still beautiful, men would write epitaphs to me.

LADY ROCHFORD: In Latin, Greek, French and

407

English—but *you* would not read them. So come now, let me hear no more of epitaphs and deaths. Smile—think on all the pleasant things in life—

(*The two ladies-in-waiting bustle breathlessly into the bedroom and curtsey.*)

FIRST LADY: Your Majesty—

CATHERINE: Well?

FIRST LADY: Master Culpeper is in the anteroom. He wishes to speak with you.

LADY ROCHFORD: At this hour?

SECOND LADY: Something concerning the King.

CATHERINE: Let him come in.

FIRST LADY: Here? To the bedroom?

CATHERINE: Do as I say.

(*The two ladies go out. Lady Rochford prepares to cover the Queen's present state of undress, but the Queen waves her away. Lady Rochford seems to understand. Culpeper enters.*)

It is very late, Master Culpeper.

CULPEPER: I have been with the King.

CATHERINE: I left the King at supper three hours ago.

CULPEPER: He is still at supper. The hall was hot and the wine strong.

CATHERINE: He has fallen asleep at the table?

CULPEPER: Yes.

CATHERINE: Then why come to me? This is the third time in as many ways. Surely you know what to do by now?

CULPEPER: His face is very flushed and his breathing seems to be difficult.

CATHERINE: Then leave him in his chair . . . Lady Rochford, go down to the hall. Let some of his Guard lash their pikes under his chair and let them carry him to his own apartments.

CULPEPER: Not here?

CATHERINE: No. You understand me, Lady Rochford?

LADY ROCHFORD: Yes, Majesty—

CATHERINE: Then do as I say—Go—(*Lady Rochford reluctantly goes. Culpeper bows and prepares to follow her.*)—Master Culpeper—

CULPEPER: Majesty?

CATHERINE: Stay—I wish you to do me a service.

CULPEPER: Whatever you will.

CATHERINE: The King trusts you—

CULPEPER: I am happy to think so.

CATHERINE: I am certain he does. He has spoken of your devotion many times—and always with feeling. He is pleased to have the affection and company of a younger man.

CULPEPER: I try to be of use.

CATHERINE: You are with the King more frequently

than any other gentleman of the Household. Why, I suspect you see more of him than even I do! And, therefore, I would be obliged to you, Master Culpeper, if you could see your way to being more conscious of the King's age and health. You are a young man. Your prowess in the field or at the table is a reminder to him of his own powers when he was your age. He is determined to keep pace with you— but in so doing, he is near to killing himself . . . I would not have that happen for the world.

CULPEPER: Nor I, Majesty.

CATHERINE: Then, for my sake, remember his age and try to curb yourself . . . Lord! You must forgive me, Master Culpeper. I am lecturing you like an old schoolmaster! And here am I only a year out of the schoolroom! Yet in that year, believe me, I have learned more than is in all the libraries of Europe . . . I feel as wise—and as old—as a desert hermit . . . and as alone . . .

CULPEPER: London is no desert.

CATHERINE: It is to me.

CULPEPER: I do not understand. Alone? But you are surrounded with friends, servants and every luxury. The King worships you—

CATHERINE: But everything is so remote. Nothing really touches me. My friends must not be too familiar, for I am the Queen. The King worships me—but I want more than that. God! I am at a distance from life. I do not want to be stared at as if I was a cold marble statue. I do not want to be adored as if I was the image of a dead Saint. (*Culpeper stares at the young Queen.*) Give me your hand. (*As in a trance, he obeys. Catherine takes his hand in her own and presses it to her bare shoulder.*) Is my shoulder cold like marble? Dead—like a wooden image? No—it is warm and alive like *your* hand. Hold me in your arms, Thomas . . . Hold me— convince me that I am alive—

(*Culpeper holds her. Catherine puts her arms around his neck and clings to him. She kisses him. There is a sudden rustle and the noise of someone hissing in astonishment. Culpeper turns swiftly away from the Queen—to see Lady Rochford standing watching them.*)

(*Cool.*) Have my orders been obeyed, Lady Rochford?

LADY ROCHFORD : It took eight officers of the Guard to carry his Majesty in the chair.

CATHERINE (*To Culpeper*): You will be needed below—(*Culpeper bows and prepares to leave.*) and remember your promise to me—not to encourage the King in his attempts to keep pace with you.

CULPEPER : His well-being is as dear to my heart as it is to yours.

CATHERINE : God give you good night, Master Culpeper.

CULPEPER : Good night, Majesty—

(*He goes. Lady Rochford approaches the Queen— looking at her with obvious curiosity.*)

LADY ROCHFORD : Did Master Culpeper manage to take your mind from death and epitaphs?

CATHERINE : He cheered me wonderfully.

LADY ROCHFORD : He's a gallant, handsome gentleman.

CATHERINE : Afraid of nothing, I would think.

411

LADY ROCHFORD: You'll be alone in your bed tonight, angel. Your husband will sleep sound—unless he wakes to vomit a gallon or so of wine. He reeks like an inn-keeper.

(*Lady Rochford continues undressing the Queen.*)

CATHERINE: I think he looks like the Knight in the tale of the Death of Arthur—he who loved the Queen.

LADY ROCHFORD: Not—

CATHERINE: No—Thomas Culpeper.

LADY ROCHFORD: Lancelot of the Lake.

CATHERINE: Yes—

LADY ROCHFORD: Mm—I must tell your Sir Lancelot next time we meet to remember that his namesake was more gentle and considerate—

CATHERINE: What do you mean?

LADY ROCHFORD: *Your* knight has bruised your arm—here. You see?

(*Lady Rochford chuckles while Catherine softly strokes the bruise on her upper arm.*)

22

Interior. Council Room. Day.

(*The Duke of Norfolk and Thomas Culpeper are together. An officer of Norfolk's stands silent by the door to the room—a tall, saturnine man with an impassive face and manner.*)

NORFOLK: You will leave tomorrow and be in Lincoln in time to meet the King on his return from the visit to York. You will take charge of certain documents and reports which you will personally deliver to his Majesty. You will then return here to London with the King's replies and orders.

CULPEPER: The Queen travels to Hatfield tomorrow?

NORFOLK: Yes. She is to await the King there.

CULPEPER: I had hoped to have the honour of escorting her Majesty to Hatfield.

NORFOLK: Perhaps the King will ask you to return by way of Hatfield. There has been an extraordinary stream of messages and presents for her ever since the King set out on his northern progress. Who knows? He may well decide to send you to Hatfield with yet another wagon-train of love-tokens. He is still as doting and generous as a bridegroom—(*Culpeper grunts in answer. Norfolk studies him with some curiosity.*) One of the letters you will be carrying is from the Grand Prior of the Order of St. John.

CULPEPER: Another request for money and men?

NORFOLK: Above all, for men. I wonder you were so apparently unmoved, Master Culpeper, by the Prior's Ambassador's eloquent plea before the Court.

CULPEPER: Unmoved?

NORFOLK: As I remember—it was the night following Cromwell's execution—

CULPEPER: The night of the King's marriage—

NORFOLK: I remember the conversation we had—you were rather drunk at the time—we were examining possible outlets for a young man's energy. You were looking for a crusade. What better cause than that of the gallant Knights of St. John? The Defenders of

413

Christianity against the heathen Ottomites? Or have you decided now to stay safe and secure at home?

CULPEPER: I have decided to stay here at Court, my Lord.

NORFOLK: Safe and secure?

CULPEPER: I suppose it must appear so.

NORFOLK: Very well, Master Culpeper. The correspondence for the King will be delivered to you shortly after dawn tomorrow. My officer here will bring it to you.

CULPEPER: I shall be ready.

NORFOLK: Excellent. That will be all for the moment. (*He waves his hand casually. Culpeper goes—the officer holding the door open for him.*) Stanton . . .

OFFICER: My Lord?

NORFOLK: Watch Culpeper—go after him now. See where he goes, what he does. I want a full account of every minute between now and when he leaves for Lincoln tomorrow morning.

OFFICER: I understand—

(*The officer goes. Norfolk returns to his papers.*)

23

Interior. The Queen's bedroom. Night.

(*It is night and the room is dark and shadowy—lit only by the fire. The bed is curtained. There is the sharp noise of scratching on wood, then the turning of a key in a lock.*)

414

The curtains round the bed slide back, and Catherine appears. She climbs down from the bed and pads bare-footed across to the door to the anteroom. She unbolts, and then opens the door. Culpeper appears—guided by an excited Lady Rochford.

No words are spoken. It is as if this scene has been performed many times before.

Culpeper seizes the Queen in his arms and they embrace fiercely. Lady Rochford looks on and evidently enjoys the embrace almost as much as the lovers. Catherine leads Culpeper towards the bed.)

LADY ROCHFORD (*Whispering*): All is well, my angels. I shall return an hour before dawn . . . till then . . . God bless and preserve you both . . .

(*She goes out, locking the door behind her. Catherine falls back on to the bed and pulls Culpeper down on top of her. They writhe and moan. The Queen's fingers tear at his doublet and shirt.*)

24

Interior. Outside the Queen's door. Night.

(*Lady Rochford stands by the door—listening to the sounds from within the bedroom. Then there is silence. Lady Rochford, almost reluctantly, moves away from the door and creeps away. She has not seen the tall sinister figure lurking in the shadows by the long windows. The figure steps into the dim light. It is Stanton. He settles himself to wait.*)

25

Interior. The Hall at Lambeth. Night.

(*The Dowager Duchess of Norfolk sits in her chair. Norfolk stands facing her.*)

NORFOLK: It is three months since the King returned to London. My information is that the Queen shows no sign of pregnancy, but that her liaison with Culpeper is daily becoming more reckless and increasingly obvious.

DOWAGER: Have you warned her—or spoken with the young man?

NORFOLK: I am not supposed to know.

DOWAGER: But you encouraged her.

NORFOLK: Advised her. She was, through her own fault, in great danger. I suggested a possible remedy.

DOWAGER: Every bit as dangerous.

NORFOLK: I agree. But there was no alternative. If she could have gone to the King and announced that she was carrying a child, then no rumour could have hurt her. But now, not only are the stories of her escapades at Horsham known to half the Court, but people are beginning to whisper about Culpeper.

DOWAGER: And the King?

NORFOLK: Oh, he's as blind and as much in love with her as ever. He's even thinking of possible promotion for the man who is cuckolding him!

DOWAGER: How, and when, do they manage to meet?

NORFOLK: Lady Rochford is a natural pander. If

Argus himself were to guard the Queen's apartments, she would still find a way to smuggle the young man into the Queen's bed.

(*Pause.*)

DOWAGER: What is to be done?

NORFOLK: If the Queen is to fall through her own rash behaviour, then she must not bring us down with her. Our collective security is my first consideration. The safety of the Howards is my primary duty.

(*A knock. As the officer enters.*) What is it Stanton?

OFFICER: My Lord Duke, my Lady—

NORFOLK: Well, what news from Horsham?

DOWAGER: Horsham?

NORFOLK: I ordered my officer—Master Stanton here—to make certain enquiries.

OFFICER: I fear I was too late for any enquiries, my Lord.

NORFOLK: What do you mean?

OFFICER: Others had been there before me on much the same errand. A priest and two gentlemen—servants of the Archbishop.

NORFOLK: What did they discover?

OFFICER: They questioned Anne Carey—also one John Lassells.

NORFOLK: Who?

OFFICER: Lassell's sister-in-law is a woman called Mary Hall.

DOWAGER: A servant of mine at Horsham. One of her duties was to attend Catherine—

OFFICER: They took sworn dispositions from Anne Carey and from Lassells and Hall. The priest returned to Canterbury. The gentlemen set out to Winchester. I believe they are looking for the Queen's secretary—Francis Dereham.

(*Norfolk considers for a moment, then*)

NORFOLK: I shall speak to the King tonight.

DOWAGER: And Catherine?

NORFOLK: I can do nothing. If I shirk telling the King then he will surely hear it from the Archbishop. I must be first—

26

Interior. The King's bedroom. Night.

(*The King is sitting with his hands covering his face. Then, slowly, he lowers his hands and lifts his head. We see that Norfolk is standing near the King.*)

NORFOLK: It breaks my heart to have to tell you of her infamy, your Majesty. I feel a heavy burden of guilt, for, but for me, you might never have seen her.

HENRY: Would to God that I had not!

NORFOLK: I believed her chaste.

HENRY: So she surely seemed to all the world. So young, so beautiful; yet so corrupt. You must not blame yourself, Norfolk. We were all blind.

NORFOLK: This news has broken me, your Majesty.

HENRY: No . . . I will need all your strength to help me. I should be angry. I should be terrible in my revenge. But, strangely, I am only perplexed. I called her 'my rose without a thorn'. She was my young gentle girl. Her hands soothed and healed me. What must I do with her?

NORFOLK: She lived most corruptly and sensually before she married you, yet she presented herself to you as an innocent. She has committed adultery. She must go to the block.

(*Henry bows his head.*)

HENRY: So young—

NORFOLK: She lived most corruptly and sensually maliciously caused you harm. Death is the only proper verdict.

HENRY: Then so be it—I beg you, Norfolk, be responsible for the necessary interrogations and the eventual punishments.

NORFOLK: Orders have already been given for the arrest of Mannox and Dereham.

HENRY: And Thomas Culpeper?

NORFOLK: My officers conveyed him to the Tower earlier tonight.

HENRY: Catherine?

NORFOLK: I did not wish to act until you knew of her guilt.

HENRY: I will not speak with her.

NORFOLK: She will surely beg to see you.

HENRY: I could not face her. Do whatever you think fit, Norfolk. I must leave everything to you. Were she

419

to throw herself on my mercy, kneel and weep at my feet, then I do not know what I should do—strangle her with my own hands; or weep with her . . . weep and forgive her . . . Go now. Do what must be done—

(*Norfolk goes. The King sits alone for a moment, then gets to his feet. He takes a step then shouts.*)

Will, bring me a stick! (*Very loud.*)

27

Interior. The Queen's bedroom. Night.

(*Catherine is lying in the bed. She is awake and anxious.*

There is a scratching at the anteroom door, then the sound of the key in the lock.

Catherine hurries from the bed to unbolt the door.

Lady Rochford appears and cautiously closes the door behind her.)

CATHERINE: Thomas?

LADY ROCHFORD: He was not there.

CATHERINE: You did not wait long enough.

LADY ROCHFORD: For nearly an hour.

CATHERINE: Then where—

LADY ROCHFORD: He has not been seen tonight.

CATHERINE: But he was to attend the King.

LADY ROCHFORD: The King is with your uncle. They have been alone together for more than two hours.

CATHERINE: Some business of State?

LADY ROCHFORD: Who knows . . . There, my angel. Be cheerful. Perhaps the King has sent Master Culpeper on some urgent errand. Perhaps he had no time, or thought it dangerous, to send you word.

CATHERINE: Pray heaven it is so.

LADY ROCHFORD: Amen to that.

(*There is a sudden scratching at the door.*)

CATHERINE: Thomas!

(*She hurries to unbolt the door.*)

LADY ROCHFORD: There! All is well, my angel!

CATHERINE: I would die—

(*She opens the door—and is face to face with the grim figure of the officer Stanton. She backs slowly away. Norfolk enters from behind his officer. From the anteroom comes the rattle of weapons.*)

NORFOLK: Your Majesty . . . I am ordered by the King to arrest you—together with Lady Rochford—and to convey you both to Syon House . . . at once.

CATHERINE: Arrest?

NORFOLK: On a charge of High Treason.

(*Lady Rochford screams.*)

CATHERINE: I wish to speak to the King.

NORFOLK: He will not see you.

Catherine turns to the anteroom, but Stanton bars the way. Swiftly, she runs across to the second door, flings back the bolt and hurls open the door. A large

421

halberd blocks her exit. The shadow of the halberd looms over her like the shadow of an executioner's axe. Catherine stands and shrieks. Her screams of terror echo again and again.)

28

Interior. Cell.

(A grim, dark place. Two broken men lie together in the straw and filth. They are unkempt, bruised and dirty. They have been racked, and their swollen joints are only crudely bandaged. Dereham is still strangely calm. Culpeper is plainly terrified. He trembles violently and mutters continuously.)

CULPEPER: God have mercy . . . God have mercy . . . God have mercy . . .

DEREHAM: Too late for any mercy. Be grateful the King remembered you at the end and that you are to die as a gentleman. If you must pray, pray for me. We share the same scaffold tomorrow but for you the pain will be brief.

CULPEPER: Still pain—however brief. Still *death*.

DEREHAM: You bow your head and, within a 'Hail Mary', it is all over. For me, because I was only a Secretary, I have to face the rope, the disembowelling knife, and *then* the axe . . . I *shall* know pain, Master Culpeper. You suffered on the rack, think how I shall suffer tomorrow—(*Culpeper moans.*)—God, man! If any one had cause to moan and curse heaven, it should be me! My offence was to love a girl who, by chance, became a wife of a king. But you knowingly committed adultery with a *queen*! I should rant at fate, but surely you should be patient and resigned. You are *guilty*!

CULPEPER: She tempted me! She is a witch!

DEREHAM: You were ready and eager to be tempted.

CULPEPER: She is evil!

DEREHAM: No. Evil never . . . Shallow, vain, hot, stupid, but never evil.

CULPEPER: You forgive her?

DEREHAM: I have no feeling left in me. Strangely, I find it impossible to realize that I am to die tomorrow morning, for something so ordinary that happens everywhere and all the time. I climbed her wall. I loved her, and now I am condemned to death for such a little sin—

CULPEPER: When you heard she was to marry the King, you should have left England.

DEREHAM: Yes. It would have been sensible.

CULPEPER: Sensible! I swear you will be a clerk to the very end. Come, admit it was impossible to rid your brain of the memory of those few nights. She dazzled you then, she still does. You will remember her even as they cut out your bowels.

DEREHAM: Yes.

CULPEPER: Just as I will remember her—and curse her.

(*A silence. Culpeper returns to his prayer.*)

CULPEPER: God have mercy . . . God have mercy . . . God have mercy.

(*Dereham leans back in the foul straw. He closes his eyes.*)

DEREHAM (*A whisper*): Catherine ... Catherine ...
Catherine ...

29

Interior. Queen's prison. Day.

(*A pale Catherine, dressed in black velvet, sits listening to Norfolk.*)

NORFOLK: You will be taken down river to the Tower. The curious no doubt will be there to stare at you. It is, after all, a public occasion—and they always feel cheated because they are not allowed to witness the concluding ceremonial. I suggest, therefore, that you dress discreetly and conduct yourself with the dignity befitting your rank.

CATHERINE: And family ...

NORFOLK: Yes ... and family.

CATHERINE: I shall wear this.

NORFOLK: Admirable ... I should caution you that one stage of the journey might prove emotionally trying. The barges will, of course, pass under London Bridge.

CATHERINE: Well?

NORFOLK: The remains of Dereham and the head of Culpeper are impaled on the bridge.

(*Catherine shudders.*)

CATHERINE: How long shall I be in the Tower?

NORFOLK: Three or four days—no longer.

CATHERINE: When will I know the day, and time?

NORFOLK: The preceding night. You understand there will be only a few onlookers permitted—the Council, certain foreign ambassadors—

CATHERINE: *You* will be there?

NORFOLK: Yes. It is my duty—you will be allowed to speak.

CATHERINE: I have already prepared a short speech. And never fear, Uncle, I intend to ask my hearers to implore his Majesty not to impute my crime to my kindred and family.

NORFOLK: Excellent.

CATHERINE: I have also written to his Majesty, as you suggested—a statement of my guilt. That, I think, is what you desired?

NORFOLK: Lady Rochford is to die with you. My mother is confined to Lambeth. For the moment, the King has taken no action against others of our family. But who knows which way he will look...?

CATHERINE: When I am dead?... What will you do?

NORFOLK: I shall resign certain of my powers and responsibilities. And I shall leave London for a while—to visit my estates and properties in the country. I shall wait and see if two or three months will cure the King's present mood. At the moment he is stunned; unwilling to blame anyone, unwilling to do anything. But that mood may well change to one of anger—I shall wait and see. This is as much *my* tragedy as yours, Catherine. I had hoped to live to see you produce a son, a *Howard* King of England. But it was not to be. Now there is only one ambition left me.

CATHERINE: What is that?

NORFOLK: To die in my bed ... (*He takes the letter*.) Now I must report to the King.

CATHERINE: One favour, Uncle.

NORFOLK: Well?

CATHERINE: Would your men provide me with a block—here in my room? I am told Francis, and Thomas both died well—

NORFOLK: Bravely—I can vouch for that.

CATHERINE: I am very much afraid. I would like to try the block, kneel before it. Rest my head on it. Then, on the morning, perhaps it will not seem so terrible.

NORFOLK: My officer will have one brought to you—

(*He goes. Catherine is alone. Like a young girl rehearsing an entrance to a ballroom before a mirror, she begins to go through her planned routine for her execution. She walks upright and bravely. She looks round the imaginary group of nobles and ambassadors. She seems in a trance—almost ecstatic with the triumphant fervour of a martyr.*)

CATHERINE: My Lords ... I openly confess and acknowledge the great crime of which I have been guilty against the most high God and a kind Prince ... I am a Howard, yet beg you all to implore his Majesty not to impute my crime to my whole kindred and family. I desire all Christian people to take regard of my worthy and just punishment, for I have sinned against God in breaking his commandments, against the King's Royal Majesty very dangerously. Pray for me—

(*She kneels, and lifts her hair forward over her face exposing her white neck. She stretches out her right hand.*)

30

Interior. King's bedroom. Day.

(*The King sits morosely in his chair. His leg rests on a stool. The same two surgeons are with him. Norfolk watches as the King finishes reading Catherine's letter. It slips from his podgy hands on to the floor.*)

HENRY: Poor innocent—

NORFOLK: She was corrupt.

HENRY: No ... those around her infected her. I truly believe that she could have been perfect, a paragon without blemish. I should not have married her; I should have been content to *admire* her. When is she to die?

NORFOLK: The thirteenth, Majesty—at nine in the morning.

HENRY: You are leaving London after the execution?

NORFOLK: With your Majesty's permission. I understand that you wish to go to Hampton Court. I thought I would travel to my estates in the North—

HENRY: You have my permission to leave immediately.

NORFOLK: It is my duty to attend the Tower—

HENRY: Immediately, I say. Now. Tonight.

NORFOLK: As you wish, Majesty.

(*Nervous, for the first time, he bows and prepares to go.*)

HENRY: And, Norfolk—

(*Norfolk turns back.*)

NORFOLK: Majesty?

HENRY (*Slow and deliberate*): For your own especial safety, you would do well to *stay* in the North, or the South, or West, or wherever you will, for the rest of your days. You are the source of corruption, Norfolk. You are the disease. I never wish to speak with you, or look on you, again. If I do speak, it will be to condemn you: if I do see you, I will only look on your head! (*Norfolk goes. The King strokes his bandaged leg. He glares at the two surgeons.*) Very well—unwind the bandages. Prepare your knives. Cut as deep as you wish—I shall feel *nothing*.

(*Somers enters and crouches by Henry who puts his hands on Somers' shoulder without looking at him.*)

(*Fade out.*)

Catherine Parr

JOHN PREBBLE

Catherine Parr was first presented by BBC Television on 5 February 1970 with the following:

HENRY VIII	*Keith Michell*
WILL SOMERS	*Howard Goorney*
CATHERINE PARR	*Rosalie Crutchley*
SIR THOMAS SEYMOUR	*John Ronane*
LORD HERTFORD	*Daniel Moynihan*
STEPHEN GARDINER	*Basil Dignam*
SIR THOMAS WRIOTHESLEY	
	Patrick Godfrey
CHAPUYS	*Edward Atienza*
THOMAS CRANMER	*Bernard Hepton*
PRINCESS MARY	*Alison Frazer*
LADY LANE	*Karen Ford*
ANTHONY KNEVET	*Jim Kennedy*
ANNE ASKEW	*Elizabeth Bell*

Produced by Ronald Travers and Mark Shivas
Directed by Naomi Capon
Designed by Peter Seddon

Characters

CATHERINE PARR
HENRY VIII
SIR THOMAS SEYMOUR
STEPHEN GARDINER, *Bishop of Winchester*
THOMAS CRANMER, *Archbishop of Canterbury*
SIR THOMAS WRIOTHESLEY, *Lord Chancellor*
CHAPUYS, *The Imperial Ambassador*
EDWARD, EARL OF HERTFORD, *Seymour's brother*
WILL SOMERS, *The King's Fool*
ANNE ASKEW, *A Heretic*
LADY LANE, *One of Catherine's Ladies*
ANTHONY KNEVET, *A lieutenant at the Tower*
PRINCESS MARY, *The King's daughter*
WILLIAM, BARON PARR, *Catherine's brother*
SIR WILLIAM PAGET, *The King's Secretary*
BUCKLER, *Catherine's Secretary*

Non-speaking:

PRINCE EDWARD, *The King's son*
PRINCESS ELIZABETH, *The King's daughter*
PHYSICIAN
EXECUTIONER
LADIES, GENTLEMEN, SERVANTS, GUARDS, ETC.

Sets

Interiors:

The King's privy chamber at Hampton Court
Anteroom to the privy chamber
The King's bedchamber
Outside the bedchamber door
A room in the gate house at Hampton Court
The Queen's Chamber
A corridor in Hampton Court
Gardiner's chamber at Hampton Court
Corridor outside Gardiner's chamber
A dungeon at the Tower of London.

Exteriors:

Gardens, gate-house, courtyard at Hampton Court
Outside the Upper Oratory
Wooded country beyond Hampton
Bell-tower, Hampton Court

Period

From July 1543 to January 1547

16. *Catherine Parr (Rosalie Crutchley) hawking with Henry and (far left) Thomas Seymour (John Ronane)*

17. *Henry and Catherine Parr on horseback*

1

Interior. The King's privy chamber, Hampton Court. Day.

(*Low angle. The King's Fool, Will Somers, is asleep, or pretending to sleep, his back against the side of a chair.*

Titles: Catherine Parr by John Prebble

He moves, snuffles, settles more comfortably. There is a stout stick leaning against the chair beside him. It is grasped by a thick hand that comes into shot. Somers, suddenly awakened by the violent trembling of the stick, stares at it with interest, approvingly, head cocked like a bird's.

Pan from the stick to take in a pair of legs, grossly swollen and bandaged beneath the hose. They, too, tremble as a great strain is placed upon them.

Pan up slowly to the owner of the legs—King Henry VIII.

Take out titles.

He looks older than he is, the fringe of his chin-beard and the sparse hair on his uncovered head are white. His body is as gross as his legs. His eyes bulge and stare above his puffing cheeks. And now he is upright. His lips twist with a hard grin at this small triumph over infirmity.

Two shot Henry and Somers. The Fool claps his hands with delight. Henry looks down at him indulgently.)

HENRY: Good fool . . . am I now supposed to entertain you?

435

SOMERS: Aye, Majesty, for fools we both are. Though which is the greater, God knows.

HENRY: No riddles, Will.

SOMERS: A problem of theology sire. Who will fail to pass Saint Peter's muster, a King's Fool or a foolish King?

HENRY: Am I being foolish, Will?

SOMERS (*Rising*): Cousin Hal . . . the question is: Will you be foolish?

HENRY (*Turning away*): Hold your tongue, fellow. You're losing your wit with age.

SOMERS: I've wit enough to keep my head beneath cap and bells. (*An appeal.*) And fool enough to hope for your Majesty's continuing love—

(*Henry does not respond, even when Somers shakes his head hopefully, jingling the bells. Henry takes his own cap from the post of the chair and looks at it, as if he saw some resemblance between it and a fool's cap. He turns back to Somers, pulling the cap over his thin hair. His voice is now kindly, he has understood Somer's appeal.*)

HENRY: Don't be afraid of her, Will. This one shall not drive you from my side. (*A beat, a smile of gratitude, Somers drops on his knees before Henry, seizing the King's hand and pressing it to his lips.*) No . . . no . . . no . . . get up, Will. It makes my knees ache to see you there. Get up and see who's outside.

(*Somers rises. Pan his skipping move to the door. He opens it slightly and peers out. Cut to:*)

2

Interior. Anteroom beyond the privy chamber. Day.

(Close shot Somers, peering out of the door. Cut to: Somers' point of view. The narrow ante-chamber, a halberdier in the foreground and beyond him, by the tall windows, two groups, separated as much by mutual antipathy as by space. They all turn to face the door Somers has opened, their faces expectant. Cut to:

First group—four men: Stephen Gardiner the Bishop of Winchester; Sir Thomas Wriothesley the Lord Chancellor; Sir William Paget the King's secretary; and an aged, crippled exquisite who is leaning on a cane with an expression of shrewd boredom— Chapuys, the Imperial Ambassador. Cut to:

Somers, who sticks out his tongue with cheerful insolence, and looks away to the second group. Cut to:

Second group—four men: Archbishop Cranmer of Canterbury; the young, arrogant and flamboyantly handsome Sir Thomas Seymour; his brother Lord Hertford, and a sly-faced, nervous man, Lord Parr. Pan from them to a woman, looking out of the window calmly. She is Parr's sister, Catherine, Lady Latimer—a woman of medium height, mature of figure, with a sweet, open face and bold eyebrows. Cut to:

Somers, staring sober-faced at Catherine. He frowns and shakes his head. From outside a shout from Henry:)

HENRY (*Voice*): Will ... !

(As Somers turns, cut to:)

3

Interior. The King's privy chamber. Day.

(Henry in foreground. Somers closing the door beyond.)

HENRY: Who's there, Will?

SOMERS: Two black crows. A peacock or two. Sundry sparrows and a dove.

HENRY *(A smile)*: Then ask Sir William Paget to bring in the dove.

(As Somers nods and goes out, Henry limps towards the window. He becomes aware of the stick on which he is leaning, and, on impulse, throws it from him in disgust. At the window he looks into a mirror of polished metal, preening himself, fluffing out his beard. A change in his expression as he sees what he really looks like. His expression sags, from bitterness to maudlin self-pity, and then to frustrated anger. The sound of the door behind him and :)

PAGET *(Voice)*: Your Majesty... *(As Henry swings round, group. Paget, some steps into the room, bowing. Behind him, going down in a deep curtsey, her head bent, is Catherine. Somers grinning behind.)* My Lady Latimer, your Majesty.

(His eyes on Catherine, Henry nods a curt dismissal, and Paget backs out. Henry advances to Catherine, painfully, then conquering the pain and lightening his step.)

HENRY: Madam... *(Catherine does not move, still down in her low curtsey. Behind her Somers shakes his head and waves his hand, as if urging her to rise. Henry is standing before her. He bends, as if to help*

438

her rise, but winces with pain.) By Saint Mary, madam! Must I talk to the top of your head? (*Catherine rises, looking at him calmly.*) I'd forgotten . . . (*He puts out a hand, and when she takes it, he leads her across to the window and looks at her carefully in the sunlight.*) I'd forgotten that you are beautiful.

CATHERINE: (*A flicker of a smile*): If I am, your Majesty, I cannot believe that you would forget. If you have . . . forgotten, it is because I am not, nor ever was beautiful.

(*Somers cackles appreciatively. Henry scowls at him, then looks back to Catherine, his face settling into the smile which experience long since taught him was charming and irresistible with women.*)

HENRY: Nay, madam, any maid can be called beautiful. You have a proper beauty . . . a . . . maturity. How old are you?

CATHERINE: Old enough, your Majesty, to know that I must acknowledge 'maturity' as a compliment. ,

HENRY: How old I said!

CATHERINE: Thirty-one, sire.

HENRY: You have no children?

CATHERINE: None, sire.

HENRY: Two husbands, and yet no children?

CATHERINE: No, sire.

HENRY: They were old men. That was it. They were old men?

CATHERINE: They were good men, sire.

439

HENRY: But old!

CATHERINE: Yes, sire.

HENRY (*A nod, stares at her*): I knew your father, didn't I? Sir . . . Thomas? . . . Parr of . . . ?

CATHERINE: Of Kendal, sire. He was Master of the Wards in your Majesty's youth.

HENRY: I remember. A stiff-necked Pope-Catholic. And what think you of Rome, madam?

CATHERINE (*A beat, and with calm sincerity*): It is the head-spring of all pride, your Majesty. The seat of vain glory, ambition, and hypocrisy.

HENRY (*Unimpressed*): They've taught you well. Was it Cranmer? Or those damned Seymours?

CATHERINE (*A touch of anger*): I hope the Spirit of God has led me to a proper knowledge of the truth.

HENRY: Don't be pert with me, madam! (*Appraises her figure.*) Such a body should not house a sanctimonious cleric.

CATHERINE (*Bearing his scrutiny*): As your Majesty pleases. I answered honestly.

HENRY (*Looking up to her face, his own deadpan*): And I'll hear nothing ill said of the Pope.

CATHERINE: No, sire.

HENRY: As he tolerates no slander on me. (*He waits, then a burst of laughter that dies away when it gets no response from her. Then, impatiently.*) Madam, I jested. Doesn't it amuse you?

CATHERINE: (*Calmly*): That the Pope does in fact slander your Majesty? No, sire.

(*Somers, who shakes his head vigorously, the cap of bells ringing delight. Close shot of Henry turning to Somers in a rage.*)

HENRY : Get out!

(*Full shot Somers. He shrugs. Pan him to the door. He looks back with a malicious grin and goes out. Cut to:*)

4

Interior. Anteroom beyond the privy chamber. Day.

(*As Somers comes out of the chamber, whistling. He pauses, looking. Cut to:*

Somers' point of view, down the room. The crows, peacocks and sparrows turning to look at him.

Full shot Somers, a shrug. Still whistling he moves off. As he passes a window alcove, a hand grasps him by the collar, pulling him into the alcove.

Tight two shot, Sir Thomas Seymour and Somers.)

SEYMOUR : Good-morrow, Fool.

SOMERS (*Half-throttled*): Good day to you, Sir Thomas Seymour.

SEYMOUR : What would you do for a crown.

SOMERS : Put it on my master's head, or in my purse. Which are you offering, sir?

SEYMOUR : If your tongue wags to my humour, I'll fill your purse with crowns.

SOMERS: Well said! I can sing a song, tell a story. What's your . . .

(The rest of the question is choked off by the tightening of Seymour's grip.)

SEYMOUR: What says the King to my Lady Latimer?

SOMERS *(When he can speak)*: Indeed, I'd give you a crown if I had one. You're the better hand at jesting.

(Seymour's other hand comes up and lays the edge of a dagger along Somer's throat.)

SEYMOUR *(Sweetly)*: Master Somers, did you hear my question?

SOMERS *(Bravely)*: Take my cap, sir. I abdicate. Only the greatest fool in Christendom would think of cutting the throat of the King's Fool.

(Hertford comes up, seizing Seymour's arm.)

HERTFORD: Are you mad, Thomas?

SEYMOUR *(A grin)*: Enough to let a little sawdust out of this rogue.

SOMERS: My Lord Hertford, will you ask your brother to take his tooth-pick from my throat?

HERTFORD *(A glance down the room and back, urgently)*: Thomas! *(Still grinning, Seymour releases Somers and sheathes his dagger. Somers shakes his head till the bell rings.)* Master Somers—say nothing of this.

SOMERS *(A nod)*: For you, my Lord . . . and remembering your sister.

SEYMOUR *(Angry now)*: Don't speak of her, you rogue!

SOMERS: Why not, sir? Her late Majesty the Lady Jane was gentle with such fools as the King and I. And we loved her. May I go, sirs?

HERTFORD: Thank you, Will. (*Somers goes. Hertford turns on his younger brother in cold anger.*) Must you always be play-acting? Gardiner and Wriothesley were watching.

SEYMOUR: Let them watch a man!

HERTFORD: You can't have her! Not now. Don't you know that?

SEYMOUR (*Astonished*): Do you think I'm some country swain full of jealous spite? Of course, I can't. She must marry him!

(*Cut to*:)

5

Interior. The King's privy chamber. Day.

(*Close shot of Henry.*)

HENRY: Why did you marry them?

(*Two shot of Henry and Catherine at the window.*)

CATHERINE: It was my father's wish, sire.

HENRY: And to his exchequer's credit, no doubt. Was it only duty, madam? (*When she did not answer.*) Did you love them?

CATHERINE: They were kind to me.

HENRY: Kindness warms no bed at night. Did you pity them?

CATHERINE (*Surprised*): No, sire.

(*Henry nods. He turns away from the window, winces from the pain he puts on his legs and grabs her wrist for support. For the first time, Catherine betrays alarm, and Henry sees this.*)

HENRY: Am I as old as they were?

CATHERINE (*A beat*): No, sire.

HENRY: Yet, I *am* old, madam. Look at my legs. Look at them! (*Her wrist still firmly held, her lip trembling, Catherine slowly looks down at Henry's legs. Relentlessly.*) They're gross, madam! They are monuments of filth. In summer they stink like a byre! Do you pity me?

CATHERINE (*Looking up*): No, sire.

HENRY: What colour is my hair? My beard?

(*Catherine is bending beneath the enormous weight Henry is unconsciously putting on her wrist.*)

CATHERINE: Sire . . .

HENRY: They were red. Like copper. Am I old?

CATHERINE (*Trembling*): No, sire . . .

HENRY: Am I fat?

CATHERINE (*Scarcely heard*): No, sire . . .

HENRY (*A great shout*): Madam, have you no stomach for the truth?

(*Henry throws her wrist from him, staggering. She falls on her knees, bending over, sobbing tearlessly. Henry recovers his balance and stares down at her, astonished.*)

444

Get up, madam! Madam . . .

(*Catherine does not make any effort to rise, her shoulder moving. Henry frowns, looks about him as if to call assistance, and then changes his mind. Slowly, clumsily, and with pain, he goes down on his knees beside her. He cups a hand beneath her chin, lifting her face.*)

Madam . . . Kate . . . sweet Kate . . . Don't weep.

(*Catherine, astonished at seeing him on his knees now makes an attempt to rise, but he restrains her.*)

Nay . . . we must stay here. For once I'm down it takes half my guard to set me on my feet.

CATHERINE: As your Majesty pleases.

HENRY: Aye . . . (*He fingers her gown.*) Don't wear black, Kate. Dress in brave colours. Gold and scarlet. And green and silver when we hunt . . . (*He stops, staring at her.*) Two old dotards, and now a . . . Has your body never ached for some young stripling? (*He scarcely waits for her to answer this impossible question. He seizes her shoulders, scowling, hectoring her again.*) Or has one gone before me? His name, Madam, I'll have his name! By God, I'll not be betrayed again!

CATHERINE (*A cry*): My Lord, I've betrayed no one!

HENRY (*His mood changing again*):
Kate . . . Kate . . . I could woo a woman once, with words like syrup, and be more in love with them than I was with her. (*A beat.*) Kate, I am lonely.

CATHERINE: No, sire . . .

HENRY: Do not no-sire me. Twice widowed, and you don't know what it is to be lonely?

445

CATHERINE: I know, my Lord.

HENRY: Fourteen months I've lived alone, and have no time to waste. An hour is a second, a week a day . . . (*He sighs, moving his body painfully.*) Madam . . . my knees ache. You must help me get this mountain to its feet. (*Catherine rises, and with a great effort helps Henry up. He claws at her arms for support. When he is erect, breathing heavily, he nods.*) You're strong . . . Good! (*Half turns.*) My chair! (*Catherine helps him to his chair, and he subsides into it with relief. The change in position has brought a change of mood and tone. His voice is brisk authoritative.*) A glass of wine, madam. (*Catherine moves to a dresser and fills a glass. Watching her closely.*) There are matters of policy, madam . . . And others touching my person. I ask you again, are you Pope-Catholic?

CATHERINE (*Returning with the wine*): No, sire.

(*She hands him the goblet and stands before him, her hands loosely clasped.*)

HENRY (*Testing her*): Yet I've been told otherwise. In your youth you . . .

CATHERINE: I loved darkness better than light, your Majesty. I called superstition godliness, and true holiness error.

(*Her quiet passion surprises him, but he covers it by drinking deeply. He lowers the goblet, and then slyly.*)

HENRY: Madam, I would have the Bishop of Rome my friend again. Do you know that?

CATHERINE (*A wisp of a smile*): Yes, sire.

HENRY (*Answering the smile*): Yes, Kate, his friend. Not his subject (*And then briskly.*) What are the duties of a wife, madam?

446

CATHERINE: To learn from St. Paul that she must be obedient to her husband. To keep silent in public, and to learn from her husband at home.

HENRY: And a husband? What are his duties?

CATHERINE: To love his wife, sire, as he does his own body, as Christ loved the congregation, and gave himself for it.

HENRY: And if the husband is a King?

CATHERINE: The King is God's anointed, sire. These virtues must be pre-eminent in him.

HENRY (*Suspiciously*): Are you mocking me, madam?

CATHERINE (*Surprised*): No, sire!

HENRY: Then you make dry dust of marriage. What of the flesh?

CATHERINE (*Prim*): We shouldn't be so carnal that we run headlong after desire, your Majesty. Like colts without snaffle and bridle.

HENRY (*Sourly*): Aye, they must have been old men. (*Empties the goblet.*) It's certain you're no Pope-Catholic. You talk like Cranmer.

CATHERINE: His Grace is a saintly man.

HENRY (*Grudgingly*): Aye, and a brave one. He'll need to be both. Bishop Winchester and the others will burn him if they can. (*A malicious grin.*) As he'd be pleased to burn them. (*Henry abruptly thrusts the empty goblet towards Catherine. She takes it, and moves to refill it. He stares at her back, frowning intently, and speaks more to himself.*)

I burn in the fires which lesser men light to warm

their ambitions. And fight wars to make them rich.

(*Catherine has returned to him. He stares at the goblet she holds out, but does not take it.*)

Hertford whips the Scots and empties my purse. I can fill it again by fighting the French for the Pope. And if I win he may call himself a liar and graciously admit that I am no adulterer! (*The last words are almost a snarl. He snatches the goblet, drinks and looks at Catherine over the rim.*)

Am I an adulterer, madam?

CATHERINE (*A beat*): No, sire . . .

HENRY: But . . . ? What is your but?

CATHERINE: My Lord, I . . .

HENRY Speak out! You were full enough of pious dogma just now.

CATHERINE: My Lord . . . my Lord, I do not see your children at Court.

HENRY (*Puzzled*): My children?

CATHERINE: They say you've put aside the Lady Mary and Lady Elizabeth because the sight of them troubles you.

HENRY: *They* say? Who says?

CATHERINE (*Bravely*): It is said, my Lord.

HENRY: I love my daughters! (*And then, when she does not answer, his mood changes, his voice appealing.*) I'll bring them back, Kate. If you'll mother them.

CATHERINE: Sire?

HENRY: By St. Mary, madam! Are we playing tennis? Will you marry me? (*Catherine does not answer him. She stares at him, her head up, though it is clear she is afraid.*) Well, madam? You knew I would ask you.

CATHERINE: Yes, sire.

HENRY: I told Cranmer to prepare you. And Bishop Winchester.

CATHERINE: They prayed with me, sire.

HENRY: For God! Did it need praying over?

CATHERINE: We must be led by the Spirit of God, sire.

HENRY (*Heavily*): So you've said. And to what conclusion did the Spirit of God lead you? (*She cannot answer him.*) Well, madam?

CATHERINE (*A rush*): That rather than marry you I would submit to being your mistress.

(*Close shot Henry, staring, a terrible frown on his face. It suddenly breaks. He opens his mouth in a great bellow of laughter. Cut to:*)

6

Interior. The anteroom beyond the privy chamber. Day.

(*Close shot of Gardiner turning into camera at the sound of Henry's laughter. He frowns slightly, then a thin smile. Pull back to three shot with Chapuys, who is delicately hiding a yawn, and Wriothesley who is gnawing at the forefinger of his glove.*)

449

GARDINER: She amuses him. I hadn't taken her for a wit.

WRIOTHESLEY: A comic wit that may laugh us into the Tower.

GARDINER: No, Wriothesley . . . she means no harm.

WRIOTHESLEY (*A glance over his shoulder*): She's their creature. Cranmer and the Seymours.

GARDINER: She'll warm the King's bed none the less for that. (*To Chapuys.*) If the sap rises, we may yet get him into armour and the field. The Emperor would not cavil at the source of such vigour, would he, Chapuys?

CHAPUYS (*Wearily*): My Lord Bishop of Winchester, I've told you that the compact is what matters. If your King invades France with my master, then his Imperial Majesty will persuade his Holiness to accept the divorce of Aragon. (*A bright smile.*) And you may yet be a cardinal.

GARDINER (*Stiffly*): I labour not in my own vineyard.

WRIOTHESLEY: I don't trust her.

GARDINER (*Patiently*): My Lord Chancellor, she is a good woman.

CHAPUYS: A *good* woman? Then why does Thomas Seymour desire her? (*Innocently as Gardiner looks at him sharply.*) Is it a secret?

GARDINER: From the King, yes. And must be kept so.

CHAPUYS (*Blandly*): You labour deviously in that vineyard.

WRIOTHESLEY: Gardiner, we're fools to encourage the King in this. Tell him about Seymour, and scotch them all.

GARDINER: And so we would be fools! She's pious and blameless, and answers her own conscience. She is more valuable to us as the King's wife then some you would have thrust before him. (*With a touch of anger Wriothesley opens his mouth to protest.*) Yes sir, she is! Can you not see that?

WRIOTHESLEY: I can see Hertford's ambition behind her piety. And Cranmer's heresy.

GARDINER: As is your honest custom, sir, you see all and understand nothing. She can't be brought down like those wantons Bullen and Howard, who destroyed only themselves. Or put aside like Aragon and the Flemish mare. If Heresy aspires to see her Queen, so be it, for the King knows it well enough. Yet what does not prick him now may easily be rubbed into a sore later. Thus we shall ultimately destroy all in one.

CHAPUYS: My Lord, you'll be wasted if you don't get a cardinal's hat.

(*This ironic taunt seems to embarrass Gardiner. He turns away, looking down the chamber to the other group. Cut to: Seymour, Hertford, Parr and Cranmer. Seymour is staring back at Gardiner with an arrogant frown.*)

SEYMOUR: That croaking raven's talking about us. God give me joy to open his crop!

CRANMER (*A sigh*): Control your temper, Thomas. You have too great a conceit of yourself.

SEYMOUR: And there are enough canting prelates in this kingdom to give me cause!

HERTFORD: Tom . . . be still. Cranmer gives you good advice.

451

(*Seymour turns his back on them. Parr plucks at Cranmer's sleeve nervously.*)

PARR: My Lord, will my sister agree to wed him?

CRANMER (*A smile*): The King may ask, yet it will be an order. But she'll obey willingly. She understands her duty to God and the Church.

SEYMOUR (*Turning*): She spent as much time on her knees with Gardiner as she did with you.

CRANMER: She's proof against Papistical doctrines, Thomas. And the Bishop of Winchester also directed her prayers towards marriage with the King.

SEYMOUR: Aye . . . to what end?

CRANMER: That we might betray our Faith through her. And so we will, Thomas, if we're rash and foolish.

PARR (*Looking off*): She's coming!

(*As they turn cut to: their point of view. Catherine is approaching down the anteroom. As she passes Gardiner's group they bow to her. She smiles at them without stopping. Cut to: Gardiner, Chapuys and Wriothesley, rising from their bow and looking into camera.*)

WRIOTHESLEY: She walks like a Queen already . . .

(*From inside the privy chamber an impatient bellow.*)

HENRY (*Off*): Gardiner . . . !

(*Gardiner moves hastily toward the chamber, followed by the limping Chapuys and by Wriothesley who looks back over his shoulder with a suspicious frown. Cut to: Catherine stopping before Cranmer and the others.*)

PARR: What news, Catherine?

CATHERINE: What news is there, brother?

SEYMOUR (*Impatiently*): What did the King say?

CATHERINE (*Wistfully*): That he's lonely.

SEYMOUR: Kate . . . !

CATHERINE (*Quickly to Cranmer*): Pray for me, my Lord.

CRANMER: My Lady, we've both prayed that . . .

CATHERINE: No, my Lord, for *me*!

CRANMER (*Understanding*): I will, my child.

PARR (*Peevishly*): Catherine, did you say what you were taught?

CATHERINE: Sweet brother, I would have answered as you instructed me . . . (*Then brightly to them all.*) But no, my Lords, I could not.

HERTFORD: Madam, you're a fool!

CATHERINE: Aye, my Lord, for when the King said he would marry me, I told him I'd sooner be his mistress.

(*They stare at her in astonishment. She turns away and moves off. Parr takes an angry step to follow her, but Hertford grasps his arm roughly. Still holding Parr, he looks at Cranmer, then to his brother.*)

HERTFORD: Thomas . . .

(*Seymour turns and follows Catherine. Cut to:*)

7

Interior. The King's privy chamber. Day.

(Henry looking up into camera from some papers in his hand.)

HENRY: Twenty-five thousand Horse and Foot! *(Throws down the papers.)* Your master asks a lot of my kingdom, Chapuys!

(Cut to Chapuys leaning painfully on his cane before Henry's chair. Wriothesley behind him. Gardiner bends to pick up the papers and places them on a table beside the King's chair.)

CHAPUYS: He promises no less himself, your Majesty. And he has acknowledged your . . .

HENRY *(With malice)*: Does your leg pain you? *(Chapuys bows silently in agreement, but says nothing.)* Would you sit in your master's presence?

CHAPUYS: No, your Majesty.

HENRY: Would you sit in mine?

CHAPUYS: If your Majesty wishes.

HENRY *(Enjoying this)*: We must endure our infirmities, Chapuys.

CHAPUYS: I hope I may do so with your Majesty's fortitude.

HENRY *(A grunt)*: What has the Emperor acknowledged?

CHAPUYS: Your Majesty's claim to Boulogne, Montreuil and Thérouenne.

HENRY: If I take them from the French, of course.

CHAPUYS: When your Majesty does.

HENRY: And the Pope? Will he acknowledge me as the sovereign head of the English Church? No less?

CHAPUYS: My master is in Rome. He will inform his Holiness.

HENRY: If I wed again, I want no snivelling priest— here or in Rome—crying 'Adulterer!' at me.

CHAPUYS: Twenty-five thousand men, under the banner of the Church, should be your guarantee, sire.

HENRY: Enough for Rome to accept my divorce from Aragon?

GARDINER (*Quickly*): Majesty... (*As Henry turns to him.*) Your Majesty... The Six Articles passed by your Majesty's Parliament are cogent proof of your desire to follow...

HENRY: Are they enough, Chapuys?

CHAPUYS: With respect, your Majesty ... these ... Six Articles ... were approved by you four years ago. They have yet to be enforced. The Church in England does not accept the Sacrament in its fullest sense. It does not regard confession as compulsory. It does not permit private masses, or impose celibacy upon its clergy...

HENRY (*A grin*): Cranmer's wife and children. They irk your flesh, don't they, Gardiner?

GARDINER: Sire ... !

HENRY (*To Chapuys*): I should enforce the Articles?

CHAPUYS: Your Majesty spoke of marrying again...

HENRY: A good and wholesome widow.

GARDINER: I'm sure your Majesty never had a wife more agreeable to your heart than Lady Latimer will prove to be.

HENRY: She's no Pope-Catholic, Chapuys.

CHAPUYS: Your Majesty's consort, as much as your people, will surely observe these Articles you have enforced.

(*Henry says nothing. He chews on a thumb-nail, staring at Chapuys. Then he looks at Gardiner, who speaks as if on cue.*)

GARDINER: God send you both long life, and much joy in each other.

HENRY: Long life we may indeed expect from God. The joy in each other must be of our own making. (*And then another grin.*) But what if she has refused me?

(*Cut to:*)

8

Exterior. The gardens at Hampton Court. Day.

(*Seymour is running up an avenue of yew towards camera. He stops and looks to his left. As he looks to his right and smiles. Cut to: Long shot his point of view. Catherine is sitting on the wall of a pool, back to camera. Cut to: Catherine holding a small book of devotions, and reading intently. Seymour comes into shot, a beat, and he sits beside her. He closes the book in her lap and takes her hands.*)

SEYMOUR (*Chidingly*): Kate . . .

CATHERINE: I thought your brother would pursue me himself, and talk of duty. Or that he'd send mine to scold me. Are you a volunteer?

SEYMOUR: I came on my own prompting.

CATHERINE: Thomas, why can you never be honest?

SEYMOUR: I would have you wed the King. What could be more honest than that?

CATHERINE: A rose you sent me once. When my Lord Latimer died. You sent me a rose, and walked beside me at Court. Touching your sword. You sang to me and played the lute.

SEYMOUR (*Releasing her hands*): If you wish me to say I love you, I will. But if you love me, Kate, you must wed the King.

CATHERINE: I'd rather your brother had come. Or Cranmer. They'd have only talked of the love of God.

SEYMOUR (*Crudely*): And if the sight of the King offends you, close your eyes!

CATHERINE (*Gently*): Thomas . .

SEYMOUR: There'll be more offence in the fires which Gardiner will light at Smithfield. What's an old man's body to that blasphemy?

CATHERINE: Are you afraid?

SEYMOUR (*Withdrawing*): Madam!

CATHERINE: Or are you bold enough to think I'd turn my marriage ring into a coronet for you? (*Hand on his arm.*) Thomas, the sight of the King doesn't offend me. He's old, and lonely.

SEYMOUR: Then marry him in pity, madam!

CATHERINE: And if I won't, would you marry me, Thomas?

SEYMOUR (*A long, scowling beat*): I love you. I've always loved you. But before God, Kate, I tell you this. If I marry you now you've refused him, I shall in time hate you!

(*Close shot Catherine, there are tears in her eyes now.*)

CATHERINE: I'd not expected more. Be easy Thomas. I told the King that I would wed him.

(*Two shot favouring Seymour. With a smile of almost boyish delight, he seizes her hands and presses them to his lips.*

Cut to:)

9

Exterior. Outside the upper oratory, Hampton Court. Day.

(*Full shot as the double doors from the corridor to the oratory are swung open from the inside by two Halberdiers. Somers bursts out, turning jingling cartwheels past the camera.*

He is followed by Henry and Catherine. The King walks slowly, in a kind of majestic agony, his great body swinging from side to side. There is a simple, almost sly smile on his face, and his eyes are turned to Catherine whose hand rests on his arm. Her face is calm, empty.

Behind them, in his canonicals, is Gardiner who has just celebrated the marriage. He is followed by the

King's children. The boy Edward first, and then Mary and Elizabeth, walking together.

Finally a few ladies and gentlemen, among whom is Seymour. He steps away into a window alcove.

Seymour stares at the departing wedding group. He raises a pomander of gold to his nostrils and breathes it, one corner of his mouth lifting.

Mix to:)

10

Interior. The King's bedchamber, Hampton Court. Night.

(Henry, elephantine in a nightshirt and nightcap, sitting up in bed with his back against the pillows. On his face is a scowl of disappointment and suspicion, and his eyes are following somebody about the room.

Cut to:

Catherine, Henry's point of view. In a fur-trimmed red gown she is fussing about the room, picking up Henry's discarded clothing. Pan her to the bed with a short cloak which she puts about his shoulders. He pushes it from him angrily.

She takes a cup of wine from the table nearby and hands it to him. He takes it and without drinking looks at her over the rim.)

HENRY: Madam, do you think I wed a nurse this morning?

CATHERINE: Drink the wine, my Lord. It will be cold tonight.

HENRY (*Darkly*): Aye . . . no doubt.

(*And he drinks. Catherine sits beside the bed on a small chair, taking a small manuscript book from the table. She opens it, and then looks up to him.*)

CATHERINE: My Lord, I would ask a favour.

HENRY (*Cocking an eye*): Is it jewels?

CATHERINE: No, my Lord, I want no jewels. But the ladies of my privy chamber . . .

HENRY: You haven't any.

CATHERINE: No, my Lord, I haven't. Have you finished the wine?

HENRY: No.

CATHERINE: It's too hot, perhaps?

HENRY: Don't cosset me, madam. What of your ladies?

CATHERINE: I wish to choose them myself.

HENRY (*Suspicious again*): Some withered lemons, no doubt?

CATHERINE: By your favour, my Lord. I would have my sister, the Lady Herbert.

HENRY (*A sigh*): Aye. I know.

CATHERINE: And my cousin, german, the Lady Lane.

HENRY (*Brightening*): A sweet lass. I remember.

CATHERINE: Who loves young Knevet, a lieutenant at the Tower.

HENRY: Kate, now that we're speaking of love . . .

CATHERINE: And lastly the Lady Tyrwhitt.

HENRY: A dragon.

CATHERINE: A good heart, sire. May they serve me?

HENRY (*A sigh*): Aye . . . (*Catherine opens the little book and begins to read.*) But speaking of serving . . . (*And then, astonished.*) What are you doing now?

CATHERINE: Reading, my Lord.

HENRY: By Saint Mary, you try my patience . . .

CATHERINE: They're some pieties of my own composition. I've called them *Lamentations of a sinner.*

HENRY: And what in the name of God, sweet Kate, can you know of sin?

CATHERINE: Shall I read to you, my Lord?

HENRY: Aye, read to me. I've forgotten what else I had in mind.

CATHERINE (*Reading*): 'Mine evils and miseries are so many, and so great, that they can accuse me even to my face. Oh, how miserably and wretchedly am I confounded, when for the multitude and greatness of my sins I am compelled to accuse myself?' (*Close shot Henry staring with growing bewilderment.*) 'Was it not a marvellous unkindness when God did speak to me, that I would not answer him . . .'

(*Two shot as Henry leans forward and grasps Catherine's hand.*)

HENRY: Kate . . . Kate, my wife . . .

CATHERINE: My Lord?

HENRY: Is it not also a marvellous unkindness when the King your husband did speak to you, and you would not answer?

CATHERINE: I've displeased you, my Lord?

HENRY: Sweet Kate, how can I be displeased with the journey when I've yet to set out?

CATHERINE: Will you take some more wine, my Lord?

(*With a quick, brutal movement, Henry pulls her from the chair to the bed by his side.*)

HENRY: Madam, I would remind you of a promise you made when we were wed today.

CATHERINE: My Lord?

HENRY: It was, if you recall, to be 'bon air and buxom in bed'.

CATHERINE (*Almost inaudible*): Sire . . .

HENRY (*His face gentling, his voice soft*): I disgust you, Kate. I am gross. I'm old. I disgust you.

CATHERINE (*A beat*): No, my Lord . . .

HENRY: Then be not afraid of me. There's nothing to fear in love, Kate. I'm an old campaigner, and couch a lance like a gentleman.

(*Slowly Henry pulls her down to him, his arms encircling her.*

Mix to:)

11

Interior. Outside the bedchamber door. Later.

(High angle. Somers, arms folded, mouth open, as he leans against the jamb asleep. Behind him the door opens, revealing the skirt of Catherine's nightgown, her bare feet.)

CATHERINE (*Voice, softly*): Master Somers . . . (*And again.*) Master Somers!

(Somers awakes, looks up and frowns. As he gets to his feet. Two shot Catherine and Somers. Her hair is loose, falling over her shoulders.)

SOMERS: My Lady?

CATHERINE: The King is fatigued . . .

(Cut to:)

12

Interior. The King's bedchamber. Night.

(Close shot Henry, beard and hair ruffled, his eyes bright. He looks off and calls impatiently.)

HENRY: Kate . . . !

(Cut to:)

13

Interior. Outside the bedchamber door. Night.

(*Two shot Catherine and Somers.*)

CATHERINE (*A smile, a glance over her shoulder*): Yes, my Lord ... (*To Somers.*) Bring his Majesty some wine. . . .

SOMERS (*A grin*): Aye, my Lady!

HENRY (*Off*): Kate!

(*Catherine turns to the door. As it closes behind her cut to :*)

14

Exterior. Countryside near Hampton Court. Day.

(*Low angle, Henry on a horse, his right arm crooked, a hooded falcon on his fist. As the shot opens he is unslipping the lace of the hood and yelling.*)

HENRY: A la volée!

(*The falcon goes up. Cut to: Mounted group. Henry, Catherine, Hertford and others. They are looking up, their eyes following the climb of the falcon, and dropping as the bird stoops.*)

She stoops!

(*Henry plunges his spurs into his horse and moves off. The rest follow. Pan them away. Cut to: High angle from hillside. Below, the Royal Party is streaming away. Pan right to Seymour, also mounted, biting at his gauntlet and looking down to the riders. He moves down the hillside. Pan with him and Mix to: Full shot a glade. Catherine is approaching camera alone. She hears hooves behind her and pulls in her horse, turning it. Cut to: Seymour rides up to Catherine and halts beside her. She is alarmed, looks over her shoulder, and is about to ride off, when he takes her bridle, restraining her. He smiles at her boldly, for a moment or two, then looks down the glade.)*

SEYMOUR: You've put life into him, I'll swear to that. This is the first time he's been in the saddle for a year or more. (*Turning to her.*) Are you happy?

CATHERINE: I'm content, Thomas.

SEYMOUR: He doesn't abuse you?

CATHERINE: He's gentle.

SEYMOUR: Gentle? That mountain of lard and stinking sores!

(In a cold fury, Catherine raises her crop to strike him. He catches her arm, bringing his horse close to hers. A beat. He releases her wrist and slips an arm about her waist, looking into her eyes.)

Fore God, I believe he's put life into you too! (*He laughs, releasing her.*) Did you think I'd come to abduct you, Kate?

CATHERINE: What do you want?

SEYMOUR: To remind you that you're no bumpkin's wife.

CATHERINE: You should remind yourself of that!

SEYMOUR: We made you a queen, Kate. Have you forgotten you stand between us and the Pope-Catholic?

CATHERINE: I'll not plot for you.

SEYMOUR (*Growing anger*): The King goes to war to win himself the Pope's pardon. Will you see us burn and do nothing?

CATHERINE: You burn already, with ambition.

SEYMOUR: If he dies in Flanders . . .

CATHERINE: No!

SEYMOUR (*Surprised*): He means that much? (*A shrug.*) So much the better. But if he dies, Kate, before you've done your work . . .

CATHERINE: I'll do no work!

SEYMOUR (*Persisting*): . . . Gardiner will have young Edward set aside and the crown on Mary's cunning head.

CATHERINE: She would not . . .

SEYMOUR: She would. And fill the kingdom with priests. They'd send you to the stake, my Lady, with the rest of us.

CATHERINE: He won't die!

SEYMOUR: Not yet, please God. Not before you've persuaded him to name my brother Protector of Edward, and myself his Master of Horse. (*When she says nothing, his tone changes.*) Kate . . . are you out of love with those who cherish you?

(*Catherine stares at him with anger and contempt for this cynical appeal. From off there is the sound of hooves. They turn to it.*)

CATHERINE: Gracious Mother of God!

(Cut to: Their point of view. Henry is riding up with an equerry. Cut to: Group, as Henry comes up, his face blank with suspicion and anger.)

HENRY: What dalliance is this?

SEYMOUR *(Pulling off his hat and bending over his saddle)*: Your Majesty ...

HENRY: Aye, my Majesty ... and what assignation have you with my Majesty's wife, Sirrah?

CATHERINE: My Lord ...

HENRY: Be quiet, madam!

CATHERINE: Nay, sire, I will not!

HENRY *(Astonished by her defiance)*: Madam!

CATHERINE: I'll speak before you do your conscience hurt.

HENRY: You talk of *my* conscience?

CATHERINE: I do, for it's as sacred to me as my own.

HENRY *(A glowering frown at Seymour, then to Catherine)*: Well?

CATHERINE: This gentleman ...

HENRY: This *gentleman* ...

SEYMOUR: By God's most precious soul ... !

HENRY: Don't browbeat me with your braggart oaths! Haven't I made you rich enough? Have I filled your purse with monk's gold so that you may now covet my wife?

CATHERINE: Henry ... !

467

HENRY: Madam! That name is for our closet only.

CATHERINE: My Lord . . . this gentleman came to me that I might plead with you on his behalf.

HENRY: Hah!

CATHERINE: It's true, my Lord. He wishes to serve you, and begged me secure him some post abroad in your cause.

(*Close shot Seymour, astonishment and then anger. Henry is now less certain of his suspicions. He looks from Catherine to Seymour, studying him keenly.*)

HENRY: Abroad you say?

SEYMOUR (*Making the best of it*): I tire of England, your Majesty.

HENRY: Or a woman? Eh?

SEYMOUR: I wish to serve your Majesty.

HENRY (*Turning to Catherine and taking her bridle:*) Sweet Kate . . . such things need not concern you.

CATHERINE: My Lord . . .

HENRY: No, come away . . . the hawks aren't taking the lure. Come and charm them.

CATHERINE (*Firmly*): My Lord, I beseech you, send this eager gentleman where he desires.

HENRY (*Sensing something in her tone*): Has he offended you?

CATHERINE: No, my Lord, but we shall surely offend him if we reject his honest loyalty.

HENRY (*At last*): So be it. (*Turns to Seymour.*) Will you leave this week. (*Speechless with chagrin,*

Seymour can only bow.) You may go with Paget to
the Emperor. And secure quarters for my Army.

(*Close shot Catherine, a small cold smile of unforgiv-
ing triumph. Group, as Henry, Catherine and the
equerry ride off, leaving Seymour bent over his
saddle in a bow. Seymour straightens his body, looking off. His lips are drawn back over his teeth in a
snarl of fury and frustration. He swings his horse
about savagely and strikes it with his crop, as it
gallops off down the glade. Hold on it and mix to:*)

15

Exterior. The gatehouse, Hampton Court. Day.

*Low angle, trumpeter, raising his trumpet to his lips.
As he sounds a bright call pan up along the instru-
ment to:*

*Low angle, Henry. He is suspended by a rope from a
scaffold. He wears full body-armour except for his
helmet, and his white-fringed face is flushed above
the lobster-shell of his cuirass. His fat legs, in their
shining greaves, are straddled wide.*

Cut to:

Man at a winch. He looks up, and begins to unwind.

Cut to:

*Low angle, Henry as he comes slowly down, legs
wide, into the bucket saddle of a great shire warhorse.
A servant stands at the horse's head, holding it
steady.*

Cut to:

Group before the gatehouse. Beyond Henry are other riders, and fluttering pennons—a suggestive angle this of an Army ready, out of sight.

By the horse is Catherine. She is holding young Edward's hand, and has the other arm about Elizabeth's shoulders. Mary stands behind them, and some paces back are Catherine's ladies.

There is a noise of many voices off, the sound of hooves, barking of dogs and whinnying.

As Henry gathers the reins with a smile of satisfaction, and the trumpeter sounds again.

Cut to:

16

Interior. A room in the gatehouse, Hampton Court. Day.

(Two shot at an open lattice window—Gardiner and Chapuys. They are looking down at the scene below. As the sound of the trumpet fades away, and is followed by a distant roll of drums, Chapuys smiles at Gardiner.)

CHAPUYS: You were right, Bishop. It's taken a year or more, but she's made a warrior of him. In faith, King and horse are a mighty host in themselves.

GARDINER: She is the Devil's agent.

CHAPUYS: Not yours, my Lord?

GARDINER: No, sir. The Devil's. And for the glory of God I would not have it otherwise. She has ordered a translation of Erasmus' paraphrases on the Testament, and persuaded the King that it should be placed in every parish church. (*Looks down through the window.*) Cranmer and Latimer grow bold in her shadow.

CHAPUYS: You've not been idle, yourself, my Lord. I saw the ashes at Smithfield on my way here. Who were they?

GARDINER (*A shrug*): They were guilty of keeping heretical books.

(*Chapuys raises a pomander to his nose with a faint expression of disgust, and looks out of the window again.*

Cut to:)

17

Exterior. The gatehouse, Hampton Court. Day.

(*Catherine is now standing by Henry's stirrup. He smiles at her.*)

HENRY: Take counsel with Cranmer when I am in Flanders. Wriothesley is a dullard, but if used wisely he's a diligent Chancellor.

CATHERINE: And Bishop Gardiner?

HENRY (*A little coldly*): He's God's servant, and mine.

CATHERINE: Who burns men for keeping books . . .

HENRY (*Gently remonstrating*): Kate . . . Kate . . . (*He turns from Catherine, looking off and lifting himself as best he can in the saddle. He calls.*) Be it known . . . ! And ordered by me . . . ! That in my absence this kingdom shall be ruled as Regent by my Sovereign Lady the Queen!

(*Cut to:*)

18

Interior. A room in the gatehouse, Hampton Court. Day.

(*Two shot, Chapuys and Gardiner listening to the King.*)

HENRY (*Voice over*): Into her hands I entrust the safety of my people, the honour of my name, and the good keeping and education of my children!

(*A trumpet, the sound of cheering off. When they die away, Chapuys turns to Gardiner.*)

CHAPUYS: The education of his children ... perhaps you should tell the King to study his wife's library.

GARDINER: She will betray herself.

CHAPUYS (*Curious*): And would you burn her, my Lord?

GARDINER: To save the Church? Yes. And I would weep for her.

CHAPUYS: Your compassion humbles me, my Lord.

(*As Chapuys raises the pomander to his nose again. Cut to:*)

19

Exterior. The gatehouse, Hampton Court. Day.

(*Henry is holding his son, Edward, high in the air. A beat, he kisses the boy on both cheeks and lowers him.*

Catherine holds the King's helmet, a servant takes the boy from Henry and moves off.

Catherine hands Henry the helmet which he crooks in his arm. He puts out a hand.)

HENRY : Fare well, sweet heart.

CATHERINE (*Taking Henry's hand and pressing it to her cheek*): God keep you, my Lord!

(*Henry gently releases his hand and gathers the reigns. The great horse backs ponderously and turns. Trumpets sound again off. Full shot Catherine. Tears in her eyes as she looks into camera. She puts out her arms and gathers Edward and Elizabeth to her side. Slow mix to:*)

20

Interior. The Queen's Chamber, Hampton Court. Night.

(*Buckler, the Queen's secretary, is seated at a small table, scratching on paper with a quill. A candle beside him. He finishes, looks up into camera, dipping the quill into an ink-horn.*)

BUCKLER : My Lady . . . ? (*Catherine is seated beside the table. She is bending over to Elizabeth, who is seated on the floor at her feet guiding the girl's fingers at her needlework. Edward is also on the floor, asleep, his head against Catherine's gown. Beyond, Mary sits erect in a chair, reading. And beside her is Lady Lane. Again* :) My Lady . . . !

(*Catherine smiles at Elizabeth and looks up to Buckler, her hand going to Edward's head and resting there gently.*)

CATHERINE : Your pardon, Master Buckler . . . we'll continue . . . (*A thought, she dictates.*) 'It is now many months since your Majesty . . .' No, strike that out. 'This distance of time and days is so long and so many . . . yet the want of your Majesty's presence is such that I can take no pleasure in anything . . .'

BUCKLER (*Finishes, looks up*): Yes, my Lady?

CATHERINE (*Continuing to dictate*): 'Thus, my sweet Lord, love and affection compel me to desire your presence . . .' (*Edward stirs and sighs. Catherine looks down at him, smiling. She bends, gathering him in her arms and looking across the room to Lady Lane, who rises and comes to her. Catherine kisses the sleepy boy on the lips.*)

God rest you, Edward. (*A beat, then Edward quickly throws his arms about her neck, hugging her, and as quickly releasing her. Lady Lane takes him away. Elizabeth has also risen, and now she places her embroidery on the table, where Buckler irritably moves it out of his way. Elizabeth, smiling, presents her cheek to Catherine. Kissing her.*) God rest you, Elizabeth.

Another smile, Elizabeth curtseys low, and leaves. All this has been watched by Mary with a calm unemotional stare. As if she is aware of what the Princess is thinking, Catherine gives her a bright, warm smile, before turning back to Buckler.) Again, your pardon, Master Secretary . . . I shall persevere . . . (*A thought, and then.*) 'God, the knower of secrets can judge these words to be not only written with ink, but most truly impressed upon my heart . . .'

(*Mary, turns back to her book. Catherine watches Buckler's scratching pen. Door is opened by a servant.*)

SERVANT: Madam . . .

(*Two shot Buckler and Catherine. As they look towards the door, Buckler puts down the pen with an exclamation of disgust. Full shot door, as Seymour pushes past the servant. Pan him across the room to Catherine. He carries his feathered hat in his hand. His clothes and high riding boots are stained with mud. He strides to Catherine and goes down on one knee, his head bent.*)

SEYMOUR: Your Majesty . . .

(*Close shot Catherine, her face calm and still with the sudden shock of his appearance. And then.*)

CATHERINE: What does this mean, Sir Thomas?

SEYMOUR (*Rising. A glance at Buckler and Mary, then to Catherine*): Your Majesty's pardon for this intrusion. I come to you from the King . . . (*He pulls a letter from the cuff of his gauntlet and holds it out. As she takes it.*) And more, by word of mouth, for your ear alone. (*Catherine is looking down at the letter. She does not speak. Seymour turns impatiently to Buckler.*) Sir . . . if you please! (*Buckler rises, clucking to himself, gathering papers. He bobs a bow to the Queen, glowers at Seymour and leaves. Seymour turns and looks at Mary, who has remained seated. To Catherine, eyes on Mary.*) Madam . . . (*Now Catherine looks up, follows Seymour's eyes to Mary. She frowns. His eyes still on Mary.*) For your ears alone, madam.

CATHERINE: Mary... (*Mary rises and comes to Catherine, presenting her cheek. Kissing it.*) God rest you, Mary. (*And she places her hand gentle, kindly, on Mary's other cheek for a second.*)

Mary goes, after one long, cold look at Seymour. His eyes follow her to the door, then he swings round, dropping on his knee again before Catherine.)

SEYMOUR: Two years!

(*He lifts the hem of her skirt and kisses it.*)

CATHERINE (*Coldly and unmoved*): Get up! (*Seymour rises, smiling.*) You're still mad and reckless. What message have you from the King?

SEYMOUR: None but that love-note... (*A nod to the letter, and then, when she is about to protest.*) I would see you alone, that's all. I've ridden from Dover since morning, and in no mood to wait on you like a servant. Kate, you've become a beauty... !

CATHERINE: How is the King?

SEYMOUR (*A grin*): In a black humour. He serves his Popish masters like a Paladin. Captures a town or two, and is given the plates to lick afterwards. A faithful dog.

CATHERINE (*Rising*): You're the dog!

SEYMOUR: I'm an Englishman! And one with no taste for a sick King's fan...

CATHERINE (*Quickly*): He's ill?

SEYMOUR: Ill? No. Camp-fever and aching bones. But not ill. Just older than he thinks.

CATHERINE: Poor Henry!

SEYMOUR: Poor England! Kate ... Have you no notion of what is happening?

CATHERINE: He's ill!

SEYMOUR: By God's most precious soul! Madam . . . He's in debt to the Emperor and the Pope-Catholics. They demand an end to what they call his soft treatment of our Church. They want more of Gardiner's fires, and there's talk . . . (*He stops, looking at her.*) There's talk of him taking a new queen.

CATHERINE (*She sits slowly, staring at him*): A new queen . . . ? He would set me aside?

SEYMOUR: There's no danger of it ... yet. He all but throttled the fool who spoke of it openly. But Kate . . . when he comes, you must pers . . .

CATHERINE (*Rising again quickly*): He's coming?

SEYMOUR: By tomorrow's tide from Boulogne. He'll be here the day after.

(*Close shot of Catherine.*)

CATHERINE: Oh, Thomas . . . Blessed be God! My Lord is coming home!

(*Cut to:*)

21

Interior. A corridor in Hampton Court. Day.

(*Long shot as the doors burst open at the end of the corridor, and Henry comes through them with a bellow.*)

HENRY: Kate . . . ! (*Two halberdiers by the windows spring to attention. Henry advances on camera stumbling, staggering, discarding cap, gauntlets, cloak and sword. Two terrified servants follow, picking them up. Pan Henry by to the door of Catherine's chamber.*) Kate . . . !

(*Hardly pausing, he flings it open and enters. Cut to*:)

22

Interior. The Queen's chamber, Hampton Court Day.

(*Henry standing in the open door in the background. Catherine in foreground, her back to camera. A beat as they stare at each other and say nothing. Then Henry slams the door behind him. Full shot Catherine. She is smiling, her eyes wet.*)

CATHERINE: My Lord . . . (*She goes down on the floor, her head bowed. Two shot, as Henry limps towards her and looks down. He is tired and travel-stained. He bends—with pain—taking her shoulders and raising her. They look into each others eyes and then he suddenly embraces her in a great bear-hug of rough gentleness. Hold for an instant. They do not move. Her voice muffled against him.*) Oh, my Lord . . . *Bien venu!*

HENRY (*Thickly*): Kate . . . my Lady Kate!

(*Slowly he releases the embrace, holding her arms still. She touches his face with her hand.*)

CATHERINE: My Lord . . . you are ill?

HENRY: Tired. No more . . . (*But he allows her to take him to a chair. He slumps in it with a great sigh, his eyes closing. She crouches beside him, loosening his* *shoes. He opens his eyes and looks down at her. In a* *passion of longing, that can do no more at this* *moment than move his hand, he locks his fist in her* *hair. It falls about her shoulders and she looks up,* *smiling. He answers the smile. There is no need for* *words, and then*:) I would sleep . . .

CATHERINE: Yes, my Lord.

HENRY: And then eat.

(*Cut to*:)

23

Interior. The King's privy chamber, Hampton Court. *Evening.*

(*Close shot a roast bird on a silver plate. Henry's* *hands come into shot, one holding the bird, the other* *sawing off a leg with a knife. Pull back to two shot of* *Henry and Catherine. He sits alone at a small table,* *wearing a fur robe, eating heartily, but delicately, and* *with frequent use of a napkin. Catherine sits beside* *the table, watching him with simple pleasure.*)

HENRY: Did they . . . (*Swallowing, then using the nap-* *kin.*) Did they tell you? How I took Boulogne?

CATHERINE (*Proudly*): Yes, my Lord.

HENRY: By land and sea. While the Emperor's men were robbing farm-yards. And looting the Dauphin's train at Chateau Thierry. (*A grin, relishing the* *memory.*) I was two days in armour, Kate. Are you proud of this old body of mine?

CATHERINE (*An affectionate smile*): I am proud of

479

you, Henry. (*And then, concerned.*) But my Lord, it has made you ill . . .

HENRY: I could have had Boulogne twenty years ago, but for Wolsey! (*His face clouds suddenly.*) Has Cranmer come?

CATHERINE: No, my Lord.

HENRY: Or Gardiner? I sent word from Dover to get them out of their beds.

CATHERINE: No, my Lord.

HENRY (*Staring at the table with a frown, he turns the knife slowly in his hand, and then stabs the point angrily into the table*): I've been cheated, Kate.

CATHERINE: My Lord!

HENRY: Four days after I took Boulogne, the Emperor signed a treaty with France. He told me he would and I dared him to.

CATHERINE: But why, my Lord?

HENRY: He would have France as his ally now. To crush the Lutherans in his own provinces. (*Looks at her.*) I've kept my bond. They've cheated me! (*Then a shout*). What has Gardiner been doing?

CATHERINE (*Seizing this opportunity boldly*: My Lord, the Bishop of Winchester has been burning heretics.

HENRY (*Puzzled*): So he lights faggots under a shop-keeper or two. And puts a scholar to the rack. But he's my minister of state and . . .

CATHERINE: He strikes at Cranmer through them. And at me.

HENRY: You?

CATHERINE: At me, my Lord.

HENRY (*Swinging round to her and grasping her wrist fiercely*): For what reason, madam?

CATHERINE (*Wincing*): None, my Lord.

HENRY: Must I ask him?

CATHERINE: As your Majesty pleases.

HENRY: I'm not pleased. But, madam, as it pleases you, for what reason?

CATHERINE: He has brought some of my ladies before your council for examination.

HENRY (*Still holding her*): So?

CATHERINE: He accused them of keeping forbidden books. He asked them what I read, what I said, what I am teaching your Majesty's children.

HENRY: What do you teach them, madam?

CATHERINE: To love the charity and goodness of God. To follow His doctrine. To love you and obey you as I do.

(*Henry stares at her. He looks down at the hand he holds, and is suddenly aware of the fierceness of his grip. Impulsively he relaxes the grasp, bends his head and tenderly kisses her open palm.*)

HENRY (*When he looks up, his voice now gentle and loving*): I would as lief be a country gentleman, with a good wife and a hundred acres. And a hand's-span of stout sons to hunt with me. Would you like that, Kate?

CATHERINE: No, my Lord. I would have you King.

HENRY: And thus be Queen.

CATHERINE: And thus love my husband and my country in one gentle soul.

HENRY (*A beat*): Trust no one, Kate . . . no one . . .

CATHERINE: Yet I must trust you, my Lord.

(*A knock at the door. As Henry turns, cut to: Full shot. Behind a bowing servant is Gardiner. He comes forward, the servant retiring. Pan Gardiner to Henry and Catherine.*)

GARDINER (*Bowing*): I rejoice to see your Majesty in such health . . .

HENRY: Where's Cranmer?

GARDINER (*A twist of his lips*): His Grace is . . . ill, sire.

HENRY: If he won't come, then truly he's ill. He's not afraid of you, Gardiner.

GARDINER: All men must fear God's displeasure. And their King's.

HENRY: Am I displeased with him?

(*Gardiner says nothing, but glances uncertainly at Catherine.*)

The Queen stays.

GARDINER (*A bow*): Majesty . . .

HENRY: The Emperor's made peace with France.

GARDINER: And will move with them against the Lutherans.

HENRY: What of his bond to me?

GARDINER (*Gloomily*): Sire, what honour is there in the world now all men are turned against us? We are at war still with France and Scotland, and . . .

HENRY (*Brightening*): Hah, Scotland! Hertford teaches them a lesson. Seven towns, seven monasteries destroyed. Ten score villages and thirteen mills . . .

GARDINER: Your Majesty . . . ! (*And then, gentler.*) Your Majesty, the Pope has been displeased by Hertford's work in Scotland. The Emperor is no longer your friend and ally . . .

HENRY (*Blustering*): I know all this!

GARDINER: It is my duty to tell your Majesty that, in the opinion of your Council, any weakness toward heresy in England may encourage the Emperor and France to move against you. There is a French fleet off the Isle of Wight, and your . . .

HENRY: The opinion of my Council?

GARDINER: Of those who are your Majesty's true and loyal . . .

HENRY (*Sarcastically*): But not Cranmer, of course.

GARDINER (*Suddenly bold*): He should appear before the rest of the Council to answer charges against him!

HENRY: What charges?

GARDINER: His tenderness toward the heretics. His opposition to the Six Articles which your . . .

HENRY: Your witnesses?

GARDINER (*A thin smile*): Sire, no one dares give evidence against a member of your Privy Council whilst he is still free to proceed against them.

CATHERINE: My Lord . . .

HENRY: Be still, madam! (*To Gardiner.*) You would send an Archbishop to the Tower?

GARDINER: Your Majesty, I would consider it my duty to deliver my brother to the stake if he offended God. And thereby be assured of his salvation.

CATHERINE: My Lord, I beseech you! Speak with Cranmer first!

GARDINER (*A polite smile*): My Lady's gentle concern for His Grace is well known, and to her cre . . .

HENRY (*A bellow*): Sirrah!

GARDINER (*Unfrightened*): Your Majesty . . . I did but recall your own words. That affairs of State and Church should best concern the minds of men, and not the hearts of women.

(*Henry for a moment says nothing. He gnaws at a finger-nail, looking from one to the other, and then curtly*:)

HENRY: Very well. He may be examined. But be sure you're right, Sir Bishop. (*A sharp intake of breath from Catherine.*) Now leave us a while. But wait on me. We'll speak later. (*Gardiner bows and goes. Henry looks at Catherine's tight, angry face, and he frowns.*) Madam, will you now dispute with me?

CATHERINE: No, my Lord.

HENRY: Your face is as long as a barber's pole, and your expression as sour as vinegar.

CATHERINE: I'm afraid of him.

HENRY (*A shrug*): Because he examined your foolish ladies?

CATHERINE: And more, my Lord. He arrested a priest from my chapel, and several choristers. His officers have searched my chambers for books ... (*She waits for his protest and is surprised when he appears unmoved.*) My Lord, will you abandon Cranmer?

HENRY (*Begins to tug at a ring on his finger*): If I'm to have every Popish prince at my throat, I may need the friendship of the German Lutherans (*The ring has come off. He looks up at her, a smile.*) And they would trust Cranmer. (*Holds out the ring.*) Send this to him.

CATHERINE (*Taking it*): My Lord?

HENRY: When the Council call him, let him show them that. As a token that they may not proceed without my presence.

CATHERINE (*Puzzled*): When will that be, my Lord?

HENRY: Why, madam, when I choose. (*He smiles at her.*) That's kingly craft, my Lady. I give Gardiner his way, and keep my arm about Cranmer. And thus have two servants still. Two legs upon which, like Colossus, I can straddle this contentious kingdom.

CATHERINE (*Dropping on her knees before him*): My Lord ...

HENRY (*Leaning forward and cupping her chin*): But hark ye, Kate ... (*His voice harder now, almost a threat.*) Remember Saint Paul. Do not dispute with me on matters that are not your concern!

(*Mix to:*)

485

24

Interior. A dungeon at the Tower. Night.

(*High angle close shot, a woman called Anne Askew. Her face is wet with sweat, her hair clinging to her cheeks and forehead. She is unconscious, eyes closed, lips drawn back in an immobilized spasm of agony. Water is thrown upon her, and as her eyes open pull back to group about the rack on which she is stretched. By the wheel an executioner has just thrown the water on her. Beside him stands Anthony Knevet, a young lieutenant of the Tower. He turns towards two men in the background. Wrapped in cloaks against the cold of the dungeon, they are Gardiner and Wriothesley. They are whispering together.*)

KNEVET: My Lords . . . !

(*Two shot of Gardiner and Wriothesley.*)

WRIOTHESLEY: They took a boat on the Thames. Alone. Except for the waterman.

GARDINER: Did you examine the fellow?

WRIOTHESLEY: He said the King jested with Cranmer, 'saying he knew now who was the greatest heretic in Kent. He pulled the depositions we prepared from his sleeve, and showed them to Cranmer.

GARDINER: And then?

WRIOTHESLEY: And then the King told Cranmer to fear nothing while the whole cause was in his hands.

(*Cut to Knevet. He looks down at Anne Askew, a glance of compassion, and then, raising his voice.*)

KNEVET: My Lords . . . She's recovered her senses.

486

(*Two shot Gardiner and Wriothesley.*)

GARDINER (*A look towards Knevet*): We're coming, Master Knevet ... (*To Wriothesley.*) It's the Queen's work.

WRIOTHESLEY: Then we're lost.

GARDINER: No ... She's begun her own betrayal, that's all ... (*Looks off to the rack.*) And needs but a little help from us to complete it. (*Pan them away towards the rack. Cut to: Low angle as Gardiner kneels beside Anne Askew. He wipes her face gently, and she looks at him with wild eyes.*)

(*Softly.*) Mistress Askew ... Will you now confess?

ANNE ASKEW (*Her voice harsh and strained by pain.*) I'll confess my sins to God, and He will hear me with favour, for I am unjustly persecuted!

GARDINER: Will you die so perversely?

ANNE ASKEW: Nay, in innocence! Oh, ye of little faith, can you know the truth?

GARDINER: Madam, who taught you these responses?

ANNE ASKEW: The voice of God whose hand protects me!

(*Full shot group.*)

WRIOTHESLEY: The witch blasphemes!

(*Wriothesley pushes the Executioner aside and grasps the wheel. He turns it a notch. Anne Askew screams. Gardiner looks up and waves an impatient hand. Wriothesley steps away. Gardiner again wipes the woman's face.*)

GARDINER: Mistress Askew, how old are you?

KNEVET: She's twenty-five, my Lord.

GARDINER: And of gentle birth?

ANNE ASKEW: I am born of God's family.

GARDINER: As are we all ... in His sight. Do you know your husband has abandoned you because of your heresy?

ANNE ASKEW: I forgive him!

GARDINER: That heresy having been proved by witnesses?

ANNE ASKEW: I forgive them.

GARDINER: Mistress Askew ... I would be your friend.

ANNE ASKEW: Thus said Judas!

(*Wriothesley makes an angry movement towards the wheel again, but is stopped by Gardiner.*)

GARDINER: Your sins are great, mistress, and you have been condemned ... My child, I can yet secure you the King's pardon.

ANNE ASKEW: I shall not deny the Lord to save myself!

GARDINER: You sent books to the Queen's ladies?

ANNE ASKEW (*A great cry of agony*): I wish to die! Let me die!

GARDINER: My child, it's in the confession you made upon your first examination.

ANNE ASKEW: No . . .

GARDINER: It is recorded.

ANNE ASKEW: Oh, good Christ, succour me!

(*Gardiner sits back and nods to the Executioner, who turns the wheel slightly. There is a great sigh from Anne Askew. Close shot Knevet, reacting with horror and compassion. Two shot Gardiner and Anne Askew as he leans over her, and once more wipes her face.*)

GARDINER: Did you not send books to the Queen also? Did she not smile upon you and call you her friend, and ask you to debate with her?

ANNE ASKEW: I will . . . tell you . . .

GARDINER (*A sharp look up to the others then back to her*): Yes, my child?

ANNE ASKEW: . . . nothing.

(*And she faints again. Gardiner stands up slowly. Pull back to group. Gardiner wipes his hands carefully on the cloth, staring down at the unconscious woman. He lets the cloth fall to the floor and turns to Knevet.*)

GARDINER: She was beautiful?

KNEVET (*Bitterly*): Aye, my Lord! She was beautiful.

GARDINER (*A keen look at the young man, and then to Wriothesley*): Let this officer be relieved of his duty here.

KNEVET (*Grateful*): Thank you, my Lord!

WRIOTHESLEY: And the woman?

GARDINER: She'll admit nothing.

WRIOTHESLEY: I'll turn the wheel again and . . .

489

GARDINER: No! She's in an ecstasy of sin. Would you encourage her? She's condemned, and she'll burn. (*He turns away towards the door, and then pauses by Knevet.*) There is truth in pain, Master Knevet. And salvation in fire for the sinner. Don't reproach yourself.

KNEVET (*Tightly*): No, my Lord.

GARDINER: There's some dalliance between you and one of the Queen's ladies?

KNEVET: Yes, my Lord. The Lady Lane.

GARDINER (*Smiling*): Then tell her what has occurred here.

KNEVET: My Lord! I could not . . .

GARDINER: You're troubled, my son. Then why not find heart's-ease by talking about it with your love?

KNEVET: Yes, my Lord.

(*Gardiner smiles, and gently pats Knevet's shoulder. As he then moves away, mix to:*)

25

Exterior. The gardens at Hampton Court. Day.

(*Close shot Catherine, her pale face registering shock and grief.*)

CATHERINE: Master Knevet saw this?

(*Two shot Catherine and Lady Lane. They are sitting on a bench by a box hedge, each holding a piece of embroidery on which they have been working.*)

LADY LANE: Yes, my Lady.

CATHERINE: And he's an honest man?

LADY LANE: Indeed, my Lady, and much troubled.

(*Catherine turns her head slowly to look off. Cut to her point of view. In the middle distance a group. Henry seated on a chair, Gardiner standing beside him, and two gentlemen behind the chair. Two shot Catherine and Lady Lane. Still looking off Catherine rises; putting out a restraining hand when Lady Lane would rise too. Pan Catherine away towards the King. Cut to: Henry, frowns above his habitual finger-gnawing. At last:*)

HENRY: She confessed nothing of plots against me? Of Surrey? Or his father's complicity? (*Cut to: group. Henry's swollen legs rest on a stool. He is tired, and looks very ill. The two gentlemen are in the background out of earshot.*)

GARDINER: No, your Majesty. But she revealed much of her own heresy and that of others. Where there's heresy we find the camp-followers of treason.

(*Catherine joins them.*)

HENRY: She was put to the rack? (*To Catherine.*) Sit by me, madam.

(*Catherine sits erect on a chair beside Henry, her eyes hard on Gardiner.*)

GARDINER (*A bow to Catherine*): Twice, your Majesty. And thrice examined.

HENRY: And she is to burn?

GARDINER (*A gentle nod*): And also William Morrice, lately your Majesty's Usher. With Sir George Blagge of the Privy Chamber.

HENRY (*Unhappy*): Morrice? He was a good and simple fellow.

GARDINER: Who denounced the Mass, your Majesty. As did the woman Askew.

HENRY: But Blagge? You take away my servants, Gardiner.

GARDINER (*His eyes on Catherine*): *Fiat justitia, sire* . . .

CATHERINE (*Suddenly accepting Gardiner's challenge, and in a high, tight voice*): My Lord Bishop . . . Is it true that Sir Thomas Wriothesley turned the rack himself, and would have Mistress Askew perjure herself by accusing my ladies?

GARDINER (*Feigning hurt as he turns to the King*): Sire . . .

HENRY (*Wearily*): Be silent, madam.

CATHERINE: Nay, my good Lord, for that wouldn't silence my doubts, unless his Grace can do it for me. (*Close shot Henry, an angry look. Close shot Gardiner, a glance at Henry, then back to Catherine with a smile.*)

GARDINER (*Pleasantly*): Doubts, my Lady?

(*Close shot Catherine.*)

CATHERINE (*Boldly and unaware of the King's suspicious stare*): Aye, sir . . . That God wishes us to abuse each other so foully. That His truth can be truly discovered in the lies which a poor woman tells in agony.

(*Three shot.*)

GARDINER (*Still smiling politely*): Your Majesty knew this . . . poor woman?

CATHERINE: No, sir. But I've heard her gently spoken of.

HENRY (*Sharply*): By whom?

CATHERINE (*Surprised*): Why, by you, my Lord. You said she might be more foolish than vicious.

HENRY: By St. Mary, I did not!

CATHERINE: But you . . . (*And stops.*)

GARDINER (*Smoothly*): My Lady, perhaps the thought is your own? Perhaps compassion has betrayed you into error?

CATHERINE: God knows my sins and faults, Lord Bishop! I doubt He would agree with you and include compassion among them.

HENRY (*Irritably*): Madam, if the wicked woman was racked, it was by God's will and in God's name!

CATHERINE: I know nothing of her wickedness, my Lord. But surely it is wicked to argue that Christ's love is made manifest by the rack and the fire?

(*Henry stares at her, astounded, unable to speak. Fearing that Catherine may now see that she has gone too far, and draw back Gardiner gently urges her on.*)

GARDINER: My Lady would not agree that, in preaching her heresy openly, the woman was endangering the safety of this kingdom?

CATHERINE: She preached the Scriptures, sir. There's nothing perilous in that.

GARDINER: You've heard her preach, my Lady? Or read her writings?

CATHERINE (*A beat*): I've read something of what she's written.

HENRY: By Heaven, madam, I knew nothing of this!

CATHERINE (*Quickly*): My Lord, there never was a greater need than now for a good doctrine that will benefit all men. Must we burn those who honestly search for it?

HENRY: Aye, if they seek also to corrupt this kingdom and destroy the Throne.

CATHERINE (*Passionately*): You are our Moses who delivered us from the bondage of the Pharaoh of Rome. If there's ignorance and blindness among us still, by the truth of God's word alone should you instruct us, and set us on the path of righteousness.

HENRY (*An aloof, terrible calm*): Madam, are you teaching me my duty?

CATHERINE: My Lord, the Devil is the sower of sedition. The woman Askew loved God. How can that be treason?

HENRY (*Spacing the words*): Madam, do not dispute this with me!

(*Catherine now realizes the danger she has placed herself in. She is silent, lowering her head, yet she has not gone far enough for Gardiner.*)

GARDINER: My Lady, the woman was examined, tested and tried by Church and Law, by the high officers of God and the King your husband. Therefore, is it not impertinent for a woman to question so supreme a judgment?

CATHERINE (*She is stung into a last indiscretion by the taunt*): Sir, the Pharisees also waxed haughty and proud, taking themselves to be men of greater virtue because of their rank!

GARDINER (*Innocently*): Am I a Pharisee, my Lady? If this be so, what must be the King whose appointed Minister I am?

CASHERINE (*Turning too late to the King.*) My Lord, I meant no offence to you . . .

HENRY: Hold your tongue! (*Catherine bows her head silently. Henry forces himself up in his chair, wincing at the pain in his legs. His face is distorted by anger and injured vanity.*) You do offend me, madam! Your pious face offends me! I am offended by your prattling, insolent tongue! (*When she does not move.*) Well, madam? Must I have my guards remove you from my sight?

(*Catherine rises, shaken. Her face white and empty, she bows deeply and leaves. Henry glowers after her, then lowers himself back into the chair with a groan of pain.*) A fine season this, when women would be clerks. And I'm to be taught my duty by my wife! (*He looks at Gardiner sourly.*) And you, sir? Are you going to be silent now?

GARINER: My Lord . . . If I cannot speak it . . . No, it's of no consequence.

HENRY: Go on.

GARDINER: Sire . . . If I cannot speak it is from astonishment . . .

HENRY: What?

GARDINER: . . . that the Queen should so far forget herself to stand in argument with you. Since your

495

Assertio on the heresies of Luther you have been above all princes in learned judgment on matters of religion.

HENRY (*Moving painfully*): My lady wife ... (*A scowl off*.) ... thinks not. There's a comfort in my old age, Gardiner. To be taught theology by a woman!

GARDINER: Sire ...

HENRY (*Turning from his self-pity*): What now?

GARDINER: Sire ... the love you bear me encourages me to speak frankly. Any prince who tolerates malapert insolence from his subjects, whatever their station, imperils not only his throne but his salvation in Christ.

HENRY (*A long hard look*): And how honest have you been with me, Sir Bishop? Did the woman Askew name the Queen?

GARDINER (*With convincing embarrassment*): Sire ... she would not deny that she had spoken with her Majesty ... (*And then, with unconvincing reassurance.*) But we know the Queen's goodness and charity. If these virtues have led her into a betrayal of your Majesty's trust, I'm sure ...

HENRY: You examined her ladies?

GARDINER (*A sigh*): I did, your Majesty. And among their papers I found much that was both controversial and heretical.

HENRY: But you found nothing against the Queen in those papers?

GARDINER (*Sadly*): Sire, there were matters both equivocal and unequivocal that require her explanation.

HENRY: Touching upon what?

496

GARDINER: Upon religion and government, your Majesty. (*He waits for comment, gets none, and continues.*) Those doctrines which we heard her Majesty stiffly maintain, do in their extremes, and among malcontents, disallow government by princes and argue that all things ought to be held in common. This is ultimate heresy, your Majesty.

HENRY: The Queen said that!

GARDINER: By implication, your Majesty, and not in full knowledge of the heresy. (*Then, blandly confident.*) But upon her examination by your Council, she'll recognize her innocent errors, and satisfy your Majesty's painful doubts.

HENRY: I've not said she may be examined.

GARDINER: No, your Majesty ... but how else—for her own salvation—can we find the root of her obstinate and perverse opposition.

HENRY (*Resentfully agreeing*): By Saint Mary, it is obstinate and perverse!

GARDINER: But in the Tower your Majesty's Council will discreetly lead her to a discovery of her innocent foolishness.

HENRY (*More surprised than angry*): The Tower?

GARDINER: For her own safety, sire. That she may have solitude to reflect, and be free of those who would influence her against you.

HENRY (*Weakening*): Is it necessary?

GARDINER: Alas, my Lord ...

HENRY (*At last*): Am I ever to be betrayed by those I love? So be it. Let her be examined.

(*Hold on Henry and mix to:*)

26

Interior. Gardiner's chamber at Hampton Court. Night.

(Close shot a signet ring being pressed into black wax at the foot of a document, and beside a larger seal of red wax below Henry's signature. A candle is fluttering on the table. Cut to: Wriothesley, looking down, the light of the candle moving over his troubled face.)

WRIOTHESLEY: I like it not.

(Two shot Gardiner and Wriothesley. The Bishop is sitting at the table, and having sealed the document is now folding it and closing it with another seal. He does not look up to Wrothesley.)

GARDINER: Your liking or not-liking is of no consequence.

WRIOTHESLEY: You go too far.

GARDINER *(Looking up)*: Too far? I tread God's path that others may follow. And those who would hinder me must be struck down in His name.

WRIOTHESLEY: But the Queen . . .

GARDINER: You were hot for her removal once. And those behind her.

WRIOTHESLEY: The King's sick to die. That he's still alive each morning is a miracle. If he dies before this is done, Cranmer and the Seymours will have our heads *(Correcting himself with a twist of a smile at Gardiner's expense.)* My head, as a gentleman. You will burn.

GARDINER *(Calmly)*: I hope I shall die in the knowledge that I have served God faithfully. (*He holds out the document.*)

WRIOTHESLEY (*Obstinately*): Find another to serve the warrant.

GARDINER: The hunt is up, my Lord Chancellor, and you are the King's huntsman.

WRIOTHESLEY: Find another.

GARDINER: If I can secure the King's warrant for his wife, I can also secure one for his Chancellor.

WRIOTHESLEY (*A beat, he surrenders, taking the warrant and thrusting it into the cuff of his gauntlet*): When shall I take her to the Tower?

GARDINER: The day after tomorrow. There is much to prepare. (*As Wriothesley still hesitates.*) Well?

WRIOTHESLEY (*Touching the warrant*): It bears the King's seal?

GARDINER: And his hand. You saw them.

WRIOTHESLEY: She is the Queen.

GARDINER (*Smiling*): There's been a great harvesting of queens in our time, Wriothesley. Were you this faint-hearted to garner Catherine Howard?

WRIOTHESLEY: The King . . .

GARDINER: . . . approaches Almighty judgment. He is afraid of death, and would transfer his sins to others before he departs. He will not change his mind.

WRIOTHESLEY (*Stubbornly*): I like it not.

499

GARDINER: So you have said. And so I shall remember.

(*Wriothesley recognizes the threat. He straightens his back and turns away to the door. Cut to*:)

27

Corridor outside Gardiner's chamber. Night.

(*Long shot, Wriothesley coming out of Gardiner's room and approaching camera, the warrant in his cuff.*

Lady Lane comes into shot from behind camera and goes down the corridor past Wriothesley. He stops; a beat, he turns about.

Close shot Wriothesley, biting his lip as he stares, and then, deciding.)

WRIOTHESLEY: My Lady . . .

(*Lady Lane, stops and turns into camera.*)

LADY LANE: Sir . . . ?

(*Two shot, Wriothesley and Lady Lane, he is foreground back to camera, she beyond. A beat, he raises a hand discreetly and she comes to him. He takes her arm and draws her into an alcove. He cannot for a moment, decide what to say. Puzzled*:)

Sir . . . ?

WRIOTHESLEY: My Lady . . . the Queen your mistress . . .

LADY LANE: Aye, sir?

WRIOTHESLEY (*Stiffly, a glance over his shoulder*): I must do my duty. I cannot escape it. But tell her . . .

LADY LANE: What shall I tell her, sir?

WRIOTHESLEY: My Lady . . . her life is in danger!

(*Cut to:*)

28

Interior. Catherine's privy chamber, Hampton Court. Night.

(*Catherine, stares into camera, her eyes wide with shock.*)

CATHERINE: No!

(*Two shot Catherine and Lady Lane.*)

LADY LANE: Madam, he showed me the warrant.

CATHERINE: Not my Lord!

LADY LANE: Alas, madam, it was signed by the King's hand.

(*Catherine turns from her, a stumbling step. She looks about her wildly. Pan her to the window, then to a wall, then aimlessly to another, her pace quickening, yet the movements have no objective, the desperation of animal seeking escape. As she moves she makes little whimpering sounds of fear. She stops suddenly, facing a wall, her back to camera. She stretches out her arms, clawing at the panelling, and then, with a terrible scream, she collapses. Hold on her and mix to:*)

29

Interior. Catherine's chamber. Twenty-four hours later.

(*Full shot the door as it opens and Cranmer and Lady Lane enter. The room is in darkness, and he holds up a candle, peering about him. Lady Lane closes the door.*)

CRANMER (*Frowning*): She's here?

LADY LANE (*Pointing off*): There, my Lord.

(*Cranmer leans forward, holding the candle up and outward. Full shot Catherine, his point of view. She is crouched in a corner like a terrified animal, her hair loosened, her gown torn. Her eyes stare back into camera, and the knuckles of one hand are held between her teeth. Two shot Cranmer and Lady Lane.*)

CRANMER (*To Catherine*): My Lady?

(*And when he gets no response, he turns to Lady Lane.*)

How Long?

LADY LANE: Since yesterday evening.

CRANMER: So long . . . ?

LADY LANE: At times she weeps. Then she cries out that she is dead. She'll have no candles, saying no one will find her in the dark.

CRANMER: Leave me with her.

LADY LANE: I dare not. That door is to the King's chamber.

CRANMER: He doesn't return from Windsor until tomorrow. Leave me with her.

(*Lady Lane goes unwillingly, and when she has gone pan Cranmer across to Catherine. For a moment he stands above her, looking down with compassion. Then he slowly goes down on his knees before her, putting the candle on the floor.*)

My Lady Catherine . . . (*Catherine is staring at the candle.*) Will you pray with me, my child?

CATHERINE: No light . . .

CRANMER: Nay, my child . . . it's only a candle and nothing to fear. You see? (*He passes his hand slowly through the flame. Catherine has watched this without emotion, and is still staring at the candle when Cranmer continues.*) Pray with me. 'Most benign Lord Jesus, grant me Thy grace that it may always work in me, and persevere with me unto the end . . .' (*Cranmer stops and now Catherine looks at him.*) It's your own prayer, Catherine. Do you remember writing it? 'Thy creature . . . ? Thy creature am I, and in Thy hands, turn me where Thou wilt.' (*There is no response from Catherine, but she stares at him intently and he continues.*) 'Lord give me grace, gladly to suffer whatsoever Thou willst shall fall upon me, and patiently to take at Thy hand the good and the bad, bitter and sweet, joy and sorrow, and for all things that shall befall unto me, heartily to thank Thee . . .' (*Close shot Catherine. As she listens, tears fill her eyes. The fear, the shock in her face relaxes. Two shot as Catherine puts her hands over her face and lowers her body until her head rests on Cranmer's knees. He puts a hand gently on her head.*) My sweet Lady, I entreat you, believe that God is strong enough to take the burden of this trouble from you.

CATHERINE (*Lifting her head*): He has . . . deserted . . . me . . .

CRANMER: He has sent this trial to test you. Will you desert Him?

CATHERINE: The *King* has abandoned me!

CRANMER: Yet the Lord is by your . . .

CATHERINE: I'm afraid!

(*Cranmer gathers her to him, stifling her shout in his gown.*)

CRANMER: Indeed we are all afraid. (*Looks down at her.*) Do you hear, my Lady? We're all afraid. (*He holds her from him by the shoulders.*) I feel the rack. I smell the fire. Madam, I, too, am afraid! (*Catherine pulls herself from his hands, pressing back against the wall.*) You are the rock on which we founder. Or may cling and be saved. (*Catherine turns from him, but he grasps her again, almost brutally this time.*) Will *you* abandon *us*? God forgive you if you do, my Lady, for *you* are thereby damned!

(*With an inarticulate cry, Catherine again pulls herself free of his hands. She claws her way up the wall, and cringes against it, staring at him. Slowly Cranmer rises too.*)

CATHERINE (*Lost*): Save me . . .

CRANMER: You must save yourself! (*And then gently.*) Catherine . . . I'll pray for you.

CATHERINE (*Fiercely*): When I burn!

CRANMER: Most surely then. For I shall be beside you in the flames.

CATHERINE (*Wildly*): Oh blessed God, help me . . . !

CRANMER (*Relentlessly now*): Do your duty to Him and He will! Save His church.

CATHERINE: I'm a woman, not a churchman!

(*Close shot Cranmer.*)

CRANMER: Then be a woman, madam! Be a woman as God's Scriptures and your own nature so instruct you!

(*Mix to:*)

30

Exterior. The gardens at Hampton Court. Day.

(*Close shot Henry, his eyes closed in drowsing rest. His cap slipping rakishly, his head sunk in his shoulders, an old man. He licks his lips and smacks them. A rumbling sigh. A shadow passes across his face.*)

CATHERINE (*Voice*): My Lord . . .

(*Henry's eyes open. He stares up and frowns. Three shot Catherine, going down in a bow before Henry. Will Somers who has been leaning, half asleep, against the King's chair, attempts to rise in respect, but Henry's hand comes down heavily on his shoulder, restraining him.*)

HENRY (*Eyes on Catherine*): Be still, Fool. Here's no rival for your wit. (*And then.*) But you may rise, madam. (*Catherine rises. Her face is drawn, her eyes shadowed. But her hair and gown are neat. Two shot Henry and Catherine. Heavily.*) You do me too much honour, madam. Don't you find more pleasure in the company of your heretical ladies?

CATHERINE: No, my Lord. Never.

HENRY: You know I'm ill?

CATHERINE (*Intensely*): Indeed, my Lord . . .

HENRY: And cared nothing!

CATHERINE: Oh, my Lord . . . I would give my own life that you might be well.

HENRY (*Grumbling on*): I'm sick at heart, too. Do you know that?

CATHERINE: My Lord, if I've done . . .

HENRY: Done? What haven't you done? By Saint Mary, I'll tell you what you've done! You've become a clerk, madam. To instruct me!

CATHERINE: No, my Lord.

HENRY: Not to be directed by me, but to instruct me! What say you to that?

CATHERINE: By your leave, my Lord, you are wrong . . .

HENRY: You see? You instruct me!

CATHERINE: No, my good Lord . . . I remind myself of your own instruction to me. That it is preposterous for a woman to take up the office of teacher to her husband.

HENRY: You argued with me. You disputed my judgment. Here, madam. In this garden!

CATHERINE (*Losing control*): No, my Lord. . . An it please you . . . I . . .

HENRY (*Shouting*). You're a clerk, madam, a clerk! You would instruct me! Me, madam, me! (*Catherine closes her eyes against this violent bluster. She sways.* Would you teach me theology, madam? Astrology,

506

perhaps? Or music? By heaven, you . . . (*And then.*) What is it, madam? Are you ill? (*Turns.*) Will!

(*Three shot as Somers leaps from the ground.*)

SOMERS: Majesty?

HENRY: A stool, you dolt! Get the Queen a stool!

(*Cut to:*)

31

Exterior. Another part of the garden. Day.

(*Close shot the warrant for Catherine's arrest being plucked from the cuff of a gauntlet. Pull back to show Wriothesley looking down at the warrant in his hand. He wears a cuirass and a feathered morion. Behind him is a file of halberdiers. He looks up into camera and raises a hand. He moves off, followed by the halberdiers.*

Cut to:*)

32

Exterior. The gardens at Hampton Court. Day.

(*Two shot Henry and Catherine. She is sitting on the stool beside his chair. He has an arm about her shoulders, and, somewhat comically and ineffectually, is waving her pomander beneath her nose.*

CATHERINE (*Stopping his hand*): Your Majesty . . .

HENRY: What makes you ill, madam? (*A flash of hope.*) Is it perhaps . . . ?

CATHERINE: No, my Lord... (*A smile.*) Though not for want of your Majesty's energy in assault.

HENRY (*A shout of delight*): Hah! (*And then frowning again. Releasing her.*) But you lectured me perversely, madam. You did obstinately instruct me!

CATHERINE (*Lowering her head*): Indeed I did, my Lord. And was in grievous default thereby. (*Looks up at him boldly.*) For God made man in His own shape and likeness, to instruct and improve women, who have such great imperfections in their creation.

HENRY: Even so, madam. My own words.

CATHERINE: Yes, my Lord.

(*Cut to:*)

33

Exterior. Another part of the garden. Day.

(*Low angle moving shot, the marching of feet of Wriothesley and the guard. They halt. Wriothesley stares off. A frown. He bites at the edge of the warrant in indecision.*

Cut to:)

34

Exterior. The gardens at Hampton Court. Day.

(*Two shot Henry and Catherine.*)

HENRY (*Turning from her petulantly*): Yet, you've hurt me, madam. I am angry.

(In the far background are Wriothesley and the guard, waiting indecisively.)

CATHERINE: Then punish me, my Lord. Because woman is made of man, so she must be governed by him.

HENRY: And you did not wish to instruct me?

(In the background Wriothesley turns and speaks to the guards. He then advances alone towards the King and Queen, and as yet unseen by them. He removes his morion and holds it in the crook of his arm.)

CATHERINE: No, my Lord. Only to talk with you. And from your learned answers to be instructed by you.

HENRY: Is it so, Kate? You meant no more than that?

CATHERINE *(A beat)*: No more than that, my Lord.

(Cut to close two shot of Henry and Catherine.)

HENRY: Then by Heaven, we're friends again, sweetheart! *(He seizes her hand.)* You bring me more joy than if a hundred thousand crowns had fallen into my lap!

(He bends over her hand, kissing the palm, the fingers with senile emotion. Cut to: Three shot. Wriothesley has arrived and stands behind Henry. Catherine looks up to him. He does not bow, but he is uneasy. Catherine, on her face is the same small, cold smile of triumph we saw when Seymour was banished to Europe. Three shot Henry senses that someone is behind him. He turns. Now Wriothesley bows, holding out the warrant.)

WRIOTHESLEY: Your Majesty . . .

(*Henry, his face distorted, his cheeks puffing as he searches for words. He releases Catherine's hand and claws at his stick and the arm of the chair, hoisting his great body to its feet by the power of his anger. Pan him up. He takes a stumbling limp toward Wriothesley who steps back in alarm.*)

HENRY (*A hiss*): Fool ... ! (*He rips the warrant in two.*) Knave! (*He tears it again, stumbles, throws the pieces at Wriothesley.*) Rogue!

WRIOTHESLEY (*Backing away*): My Lord ...

(*Henry flails at Wriothesley with his stick, misses and staggers. Wriothesley backs away again, then turns and begins to walk away rapidly, pursued by Henry, limping, shouting, swinging the stick.*)

HENRY: Beast ... ! Rogue ... ! Coward ... ! (*Suddenly he stops, as if frozen, his back to camera. He turns slowly. His eyes are wide with incredulity. His mouth opens, he fights for air and for the word that is not much more than a gurgle in his throat.*) Kate ... ?

(*As he pitches forward.
Cut to:*)

35

Exterior. Bell-Tower, Hampton Court. Day

(*Low angle, the bell as it tips and sounds one shuddering note. As it swings again and sounds cut to:*)

36

Exterior. The gatehouse, Hampton Court. Day.

(*Low angle, a horseman—it is Seymour—turning and passing through the gate at a gallop. The bell is still tolling.*

Cut to:)

37

Exterior. The courtyard, Hampton Court. Day.

(*Full shot as Seymour pulls in his horse before the door to the Palace. As he throws the rein to a groom, he looks up to the ringing bell, pulling back his lips with a grimace of distaste. He turns to the door.*

Cut to:)

38

Interior. The anteroom outside the King's chamber. Day.

(*Hertford in foreground. Beyond him, the anteroom is full of silent groups of gentlemen, Hertford is calm, gently running a thumb-nail along the line of his lower lip.*

He turns his head as, against a rustle of whispered protest, Seymour strides through the groups towards his brother.

The bell is still tolling, muted off.

Seymour grasps Hertford's arm and pulls him into a window-alcove.

Close two shot Hertford and Seymour.)

SEYMOUR: I came upon your message. Is the King dead?

HERTFORD: No.

SEYMOUR: The bell . . .

HERTFORD: I've sent word to have it stopped. It was his notion . . . (*A thin smile.*) That Heaven, perhaps, might have good warning of his imminent coming.

SEYMOUR: Nay, Hell more like. Three weeks . . . how can he still live?

HERTFORD: He could unleash his soul any hour now. What news?

SEYMOUR: Good news. London is ours.

HERTFORD: And here, at Hampton Court?

SEYMOUR: No one can leave without our pass. Is Cranmer here?

HERTFORD: And Gardiner. Each would have copyhold on the King's spirit before his body's cold.

SEYMOUR (*A grin, he slaps a glove on his palm, and pulls it through his fingers*): There's none here to stop us, brother.

HERTFORD: None. With Norfolk in the Tower, and his son Surrey already condemned.

SEYMOUR: Yet Norfolk's no Papist. He would be an ally.

HERTFORD: Or a rival, Thomas.

SEYMOUR (*Smiles, looks away, then back quickly.*) Mary?

HERTFORD: Here. Somewhere, Gardiner will make her Queen if he can. But the King has named Edward his heir. Give me twenty-four hours, Thomas, after he dies—with no word of it to the rest of the kingdom until we're ready—and I'll put the crown on the boy.

SEYMOUR: Has the King named you Regent? (*When Hertford does not answer.*) Or is it Catherine?

HERTFORD (*A thin smile*): He's forgotten her. And brother, here's the jest of it. By his own wish, he's to be buried in the chapel at Windsor, next to our sister Jane.

SEYMOUR (*A smile, then impatiently*): Why does the man hang on? How can life bear to linger in that hill of rotting flesh?

(*Cut to:*)

39

Interior. The King's privy chamber, Hampton Court. Day.

(*Henry. His back is propped against pillows, and only they are keeping him upright. His night-cap has slipped forward. His eyes are open, staring sightlessly, and his breath comes painfully and noisily through his open mouth.*

Pull back slowly. On the floor by the bed is Will Somers, staring up at Henry like a grieving dog. On the other side of the bed sits Gardiner, and beyond him, in a corner, are a physician and two gentlemen of the chamber.

Upon an incoherent rattle in Henry's throat, Gardiner leans forward, an urgent note in his voice.)

GARDINER: Your Majesty . . . ?

HENRY: Who's there?

GARDINER: Stephen Gardiner, your Majesty.

HENRY: My legs . . . (*Gardiner looks over his shoulder to the physician who comes forward to the bed, placing a hand on Henry's leg beneath the blanket.*) They burn . . . they're ice . . . they burn with ice!

(*The physician withdraws his hand. He looks at Gardiner and, with an almost imperceptible shrug, returns to the corner.*)

GARDINER: Your Majesty . . .

HENRY: Gardiner, you say?

GARDINER: Your Majesty's loving servant.

HENRY: You should've taken a wife . . . like Cranmer . . . (*A terrible cackle that might be a laugh.*) Like me . . .

GARDINER (*His voice close to panic now*): My Lord, she plots against you . . . !

HENRY (*The words striking fearful memories*): Plots? Who . . . ?

GARDINER: The Queen, my Lord.

HENRY: She's dead. Sweet Jane!

GARDINER: The Lady Catherine, my Lord. There is proof . . . (*He puts a hand inside his gown and half withdraws some papers, thinks better of it and thrusts them back*.) Your Majesty, the Council must examine her, lest you die in sin.

HENRY (*Puzzled*): Sin? I've been shriven, Sir Monk. Be gone. (*And then another obscene cackle*.) They'll burn you.

GARDINER: Your Majesty, will you name the Princess Mary your successor?

HENRY: Mary? (*Finding strength from somewhere*.) Rogues! All of you! You keep my daughter from me! Where is Mary?

GARDINER (*Rising with a smile and turning to the Gentlemen in the corner*): Send for the Lady Mary. (*Cut to*:)

40

Interior. The anteroom outside the King's chamber. Day.

(*Track before Mary as she walks down the corridor of the anteroom. She is erect and calm, dressed austerely in black, and in both hands she holds the crucifix that hangs from her neck. The waiting gentlemen bow to her, but she does not look at them. She stops at the door of the King's chamber, where Gardiner is waiting. He bows to her. Cut to: Seymour and Hertford, watching this keenly. Cut to: Two shot, Gardiner and Mary*.)

GARDINER: Be of good heart, my child. He has asked to see you alone.

MARY: And so, my Lord?

GARDINER (*A glance away to the Seymours and*

back): Madam, you are his only heir. In Law, in the sight of God.

(*Mary says nothing. She goes past Gardiner into the Chamber. Cut to: Two shot Seymour and Hertford.*)

SEYMOUR (*A smile*): I'll wager a good horse he told her she should be Queen.

HERTFORD: And so she believes. But while grief has a hold on her, she'll do what the King says.

(*Cut to:*)

41

Interior. The King's privy chamber, Hampton Court. Day.

(*Close shot, Henry's hand lying on the covers. As Mary's hand comes into shot and closes over it, pull back to two shot.*)

HENRY (*Stirring*): Mary? Are we alone?

MARY: But for your Fool.

HENRY: Will? Are you still here, good Will?

(*Cut to: Somers, on the floor by the bed. He looks up.*)

SOMERS: Aye, Cousin Hal. Always!

(*Cut to: Two shot Henry and Mary.*)

HENRY: Nay, Will ... Not always. (*Mary slips down on her knees beside the bed, lowering her head. Henry's hand searches for her, resting on her hair.*) I pray you, daughter ... (*Mary looks up, tears in her eyes.*) Your brother Edward ... He's small and young still. Try to be a mother to him.

MARY: I shall, my Lord . . .

HENRY: And honour him as King. (*Mary presses her cheek against his hand.*) Do not weep.

MARY (*Looking up and fiercely*): My Lord, live many days yet! Don't leave me alone among my enemies!

HENRY: Will! Will Somers!

(*Three shot, Somers rising.*)

SOMERS: Majesty?

HENRY: Take her out. I can bear no weeping! (*Somers goes to Mary, helping her to rise. They turn to the door. Cut to: Henry, staring up to the ceiling. At the sound of the door closing.*) My God . . . release me!

(*Pan from him to an unlit candle on the table beside the bed and mix to:*)

42

The King's privy chamber, Hampton Court. Night.

(*The same candle, now alight and half consumed. As the physician bends between candle and camera, pull back for three shot, the physician who is wiping Henry's forehead, and Cranmer standing by the bed. Henry stirs with a sigh.*)

CRANMER: My Lord . . . ?

HENRY: Is it Gardiner?

(*The physician retires.*)

CRANMER: Thomas Cranmer, your Majesty.

517

HENRY: You're all one to me now.

CRANMER: My Lord ... You asked for the Queen. She's here.

HENRY: The Queen is dead.

(*Cranmer looks back over his shoulder. Cut to: his point of view. Catherine. She stands at the end of the bed, her face full of grief. Cut to: Three shot.*)

CRANMER: My Lady ... ?

(*Cranmer steps back, and as Catherine moves to the head of the bed, going down on her knees, close on her and Henry.*)

HENRY: Who's there?

CATHERINE: Your wife, my Lord.

HENRY: Sweet Jane is dead.

CATHERINE: It's Kate, my Lord.

(*Slowly Henry turns his head to her, blinking. She moves the candle so that the light falls more strongly on her face.*)

HENRY: Kate?

CATHERINE: Aye, my Lord.

(*She raises his hand to her lips.*)

HENRY: My son ... Protect my children, Kate!

CATHERINE: As if they were my own, my Lord!

HENRY (*Staring*): Your own? (*And then, as another thought enters his wandering mind.*) Your jewels!

CATHERINE: My Lord?

HENRY: Don't let them take your jewels ... They're all thieves! (*He struggles to raise his head, looking across the room.*) Gentlemen!

CATHERINE (*Turning anxiously*): My Lords!

(*Full shot, a rustle as Cranmer, the physician and the two Gentlemen of the Chamber move to the bedside.*)

HENRY (*Staring at them, his voice stronger*): Honour this sweet lady, gentlemen. Honour her and treat her well, as if I still lived! (*The strength goes, his head drops back and he closes his eyes. Catherine looks up to the others and they retire again. Two shot Henry and Catherine. He opens his eyes and looks at her.*) Kiss me, my Lady. (*Catherine leans forward and gently kisses his cheek. As she moves back. Reassuring her.*) It's God will we should part, Kate.

(*As Catherine lowers her head, Mix to:*)

43

Interior. The anteroom outside the King's chamber. Day.

(*Low angle window. Bars of dusty sunlight dropping through the panes. Pan down them to Seymour who is staring up to the sky outside with a smile.*)

SEYMOUR: A fine morning this, for hawking.

(*Cut to: Three shot, Seymour, Hertford and Cranmer.*)

CRANMER: Thomas, you lack respect.

SEYMOUR: My Lord Archbishop, I'm honest. Why not be so yourself? Don't you feel a lightness of heart?

(*Beyond them, down the room, others still wait, but the long strain is telling. Some have their backs against the wall, heads nodding over folded arms. Others, older men, sit on chairs, head in hand.*)

HERTFORD: Be quiet! You're not a boy!

SEYMOUR: We're all boys, and soon to be released from school. It's a fine day for hawking. The bird stoops, and Gardiner's the quarry.

(*Cut to: The door of the King's Chamber as it opens and the physician comes out. Pan him across to the group by the window. He whispers in Cranmer's ear. Cranmer turns to the others.*)

CRANMER: The King is about to die, and must be told. (*He turns away towards the chamber.*)

SEYMOUR (*Holding Cranmer's arm*): Nay sir, let me tell him the gladsome news.

(*Two shot Hertford and Seymour.*)

HERTFORD (*Grasping his brother roughly by the shoulder and swinging him round*): I'll cut out that foolish tongue one day!

SEYMOUR: You'll have need of it yet, brother. Take your hand from me.

HERTFORD (*A beat, releasing him*): I'll tell the King. You bring our nephew Edward here.

(*Cut to:*)

44

Interior. The King's privy chamber, Hampton Court. Day.

(*Henry. His eyes stare at the ceiling. His mouth is open. His breathing is slow—a hoarse rattle, followed by an agonizing pause before there is another. Pull back slowly to take in Hertford approaching the bedside. Cranmer and the physician in background.*)

HERTFORD: Your Majesty (*Waits for some response from Henry, and then bluntly.*) Your Majesty, it's the judgment of your Physician that you are about to die. (*Cut to: Close two shot as Hertford goes down on one knee beside Henry.*) Is there one you would open your mind to?

(*Tighten shot as Hertford puts his ear to Henry's mouth.*)

HENRY (*After several, painful attempts, a rasping word*): Cran . . . mer . . .

(*Cut to: Cranmer, pan him to the bedside where Hertford is rising. Cranmer goes down on his knees. Cut to: Close two shot Cranmer and Henry.*)

CRANMER (*Taking Henry's hand*): My Lord . . . I beseech God to grant you the grace to say something at this your departure whereby He may be glorified and your memory blessed. (*Bends forward, and in a clear, firm voice.*) Do you die in the true faith of Christ? (*Henry's head goes back, quivering. He seems to be making a terrible effort to speak.*) Sire . . . Do you die in the true faith of Christ?

(*Cut to: Close shot Henry's hand grasping Cranmer's. It tightens and trembles. Cut to: Close*

521

shot Cranmer, looking down at his hand. Cut to: Henry, his head and shoulders rising from the pillows, pulled up by his grip on Cranmer's hand. His eyes are wild. He opens his mouth.)

HENRY (*A hoarse cry*): Monks... ! Monks... !
(*He falls back dead.*)

(*Cut to: High Angle Cranmer. He slowly releases his hand from the King's. He rises, turning to camera. There are tears in his eyes.*)

CRANMER: He pressed my hand. He died in the true faith of Christ and will enter eternal life.

(*Cut to: Somers on the floor by the bed. With a moan he buries his head in his arms. Cut to: Hertford by the door. Abruptly he opens it and goes out. Cut to:*)

45

The anteroom outside the King's Chamber. Day.

(*Hertford comes out of the chamber and closes the door behind him. He looks about him.*

Pan Hertford's point of view. Gentlemen rising, looking to camera expectantly, some taking a step forward.

End pan at the window. Seymour there, the boy Edward by his side.

Cut to:

Hertford. A beat. Pan him across to the window. He turns to face the courtiers, and he puts a hand on Edward's shoulder.)

HERTFORD: My Lord's, the King is dead.

SEYMOUR (*Placing his hand on Edward's other shoulder and in a clear bright voice*): *Vive le noble roi* Edward!

(*Cut to: Close shot Edward. He looks up first to one uncle and then to the other. On his face a lost expression of bewilderment and alarm. Slow mix to:*)

46

Interior. Catherine's privy chamber, Hampton Court. Night.

(*Catherine sits alone by a table upon which is a single branch of candles. She has an open prayer-book on her lap, but she is not looking at it.*

Cut to:

Door as it opens and Seymour enters. He closes it behind him quietly and looks across the room to Catherine, keeping one hand behind his back. Pan him to her.)

SEYMOUR: Kate . . . ? (*Catherine does not answer or look up.*) He's dead, Kate . . . (*Still Catherine does not answer. Sharply.*) Madam, the King is dead!

CATHERINE (*Looking up calmly*): Five hours ago. Did you think no one would come to tell me, Thomas? (*When he does not answer.*) Am I to be Regent?

SEYMOUR (*Surprised*): You? That's a cap for a man to wear.

CATHERINE: Or a crown for your brother.

SEYMOUR: The Council declares him Protector to-morrow.

CATHERINE: That wasn't my Lord's wish.

SEYMOUR: Your Lord's dead, and his son needs us.

CATHERINE: Edward's afraid of you. And so are his sisters.

SEYMOUR: Are you afraid of us, Kate?

CATHERINE: I fear none of you now.

(*Seymour says nothing. He stares at her. And then, diffidently almost, he takes his hand from behind his back. It is holding a red rose. He bends forward and lays it in her lap. She looks at it, and then up to him, without expression.*)

SEYMOUR: I found it in a corner of the garden. The warmth of the kitchens saved it from the frost.

CATHERINE: And your lute? Have you brought that?

SEYMOUR (*Stubbornly*): I will wed you, Kate.

CATHERINE (*Tightly*): May we bury my Lord first?

SEYMOUR: I want an answer now. When we marry may wait upon discretion.

CATHERINE: But I must say yes or no now?

SEYMOUR: You must say yes.

CATHERINE: Why?

SEYMOUR: For the safety of . . . That I may protect you, madam.

CATHERINE: And no word of love, Thomas?

SEYMOUR: I can speak of love, if you wish it. But what I offer, and the moment I choose to offer it, speak more strongly.

CATHERINE: I've had three husbands. I'm old. I'm nothing.

SEYMOUR: You're everything at this moment, Kate.

CATHERINE: To you?

SEYMOUR (*A beat*): To me, yes. But that's nothing.

CATHERINE: Are you being self-denying again, Thomas?

SEYMOUR: Our love . . .

CATHERINE: Our *love*?

SEYMOUR: . . . is nothing against your duty to Edward, to the Church, and to this Kingdom.

CATHERINE: But by good fortune I may this time satisfy both? (*Seymour stares at her doggedly, unable to fence with her bitter mockery. And then her mood changes, and becomes, in a way, an appeal for understanding.*) Thomas . . . I've been crucified on duty. To my father, and the husbands his debts chose for me. To the Church I love, and the King I came to love. To Cranmer, whose goodness and fear made me deny my conscience before the King. Thomas . . . may I not now find some duty to myself?

SEYMOUR (*Brutally unmoved*): Madam . . . I would, if I could, take a warmer companion to my bed. But by God's most precious soul, it must be you!

CATHERINE: No!

SEYMOUR (*Stepping towards her and pulling her to her feet by her wrist*): At this moment Edward's in his chamber puking with fear of my brother. Mary and Elizabeth stand over him like she-cats, daring either of us to enter.

CATHERINE: No! I will not . . .

SEYMOUR: You will! For it's you they love, and by your guidance will be ready to obey those in your favour! (*Catherine tries to pull her wrist free. Holding her to him.*) There's more, madam, if your new-found wit wants the truth plain. Without you, Mary will turn against us, and have this kingdom in civil war. Edward's sick enough to die for want of nursing. And my brother would be ready to choke Elizabeth himself if he thought a party might gather about her. (*He throws her wrist from him*). Now, Madam, what of your duty?

(*Catherine, shaken, confused, and alone. She grasps at the one thing that might make this bearable.*)

CATHERINE: Thomas . . . I would have loved you once. Before all others . . .

SEYMOUR (*Lightly*): Faith, if that's all, I can light the spark!

CATHERINE: You? After my Lord?

SEYMOUR: Who died crying for my sister Jane. (*Catherine turns her back to him quickly. He watches her impatiently.*) Well, madam?

CATHERINE (*Turning to him, her face now calm and empty*): I will marry you, Thomas.

(*Seymour steps towards her, bending on one knee and bringing the hem of her skirt to his lips. Roll credits. Mix to:*)

47

Interior. The King's privy chamber, Hampton Court. Night.

(Henry's body lying on the bed. Pull back slowly to take in Will Somers, crouched on the floor at the foot of the bed. Hold and end credits. Fade out.)